A Lizard in my Luggage

MAYFAIR TO MALLORCA IN ONE EASY MOVE

ANNA NICHOLAS

summersdale

A LIZARD IN MY LUGGAGE

Summersdale Publishers Ltd
46 West Street
Chichester
West Sussex
PO19 1RP
UK

www.summersdale.com

Printed and bound in Great Britain

ISBN: 1-84024-565-4
ISBN 13: 978-1-84024-565-3

For Marvellous Merzle,
without whom…

Contents

Acknowledgements

In having completed this book, it would be inadmissible of me not to mention a handful of kind and patient souls who have encouraged, chastised and galvanised me into action. I thank my dear friend Alice Hart-Davis and literary agent, Stephanie Cabot, for setting the ball rolling, Kate Cook for unlimited inspiration, and Paul Richards for his wisdom and editorial prowess. Thanks are extended to Guillem Puig for correcting my child-like Mallorcan, and to the one and only Sari Andreu for being Sari.

I would like to thank Roger Katz for backing an untried horse, and Pere and Margarita Serra, the proprietors of the Serra Newspaper Group, for their unwavering generosity. Also, thanks go to Ignacío Vasallo, director of Turespaña London, for his support, and to Tomás Graves for his book, *A Home in Majorca*, which acted as an excellent point of reference. A special mention must go to Debbie Seaman, author of *The Fearless Flier's Handbook* which has been my trusty companion on many a shaky flight. I am indebted to the Mallorcan community of our mountain valley for their acceptance and friendship. Finally, inestimable thanks to my sister, Cecilia, my nephew, Alexander, and to the two hillbilly boys, Alan and Oliver.

About the Author

As a freelance journalist, Anna Nicholas has contributed to titles such as the *FT*, *The Independent*, *Tatler* and the *Evening Standard* and for the last four years she has contributed a weekly column to the *Majorca Daily Bulletin*. She is a fellow of the Royal Geographical Society and has been an international invigilator for Guinness World Records. She has also organised an expedition to carry a grand piano to a remote tribe in South America, which was the subject of a BBC TV documentary.

Author's note

The local vernacular used in this book is mostly in the Mallorcan dialect. Although Mallorcan is derived from Catalan and is believed to have been spoken for more than five or six centuries, it varies greatly when written. During the Franco era, Mallorcan was forbidden in Balearic schools and this has made it an oral language, reliant on Catalan when transcribed to print. The vocabulary and spelling often vary greatly from village to village in Mallorca. I have taken advice from local language experts and so hope to have accurately transcribed the Mallorcan language to print. However, I apologise unreservedly to any fervent linguists who may care to differ.

ONE

RUBBLE

It's noon. A fat gecko, its eyes as large as marbles, locks on to me with an unblinking stare as I grapple with a crude, rusty key, the size and weight of a small hammer, just above his head. I want him to move but he hugs the wall like a watchful Spider-Man, daring me to engage key with lock. I know it's a male, a he, just by the way he surveys me. Everything in this country is machismo so why shouldn't that include geckos with big ant guts? He's looking disapprovingly at my bitten painted nails, orange kitten heels, fake designer handbag from a trip to Dubai, and thinking, for crying out loud, what's a house like this doing with a woman like that? He's a good psychologist too. He knows I don't like insects, snakes, small, fast moving vertebrates and anything with multiple legs, hairy limbs and antennae. And exactly why am I faltering at the door? Am I seriously scared of a lizard? Get a grip. I push the key firmly in the lock. Simultaneously, the reluctant, portly custodian of the house shimmies up the door and ducks into a groove in the stone wall. Vanished into a smudge of darkness. Good riddance. I shudder and attempt to turn the key. It won't shift and here

I am, up a dirt track drive in the sort of heat that could melt bones and trigger tantrums. Cicadas are hissing accusingly at me from the grey contorted olive trees and a voyeuristic frog is peering over a discarded can in an old septic water tank, willing defeat.

This is no simple Yale or Banham lock. It is blackish and seigneurial, displaying a few distinguished brown spots of corrosion at the edges, and fashioned out of wrought-iron from centuries ago. However, the key, its faithful lifelong partner, is old and battered with age and unable to engage in happy union as once it might. I use the time-honoured practice of the short tempered and impetuous, and start kicking the door. It shudders but refuses to budge. Four hundred odd years of Spanish craftsmanship and solid oak are not going to give way to a petulant, hot and bothered Londoner with a blatant disregard for anger management.

There's a strange humming in the distance, an angry, gnawing sound that grows louder until it soon explodes into a cloud of hot, powdery dust three feet from me. A young man with tight, black curly hair and a set of teeth and comely muscles normally reserved for matinee idols is silencing the engine of a motorbike and waving cheerfully at me. Oh God, who's this? Do I have to share the humiliation of being incapable of opening my own front door with a total stranger, and a foreigner to boot? He saunters over to me with a look of concern and it's not just for my sanity.

'Is problem wees door, *si?*' He sibilates his words smoothly, referring to me as senyorita, young lady, not the more matronly senyora, indicating that he's either in public relations, an inveterate liar, or in need of good specs or possibly all three. Still, he speaks some English. This will at least spare him from having to endure my spoken Spanish which has only recently graduated from *Teletubbies* greetings to vocabulary worthy of the Peter and Jane books. To make matters worse, he is speaking in

Mallorcan, the local dialect, which naturally poses even greater hazards for me.

'Well, I can't turn the key. It's stuck. Can you try?'

'No *problema*, senyorita. Is very old.'

In Mallorca nothing is a problem, until you have a problem. He wrenches the key round and it emits a squeal of anguish. Then with a quick kung fu arm movement he strikes at the door and it creaks open, allowing a shaft of ruby light to caress the marble floor. I throw him a gracious smile and push my sunglasses back over my hot, damp hair.

'Sorry, who are you?'

'Me? Oh, I friend of Miguel.'

And who is Miguel when he's at home?

'Miguel is friend of Joan who is brother of Jaume'.

The genealogy lesson doesn't stop here. 'Jaume's grandfather was doctor.'

I resist the childish urge to say, 'Doctor who?' and instead ask, 'So who is Jaume?'

He looks bemused and shrugs his lean brown shoulders.

'Jaume is builder. Jaume work on your house.'

Ah! Now, we're getting there.

'Do you work on my house?'

'No, Jaume leave kettle in field. I get for him now and go.'

I'm about to start all over again in an attempt to learn his name but stop. There are times when to question further would result in entering what my family call the twilight zone, an enchanted territory in time and space where nothing can ever make sense. It's a world of alphabetical letters in jumbled order, where cats wear hats and the distinctly odd becomes the norm. So should I discover that Jaume the Builder really is brewing Typhoo tea in the manner of his British counterparts in my field under the full strength of a fiery Mediterranean sun, I shall know not to question it.

I nod sagely at the young Adonis and leave him to amble off across the courtyard and down into the wasteland of a field with its towering weeds and sad bowed orange and lemon trees, splashed with mud and grime from countless assaults on the turf by tractors, diggers and lorries. I walk into the *entrada*, a large, semi-lit, blank white space smelling of damp paint and cicadas. How does a cicada smell? Like my *entrada*, that's how. I clip-clop over to the arched doorway leading to the back garden and terrace. It is masked by heavy wooden shutters which surprisingly give way when I lift the wrought-iron levers. The sun engulfs me and I'm momentarily blinded, then deafened by a sudden blast from my handbag as the mobile phone bursts into song. I could throttle it but instead I trill in the way a public relations professional should, with a voice brimming with false enthusiasm.

'Prudence! I was just thinking of you. I've literally just put the finishing touches to the brief and am about to wing it over to your office.' That's when I've actually written the wretched thing. 'Tomorrow? No problem, I'll e-mail it. Yes, it has turned cold, hasn't it?'

She rings off without the faintest idea that I'm speaking to her from a sweltering, empty house in the mountains of a Spanish island. Has she completely forgotten about my move or relegated the information to the back of her mind? The thought amuses me. I feel like a naughty schoolgirl playing truant and yet the work will get done, just in a different location.

Prudence Braithwaite is the officious secretary of Michael Roselock of Roselock Fine Jewellery, a client on the edge of a nervous breakdown who has disbanded half his staff through debt and has weakly left her to run his ailing ship. Neither of them has a clue what she's doing. Nor have I for that matter. Unnervingly, both persist in trying to embroil me in the mounting sagas of their company with daily hysterical calls that inevitably end with the fretful words, 'What are we going to do?' Much as I try to buoy them up, they've struck the iceberg and water's seeping in. I sigh and hurl the slim little silver spy back into my bag with venom. I call it Judas because it always betrays me. In my opinion the maniac who invented mobile phones really should have been shot at the prototype stage, preferably to the accompanying wail of a microchip pumping out a synthesised fugue.

My nameless friend pops his head round the front door, kettle in hand and yells '*Adéu!*' so loudly it rebounds around the stark walls and vaulted ceilings and makes my heart thump. A minute later I hear the familiar whining sound of the bike tearing off up the track. Once again, I'm alone with the geckos and my many hidden detractors – living creatures that crawl and creep soundlessly in the undergrowth, observing my every move. I pop my shades back on and stride out into the sun, the insecure owner of a partially restored pile in a foreign country. Here, in the craggy northwest mountains of Mallorca, I feel light-years away from my flat in central London with the shuddering, creaky cabs passing my windows and the constant judder of coaches and lorries as they thunder by, night and day. The air is still and fragrant and the lisping cicadas with their monotone pulsating beat lure me into a state of momentary calm. The house is ancient, so old that we can only trace its lineage back three hundred years. It's almost double that according to local oral tradition – neighbours, shopkeepers, bar owners and the elderly *paisanos* who eke out their days playing cards and reminiscing with their friends in the town square. Word has it that over the centuries this *finca* played home to the local priests of our village church and was once a safe house during violent Moorish assaults on the island. During that troubled time it also served as a secret chapel for devout local parishioners, a sacred place for those in peril. Let's hope the magic still works.

The view from the courtyard to the pinky-grey Tramuntana mountains is formidable if you can prise your gaze from the clutter on ground level, for the front of the house resembles a builders' merchant's, choking with boulders of yellow chalky stone, great planks of pine timber crushing small patches of yellowed weeds, wire tightly bound in prickly bales and sacks of cement spilling over on to the uneven ground in ugly ochre tinted piles. I listen for the mobile phone, now distracted by its muteness. Why isn't anyone calling me? Have the phones gone down in the office back in London? Has my battery died? Surely someone, somewhere, simply must be trying to get hold of me and where is Alan, my hardy Scot? He and our son, Ollie, were supposed to have been here eons ago, leading a procession of removal vans from the town roundabout to the house. Admittedly this is no mean feat. This *finca*, our *finca*, is set amidst a bewildering labyrinth of winding roads and tiny, narrow cobbled lanes, fields of olives, oranges and lemons and decoy houses that pop up along the way and bear a striking similarity to our own in shape or size of stone, but in fact belong to somebody else.

To add to the frustrations of the first-time visitor, the journey is beset with hazards of a Mallorcan kind: crater sized potholes from which gaping coloured pipes of an unknown nature spew forth, one-way signs which locals ignore but tourists don't, spontaneously reversing water carriers and tractors, kamikaze mangy dogs and cats that leap gamely at moving vehicles, elderly senyoras, bundled like mummies in black swaddling who topple onto the road, their walking sticks raised in perpetual protest, and finally, garrulous locals. The latter is the real bummer. Mallorcans are oblivious to the time constraints of others. They will happily slam on the brakes in the middle of moving traffic to wave or gossip with a friend in a passing car or pop out to buy a loaf from the local *supermercat*, leaving the engine running, while you sit, exasperated in their wake, unable to move, impatiently awaiting their return. Horns will start blasting after five minutes but it's all a good-natured game on the part of the locals and the offender, once armed triumphantly with bread stick, will return to the car to be greeted like a hero with wolf whistles, smiles and whoops, while the mystified foreigner looks on wretchedly, excluded from the fun but caught up in the inconvenience.

The removal vans are coming from Palma, Mallorca's capital, and were due to arrive at eleven. Anticipating the disaster if we left them to their own devices up here in the mountains, we insisted on acting as scouts, leading them to the house. Therefore, more than an hour or so ago Alan, Ollie and I sat hot and irritable in a sweltering hire car in a local lay-by waiting for them to arrive at the designated time. Foolishly, we had not reckoned on Mallorca *mañana* time which means you arrive within an hour or so of the time you originally agreed. After thirty minutes of heated discussion with Alan about their whereabouts, I had recklessly insisted on getting some provisions on foot and walking back to the *finca* alone. It was a decision made hastily and under the influence of a sadistic sun. Alan had accused me of being ridiculously impetuous and likely to end up with severe sunstroke striding out uncovered in such heat.

Ignoring his entreaties, I scrambled out of my side of the car, observing a brief exchange of stealthy and complicit looks between Ollie and his father. Crossly, I had to accept that no sooner had I left than Alan would be puffing on one of his putrid cigars and brokering a deal with Ollie to keep shtum later. Despite my spirited lectures on the subject of smoking and its dire consequences, Alan defiantly continues his tobacco habit, albeit more sneakily and, where possible, away from my prying eyes. Rather like an accomplished thief, he is good at covering his tracks and removing evidence of the crime, but the odd cellophane wrapper trapped under a car seat or cloying odour of a recently puffed Cuban delight refusing to disperse, even with the most pungent of air fresheners, often betrays him.

I certainly needed some fresh air. So, mincing like a poodle at Crufts up the precarious, stony lane which leads to the house in my slingbacks, I had practically thrown myself at the front porch, expecting a heroine's welcome from my husband and a dozen sympathetic and swarthy men carrying boxes. Instead I met with the hostility of nature, a thousand beady eyes and rustling limbs hiding in the grasses, wall crevices and murky pond, glaring at this ill-equipped and fey female from an alien universe, daring to invade their world.

This surely is the first time I have ever stood this still for so long in years. The last occasion must have been about aged six during the silent spell of a pass the parcel game. I'm not good at being slow. My sister always says I was born with the engine of a Porsche crammed into the body of a Mini. It's true, I don't like hanging around and I'm beginning to wonder what on earth I've done making this move to Mallorca. If I were in London now my ear would be superglued to an office phone, hands meanwhile tapping away on the computer keys, while I'd be mouthing instructions to someone in the office. There would be noise and manic activity, couriers arriving and taxi drivers barking down the intercom. A paper cup of cold Starbucks coffee would be perched on my desk, a blueberry muffin, hardly touched and stale, peeping out of a paper bag, ready for instant disposal in the bin. I worked it out one day, just for the hell of it. How much did I really spend at Starbucks? Way too much. Let's just leave it at that.

Five years back when Alan and I first came to Mallorca, it was like a game. We were on holiday in a rented property supposedly to relax, but within two days I was on the mobile to London making umpteen corrections to a client document, while he lay serenely by the pool with a glass of cold cava, immersed in *The Garden* magazine. Once the Scotsman has this horticultural fix in his grasp, he is immune to everything around him. As I stalked around the garden like a demented stork trilling into my mobile on some exigent business, he calmly turned the pages, seemingly without a care in the world. At one point he looked into the distance and said with a sublime smile,

'Ah, yes! *Quercus ilex* and *Prunus dulcis*, the evergreen holm oak and the almond tree.'

Then he sighed contentedly as if he had just solved the final mystery of the universe and resumed his reading.

When Toni appeared like *deus ex machina* before us in the garden, I wondered what genie I'd rubbed up the right way. Tall and bronzed with a chiselled cheek you could strike a match on, he stood smiling down at us like a benign God. I shook myself out of a sweet reverie and sized him up as a suave Spanish salesman. Despite the heat, he oozed charm not sweat, and had the effortless elan of a man with a mission in an impeccable cream linen suit and sinfully pricey looking shoes. It transpired that the owners of our holiday *finca* were putting it on the market and Toni was handling the sale. Later as we all sat mulling over a glass of wine on the spiky lawn, I was hooked.

'So you have other *fincas* for sale?'

Toni slid me a roguish grin from under a thick beetle-black fringe, 'So you want to buy?'

'No,' muttered Alan decisively.

'We'd like to look,' I interjected tetchily.

'No we don't.'

'Do.'

'Good. Well come and see me tomorrow. Here's my card.'

The following day, we found ourselves bumping up the very same track I have slogged along today. From the back of Toni's smart four-wheel drive with its spotless olive interiors and subtle scent of Dior's Eau Sauvage, I could see rising before us a vast stone wreck, beaten in, forlorn and unloved, its windows tiny black indents crossed with metal like decayed teeth in a brace. Small holes peppered the facade from which pigeons, like police marksmen, would poke their heads, ducking back in when they heard any noise. As we walked across the courtyard a metal sign hanging drunkenly on its side announced in gaudy red and rusted letters: '*CUIDADO CON EL PERRO*'.

'The dog has gone, I presume?'

'Of course,' sniggered Toni, tutting at me. 'Is probably dead.'

'The *finca*'s in a bit of a state. When was it last occupied?'

'Old people lived here, you know. Now they dead and there are, as we say, *muchas* brothers. Maybe there will be problem with *esciptura*, the title deeds of the house. Is lot of work. Come, I have many other houses with no problems.'

I shot Alan a look. 'What do you think?'

'What do you want me to think?'

'It's an incredible place.'

'Hmm, and free, I suppose?'

We explored the interior of the house, opening rotten, worm-infested shutters to let in the light. It was like a Mallorcan equivalent of Satis House in *Great Expectations* and for a moment I half expected to see a mantilla clad Senyora Havisham claw her way down the ancient, creaking staircase. Gigantic cobwebs with arthritic limbed spiders hung in loops from the ceilings, and long battalion lines of centipedes, ants, moths and beetles shrivelled with age lay perished on their backs in every room as if defeated in some ancient battle of the antennae and proboscis.

Several floors had caved in as well as part of the roof which now let in rough wedges of bright light above our heads. Old wooden beams supporting ceilings still intact had been ravaged by insects and, when poked with a stick, released small explosions of splintered wood and dust. Bizarrely, every room was sparsely furnished and decorated with random objects enshrined in dust, as if the geriatric tenants were still occupying the place but had given up on any housekeeping. Propped up against a mould-ravaged wall in the kitchen stood a rickety-legged, water-stained pine table. Choked with thick grey soot, it housed a clutter of yellowing church pamphlets curled at the edges, festering mugs with chipped rims and two empty brown beer bottles. Cheap religious memorabilia hung on the walls and lined a chipboard cabinet in the dining room and in a downstairs bedroom, above an ornate mahogany bed, a beseeching Jesus looked on, eyes upturned to his heavenly Father, rosary in hand. On a sideboard in the hall, a small metal framed print of the Madonna, her head ripped off so that the torn paper billowed around her shoulders like a snowy stole, stood stoically, awaiting its eventual fate. At the Virgin's feet, a sepia photograph of an old couple dressed in *pagès*, 'country folk' garb, and smiling shyly, lay grubby and creased. I picked it up, wiped it on my shorts and gently put it in my bag. Up on the landing we discovered a depiction of Saint Francis of Assisi, with obese and grotesque Friar Tuck dimensions, holding a mouse which he appeared to be kissing or devouring, depending on your perspective. Toni and I wandered around the dark, claustrophobic rooms upstairs, with their grimy concrete floors and small window holes obscured by black iron grills. The rooms led one to the other across the top floor of the house like a series of empty dungeons whose prisoners had escaped. Alan, who had gone ahead of us, stood transfixed at a window in his own reverie, gazing through the bars out to the garden and field beyond.

As we explored the various outhouses, we came across a table hewn out of old pine, its surface rough and dyed red, and sliced up as though Mad Max had been let loose on it. Several rusty instruments of torture, saws, knives and axes drooped from a lax piece of filthy rope overhead.

'Is slaughter table, *si*,' said Toni with mock solemnity. 'Many lives have ended here.'

'Just humans, I hope?'

'Mostly,' he grinned, 'But occasionally a pig or hen.'

The basement held the greatest revelation. Left as it must have been for twenty odd years, the air smelt dank and sweet and white paint powdered on our clothes as they scraped the inner wall on the way down the dark, crumbling steps. Lining every wall were bottle upon bottle of hand pickled preserves, olives and onions, cucumbers and tomatoes, fruits and liqueurs, all intact in simple glass bottles, their contents outliving their elderly owners. Hanging down over our heads were row upon row of dried tomatoes, basil and rosemary, cracked and gnarled with age but still holding the colour and vague aroma of their kind.

'This could make a great guest bedroom,' I mumbled to myself.

'Or a tomb,' my Scotsman rejoined laconically.

We stumbled back up into the main *entrada*, a dark hall with rank, mildewed walls and a pitted concrete floor.

'We'll take it.'

Toni examined his shoes and Alan looked at the Madonna for inspiration but she had already lost her head.

In an effort at male solidarity, Toni frowned slightly. 'Senyor, is important you see shower and toilet first.'

Alan growled almost imperceptibly. 'I didn't think there was a bathroom.'

'No. Is no bathroom. They used garden.'

We crept uncertainly behind him up the back garden to a wooden shelter covered with a dirty, rain-ravaged, pinstriped cotton curtain partially ripped off its wooden rod. It was hiding something grim within, I knew that much. A hole gaped at us from the ground. We had plumbed new lavatorial depths. And the shower?

'Is green hose over back door. Goes from drain above so when rain falls you have shower.' Nice touch.

'All mod cons,' Alan intoned dryly.

'Well, we still want it,' I persisted.

Alan fixed me with one of his cool gazes. 'Exactly which bank were you planning to raid?'

'But it's so cheap and think what you could do with all that land!'

As a keen horticulturist, he had already sussed out the landscaping possibilities for himself so wasn't going to be seduced by the insincere sales spiel of an inexpert gardener like me who couldn't tell a hibiscus from a hydrangea.

'Look, we're not buying a mule here! This is a house and we don't have the money.'

'So you like it?' I beamed victoriously.

'It's not a question of what I like. We came to Mallorca for a holiday, not a house.'

'And ended up doing the reverse. That's the thrill.'

'Anyway, what would we do with it?'

'We'll think of something.'

Toni shuffled outside the front door, too polite to interrupt a potential marital dispute. I followed him out moments later and told him that we were going to buy it. He raised his eyebrows slightly and stole a glance at my husband.

'What would you do with her?' Alan said to Toni with an exasperated grin, offering his hands out wide in a gesture of defeat. 'There's only one thing for it.'

And with that he drew a large cigar from his pocket and popped it defiantly in between his teeth, certain for once that I wouldn't dare say a word.

I'm slammed out of my reverie and back into reality with the sound of a deep rumbling far up the track. A procession of tipsy lorries are weaving their way unsteadily over pot holes, large gashes in the road and pools of muddy water left from the previous night's storm. Ollie has somehow inveigled his way into the passenger seat of the front truck and leans out of the open window quietly surveying the scene before him. Alan toots enthusiastically at me from the hire car, his eyes bright with anticipation and a wide beam on his face. Surreptitiously, head slightly lowered, he draws deeply on a cigar butt before ejecting it adroitly from the car window on nearing the house. He doesn't seem to think I've noticed. He parks the car under a carob tree, leaps out from his seat and saunters over to me across the gravel. It looks like we've arrived.

TWO

LONDON: AUGUST

Sunday 5 p.m., Oxford Street

Ed has bought me *The Fearless Flier's Handbook*. I laugh loudly.
It's the sort of puerile joke that appeals to us both. This time he
remonstrates earnestly.

'No, Scatters,' he yelps in between bouts of guffaws, using his
nickname for me from university days. 'I really think it might
help. If you've got to commute from Mallorca to London each
month, you've got to conquer your fear of flying.'

Ed is a nervous traveller and uses tranquillisers and various
potions from his mobile emergency kit, otherwise known
as MEK, to assist him in times of high stress; but then Ed's
problems are a tad more severe than mine. I mean Ed can't
get on a train without a respirator and a dozen pills from
the various pouches in his survival bag, which he carries
everywhere with him. As for the London underground, forget
it. Ed works as a producer at the BBC and is always in a state of
high anxiety when he needs to make business trips. On these
fearful occasions, he plans his route meticulously, packing his

MEK with loving care, or he doesn't go at all. Once or twice I have peeked inside this voluminous bag and registered:

Two packs of Nurofen
Inhaler x 4
Portable electric fan
Two-litre bottle of Evian water
Family size box of Kleenex
Tweezers and scissors
Plasters and bandages
Eight bottles of different coloured pills
Two small bottles of dubious liquid
Eight chocolate muffins
Packet of Jaffa Cakes
Two family size bars of Cadbury's chocolate
Tuna sandwich
Flask of coffee
Imperial mints
Copy of *Private Eye*
Book with obscure title
Portable CD player and multiple classical CDs

The MEK is no ordinary bag. It's a vortex. In the footsteps of Gladstone, Ed seems to be able to pack endless amounts of medicinal items inside his bag without ever filling the thing. Perhaps the day he tries to flat pack a mobile doctor, nurse and man of the cloth, he may come unstuck.

I look out of the window at the rain tumbling down on Oxford Street. Shoppers are fleeing for the tube stations, umbrellas to the wind. Most look beyond misery. We are sitting in Starbucks, two cappuccinos in paper cups between us. Proper china is off the menu which really irks me.

'Do you think you'll ever visit me in Mallorca?' I ask quietly.

'God. No!' he splutters into his coffee. 'You wouldn't catch me on a plane.'

I regard him with some alarm.

He quickly changes tack. 'Well, no, I mean, flying is really safe now. I'm just a bit paranoid. Hopeless really. Not brave like you.'

I open the book at a random sentence and read to him out loud: '"My fundamental goal in the Fearless Fliers course is to help people realize that they have no control over the aircraft or the pilot…" That's just great, Ed. I feel such immense relief just reading that.'

'Oh come on! You can't just pick out a line. You've got to give it a chance. You're so impetuous.'

I read on, '"Most people who develop a fear of flying are what we call worriers." You don't say?!'

'Look, if you're going to be sarcastic, I'll take it back.'

He grabs at it but I evade him. 'I think it's going to be an inspiration. I'm serious, really. Thanks, Ed.' I throw him one of my indulgent smiles which I know he hates.

How long have Ed and I known each other? It seems like a trillion years. I think I know him better than he does, and he thinks the same about me. We're both wrong, though. Ed is what others less endowed with brains would call a boffin. He's an academic with a first in English, a PhD and a swag bag of secret neuroses that the most fervent Freud couldn't unravel, though many have tried. But then that's part of his magic, his lure. Ed is naturally a dedicated hypochondriac and also has a weight problem. He starts a diet one day and eats the book the next with a generous dollop of mayonnaise. Exercise seems a complete waste of time to him when he could compose a brilliant piece of jazz on the piano, immerse himself on the Internet or consume a segment of a novel in the same time. Can I blame him? No. Ed's other problem is money. He never has any because he fritters his salary on endless phone calls to fantasy women he encounters on the web who invariably hail from the States and have names like Laurel, Roxanne, Ivy-League and Cup Cake. But at the end of the day – and God, don't I hate that phrase – Ed is the best friend you could have, with or without his foibles.

'What is it that kills, I mean, concerns you most about flying?' he stutters over a ton of chocolate cake which he tries to cram into his mouth all at once.

'Oh, everything really. First there's the random BING BING sound at the beginning of the flight when little lights start twitching up and down the cabin…'

His hazel eyes widen in horror.

'… then the surge of power as the plane takes off, wings shaking like beaten whippets, followed by a weird sound of scraping metal and a grinding noise that deepens into a violent juddering like an unstoppable pneumatic drill. Then comes a loud DONG DONG over the intercom and the air hostesses' nostrils are flared and a look of terror creeps into their eyes as they unclip their belts and…'

Ed loosens his collar. 'Stop, stop, for crying out loud! You'll give me palpitations. That's it, I'm never getting on a plane again.'

Monday 7.45 a.m., the Pimlico pad

I'm alone in my basement flat with the *Today* programme pontificating from the kitchen radio and breakfast television simpering from the bedroom. I'm already late but I can't blame it on this, my first monthly commute from Mallorca, since I arrived here yesterday afternoon. I just didn't set the alarm properly. Careering from room to room, cup of black tea in hand, I scoop up files, pens, mobile phone, diary, make-up, keys and wallet like a possessed vacuum cleaner with my free hand tipping these items messily into my handbag. I've got to get to a meeting in fifteen minutes. Should I catch a cab, or is the tube quicker? A hurried snoop under the living room blind reveals a heavy downpour outside. Ye gods! What's wrong with this country? It's always raining. This is still August, isn't it? I sift through stuff in the walk-in cupboard. No umbrella. Damn it. I rush out into the dark and windowless rectangular corridor, once described by a zealous estate agent as a dining hall. What a joke.

Swinging the bag over my shoulder, I pick up my briefcase and treble lock the front door. Our communal block has an archaic lift with creaky wrought-iron inner gates that, like a concertina, have to be pulled back to open. Although it reaches the basement and stops just outside my door and that of my neighbour, I'm not lazy enough to use it in place of the stairs. I pass the dark and creepy boiler room and bolt up the narrow steps to the main landing. It is sombre and covered with the kind of dreary, pea-green wool carpet that adorns so many of these sort of respectable central London blocks. The arched ceiling and elegant coving lend a rather faded grandeur to the place but the paintwork is slapdash and hardened dribbles of magnolia paint hang precipitously from the corners of dado rails and the skirting board is scuffed and grimy.

I just manage to reach the brightly lit communal front entrance when the lift door opens behind me and out puffs our resident Lord.

'Ah, what ho? Back from Milan are you?' He squints at me through his half-moon spectacles, a large girth and froth of navel hair peeping out from the frayed waistband of his stripy, cotton Jermyn Street pyjamas. I have never seen him wear anything else. Presumably he stops short of wearing them in the House of Lords.

'Mallorca, William.' It still feels strange calling my neighbourly Lord by his first name but he always insists.

'Marvellous place, Italy. Here for a holiday?'

'Hardly, I'm working. I'll be back and forth from Spain every month now. I'm living there but working here. A double life, William.'

He gives me a wink and bellows cheerfully, 'Good girl! Send my love to Fraser.'

I don't know who Fraser is but imagine he thinks he's my husband. Is the name Alan so hard to remember? Over the years, Lord Jim Jam, as we affectionately call him, has called him everything from Stuart to Macduff. Lord Jim Jam shuffles over to the mail tray and scrutinises each letter, holding the individual envelopes of our neighbours up to the light. I wonder if he's searching for postal orders but he catches my eye and mumbles about precautionary security measures. I fly into the weepy street, dash in front of a moving cab and brace myself when it screeches to a halt. The young cabbie clicks his teeth at me. 'You must have a good guardian angel. Roads are like glass today. Where you going then?'

'Piccadilly and don't spare the petrol.'

He looks back at me through the mirror as we speed along with a curious look on his face. 'In a hurry, are we?'

'Always.'

'Gotta take it easy or you'll do your head in.'

'Oh, I let others do that for me throughout the day.' I smile crisply at him.

My bag starts shivering at my side and I wonder if it's coming down with flu. Then I hear the familiar bawling of Judas from within. Oh here we go. 'Hello?'

It's Rachel, my saviour from the office, wondering where I am.

'No, I didn't miss the plane. Got in yesterday afternoon. I'll be there in five minutes. Can you hold the fort?'

Rachel could hold off a whole army single-handedly. She's a no-nonsense cookie, a human battery, constantly charged and in control and always even-tempered. Maybe I used to be like that once.

We've arrived. The cabbie gives me a wave and I scuttle down a cut-through into St James's and through the glass doors of Havana Leather to be greeted by camp Richard, the showroom sales manager. He's sporting tight yellow chinos and twirling towards me like a game show host with first question in hand. It turns out to be an order pad for coffee.

'Ooh. Just made it by the skin of your teeth, lovie, and you've got spots of rain on that gorgeous suit! It'll dry, don't fret.'

I won't.

'Our George is upstairs with the lovely Rachel. Can I get you a cappuccino?'

I nod, straighten my crumpled suit and walk up the marble staircase. To think that less than twenty-four hours ago I was sitting on my Mallorcan terrace watching the sun rise over the mountains.

George Myers is a forty-five year old *enfant terrible* who runs a luxury leather company beloved by the nouveau riche, idle and star-struck. His client list reads like a FTSE 100 Top Luvvies and his new-found fame has won him a clique of shiny showbiz friends who share his table at The Ivy and enjoy his generous discounts at the shop. George has been a client for 10 years and despite my unwavering cynicism in his presence, he bears me a grudging respect. When I first knew him, he ran a small leather workshop in Hackney and together we built up the brand's reputation so that it became the darling of the media. To the press I portrayed George as a cheeky East End boy who done good, sent them wooing gifts throughout the year, and wined and dined the fashion and shopping editors until their every waking thought was of Havana Leather. We jointly went on an assault of the business editors, earnestly portraying George as the best of British, humble roots but with a talent to match the best designers in Europe. In truth, he was a brilliant craftsman, a visionary in design but also a selfish and ruthless bully. He enjoyed belittling staff, threatening small suppliers and reducing his young secretary to tears. An inveterate debunker, he relished needling the fragile egos of the insecure fashionista press as they embroidered their copy with ludicrous sprinklings of hyperbole and absurd product descriptions.

'It's a WALLET, Amy!' he would blast good-naturedly over lunch with one of these thin, spectre-like scribes. 'What's a skinny-hipped, louche leather secret weapon when it's at home? Don't they teach you how to write plain English at journo school?'

It was these frequent outbursts with the press that persuaded me never to let him loose on the media alone unless bound like a mummy and wearing a yashmak for good measure.

Over the years George has become greedy. He enjoys success but, like an incurable alcoholic, he can't curb his principal vice. Spending money. Employees go without pay, invoices languish unpaid, but Greedy George continues to buy up half the goods in Bond Street, hangs out in the best dining emporiums and clubs, purchases the latest top-of-the-range four-wheel drive and every electronic gadget on the market. He has a three-storied house in South Kensington with olive green shutters and Tyrolean window boxes overflowing with lavender, which he shares with his agelastic and captious wife, Bianca, a waif-like Philippino housekeeper called Consuela and a West Highland terrier named Harris. George believes there is only room for one child in his household and he's already snaffled that role. His holidays are spent at his Tuscan villa or in luxury spas around the globe with his wife, where he convinces himself that his sumo-proportioned body is shrinking with every Ayurvedic massage. Inevitably, he returns fatter than ever.

I walk into his Philippe Starck-inspired office with its glass walls and sleek leather furnishings. Greedy George is lolling in a deep maroon leather chair holding forth while Rachel sits spellbound opposite. She's faking it. His face breaks into a grin when he sees me.

'Ah, guv! Thought you'd got on the wrong bus or should I say, plane?' Hoarse laughter.

'Where are you up to?' I exchange a furtive wink with Rachel and pull out a chair by the enormous glass meeting table.

'We're just discussing the forthcoming winter range. George has created a fascinating new product.'

I eye her carefully. She looks away. George heaves himself up and wanders over to a cardboard box on the table. He fumbles inside with his pulpy hands and throws me a plastic bag with what looks like – please God, no – a leather lizard inside. I've seen enough of the real thing in the last few weeks in Mallorca to last me several life times. 'It's a lizard.'

'Don't miss a trick, do you, guv?'

I hold it in my hand and peer into its face. It's about twelve inches long, olive green, and has black beaded eyes. The leather is soft and on the back I notice there are tiny perforations. Why? I grapple with its underbelly and spot a small Velcro strip which when ripped open reveals a netted cavity inside. I'm mystified. The neck, I notice, is hidden by what looks like a miniature collar but when squeezed it releases an internal spring and the head juts out and nods from left to right in a sinister way. I jump back.

'Well it's certainly worthy of a Stephen King movie.'

'Are you this rude to your other clients?'

'No, you have exclusive rights.'

George breaks into a chuckle. 'Since you're so bleeding thick, permit me to present my new masterpiece, The Lounge Lizard!'

Rachel is driving the point of her pen into her palm in a desperate attempt to keep a straight face.

'So, what does our lounge lizard do exactly?' I smile sweetly.

'Don't take that patronising tone with me, guv,' he gurgles with mirth. 'This is the new Nodding Dog. Everyone used to have them in their cars, didn't they?'

'No.'

'Yeh, well, Snooty Pants, I wouldn't have expected you to have one, would I?' he scoffs. 'Anyway, this isn't just a novelty toy. It's an anti-stress air freshener for cars, desks, wherever you want to put it.'

I feel inside the lizard's hollow stomach. 'Ah, I think I see. You put a pot pourri sachet in here?'

'Pot pourri sachet?! How naff can you get? No, it's a silk and muslin pouch infused with Eastern calming oils.'

'How long does it last?' I ask starchily.

'I've had one on trial in my car for a month. Losing its whiff now so I reckon we could hit the punter for a three month supply and then clobber him for some other gear when he comes back for more refills.'

I feel my lip curling at the edges. The world really has gone mad.

'It's certainly a one-off, George.'

'Come on, admit it, guv, I'm a genius?'

'Possibly.'

Greedy George frowns, 'Where's bloody Ricardo? He only had to fetch three cappuccinos for crying out loud.' He pounces on the door and shouts down the stairs, 'Oi, Twinkle Toes! Get your arse up here with those coffees.'

Soft footsteps follow and an aggrieved Richard arrives with steaming paper cups and a plate of croissants.

'Now, where were we?' Greedy George grins, smearing a croissant with a thick layer of butter and jam.

11 a.m., the City

And where did all the cabs go? It's bucketing with rain and I've just left Rachel's initialled umbrella at my last meeting place. It must have cost a fortune. Have I got time to go back for it? No. When am I going to get back to the office to clear all my e-mails? I look at my watch. I've a conference call at noon with my new

American client, Bryan Patterson of the Aphrodite Corporation, and then, horror of horrors, a meeting with Prudence Braithwaite at Roselock Fine Jewellery. Despite the company's rocky state, she and the owner, Michael Roselock, struggle on like a pair of obstinate mules. Have I the strength? Now in desperate need of an umbrella. Where's a Boots when you need one?

1.18 p.m., the West End
I scramble from the tube and up drizzly Piccadilly on foot, all the while dodging the battery of black umbrellas wielded like lethal weapons by those charging towards me along the pavement. Bedraggled and breathless I hurtle through the shiny revolving doors of the restaurant and up a flight of marble steps to the front desk. My hair's still dripping. I'm a mess and late. It's never good to keep a journalist waiting, even though I've known Dresden longer than Barbie's known Ken. A cloakroom attendant approaches me but seeing that I have neither raincoat nor umbrella, scuttles away wordlessly. A tense young woman in a dark trouser suit looks up my reservation in a black desk diary, her long blond tresses brushing the page, and with a red biro brusquely ticks off my name as if I'm a child arriving late for school. A queue has formed behind me and she's keen to move me on.

'One of my colleagues will show you through,' she says curtly without bothering to look up from her desk. Stalking towards me is a supercilious young man in a slate grey suit with crimson lining who impatiently leads me through the tables. I notice he steals a cursory, critical glance at my rain-splattered clothes. The restaurant is already crowded, but there are lone diners, the seats next to them vacant, edgily skim-reading copies of the *Evening Standard* or sipping on water, hoping that they haven't been stood up. The place is noisy with chatter, and frenetic waiters, sleek in black attire, waft by, trays held aloft. This, at least, is a place of refuge without lounge lizards and lunatics on the menu although several can be seen slumped at the tables.

'Darling!' drawls Dresden, leaping from his seat like a perky imp. 'Where have you been?' He air kisses my cheeks and then rolls his dark eyes at my dishevelled appearance. '*Quelle horreur*! No umbrella?'

I sit down quickly, aware of the titters of other diners as they study my guest with fascination. Today, Dresden Watts is coiffed to perfection, his hair in a quiff and his body enveloped in tight black leather with a jabot at the neck and white ruffs masking his wrists. A staggeringly large emerald glints from the little finger of his right hand. He is a would-be London dandy, an impresario and dilettante extraordinaire. He is also Asian and devilishly handsome. Waggling a white napkin flamboyantly at a passing waiter, he orders two glasses of Krug. I'm relieved that this lunch is on Greedy George since Dresden and I are meeting for the sole purpose of discussing Havana Leather.

'So, what's new, pussycat?' he purrs.

I fumble in my bag and throw a leather lizard across the table. He flinches and pulls back as if about to be struck by a viper. 'What is that?'

Ten minutes later Dresden is in full flow, mapping out a story he thinks will be great for the *Evening Standard* about designer leather toys for stressed executives.

'Dear George is a genius,' he enthuses, dabbing at his mouth with the corners of his napkin. 'Just think, a luscious lizard that exudes the exotic fragrance of the East.'

I observe him thoughtfully. A crazy image fills my head of a leather-clad Dresden enthroned on my Mallorcan porch, his perfectly groomed hands fondling a nodding lizard while the builders, torsos stripped bare and tools lying slack in their hands, stand entranced as they contemplate this hallowed symbol of London life. I'm jolted back to the table by the din of clattering plates and knives.

'So,' says Dresden, 'when can I interview George?'

5.30 p.m., in the office, Mayfair

I'm opening my forty-ninth e-mail of the day. The office is hot and airless and beyond the double-glazed window I can hear the drone of London traffic. The telephone rings. It's Alan in enthusiastic mode.

'It's scorching here,' he's saying. 'I've had to change my shirt twice today. Ollie's worn me out playing football all afternoon. How is it with you?'

'Stuffy and sticky. Is Ollie OK?'

'He's on great form. We're off to the beach for a quick swim and then a fish supper in the port.'

I feel a twinge of envy. I'd much rather be joining them for dinner in the local port than eating a Tesco ready meal on my own in the flat.

'Anything exciting to report?'

'Well you'll never believe it but we've been invited to a refurbishment party at the Banca March. Can you imagine that happening in London?'

I give a cynical grunt. 'I think not.'

In truth, the local Banca March cannot be described as a bank in the current British sense. Although totally up to date with the latest technology it still possesses one key ingredient now sadly missing from our own financial emporiums – humanity. It may be that in the past British banks were the same, with cheerful and understanding managers and staff who could remember your name and treated you as a friend but I've never known it in my time. In the mountains at our local branch it is like that. Ever since we moved to Mallorca and opened a bank account Tolo, the deputy manager, has been like a guardian angel, offering us advice in perfect English, accompanying us to the town's *notaría*, the notary's office, when we bought our *finca*, and turning a blind eye to the occasional blip in our account when builders' bills have, at times, overstretched our already strained finances. We know the names of all the staff, and pop by just for a chat when shopping in the town. I find it touching that we have been invited to this local celebration.

Alan's full of the joys. 'The party's not actually until October. A little do from noon it says on the invitation.'

'You will accept?'

'Of course,' says Alan with vigour. 'Tolo would be hurt if we didn't go.'

I'm sure Tolo isn't of such a sensitive disposition but I find Alan's loyalty to him rather endearing. Someone knocks gently on the half-open door. It's Rachel. I put the phone down.

'That was Alan. We've been invited to our local bank's refurb party, isn't it a hoot?'

She gives me an old-fashioned look. 'I can't think of anything more boring. Besides, I don't know a soul at my bank and certainly wouldn't want to.'

'Ah, but it's different in the mountains, Rachel. Our bank's wonderful.'

'Yeh, right,' she rasps. 'Have you been on the happy pills again?'

I poke my tongue out at her.

'Anyway, on to more pressing matters. Are you getting changed here or at the do?'

'The what?' A panic grips me. Crikey. The Cosmetic Guild's annual bash. How could I have forgotten? Isn't it tomorrow night? No, of course not. That's Patterson's media party for 300 guests and we're organising it, silly! Charismatic Bryan Patterson, Queen of the Aphrodite Corporation in New York, a client whose account my entire team would work on free of charge, given the chance.

Rachel is unperturbed. 'I'd better get one of the girls to jump in a taxi and pick up some clothes from your flat, otherwise, Cinders, you won't make it to the ball.'

I gratefully throw her my door keys while writing out instructions for whomever of my long suffering staff has agreed to accomplish the task. They'll need to find everything from jewellery and hosiery to make-up and shoes in my jumble sale of a bedroom. Mind you, they've all done it enough times.

'Oh and we've got team drinks in half an hour. I thought you might like to reassure the troops that you'll be back and forth each month now.'

I feel like Brown Owl about to deliver a campfire talk.

'Can't you do it?' I plead.

'No, that's not an option,' she thumps me lightly on the head with a file she's carrying and says with irony, 'By the way, George Myers rang to thank you for giving that lizard to Dresden. He's doing an interview with him on Friday.'

I begin to picture the headline and story:

Lounge Lizard Craze Hits London
It's only a toy, but a twelve-inch Moroccan leather lizard costing seventy-five pounds that shakes its head and exudes an intoxicating fragrance has caused hysterical scenes in the capital today. Designer George Myers of exclusive Mayfair store Havana Leather, created the lizard as an executive anti-stress device, never expecting it to develop into a craze.

'I put its success down to Posh & Becks who bought up the lot and now I'm waiting for new supplies,' said George Myers.

Angry riots erupted outside the showroom in the early hours of this morning when it became clear that new stocks would not be available until tomorrow...

A sharp cough shifts me out of my reverie.

'A penny for them,' says Rachel before closing the door.

Tuesday 2 a.m., the Pimlico pad
I'm watching the news. Actually I'm staring at BBC News 24 while propped up in my voluminous bed, a pile of annotated notes, two out-of-date copies of *Private Eye* and a *Spectator* on my lap. News is addictive and because I have no television in

Mallorca, I'm staring at the screen with the rapt attention of a voyeur at a bedroom window. I find it impossible to switch off in case I miss something, something heart-stopping, like the latest hourly bulletin about war and strife in the Middle East or wherever else the world's events have moved. In public relations circles we switch restaurants and hairdressers at the drop of a newspaper. In global politics, they swap their war terrain at the drop of a despot.

Somehow, since I was last here the news has taken on a more sinister mantle. The stories seem darker, the murders more gruesome, the violence on the streets more tangible yet, perversely my eyes are rooted to the news spot on the television screen or drinking up every last drop of ink on the page of a newspaper as if to goad myself into a state of terror. By contrast, in Mallorca the most nail-biting headline is likely to herald inclement weather, cancellation of a fiesta or inauguration of a new mayor. Perhaps our media should carry a government health warning.

I get out of bed and go over to the wardrobe. It's bulging with city battle dress; suits, a few expensive ones, and last night's cocktail dress, hooked lopsidedly on a hanger. Too much stuff. Did I ever really wear all this clobber? As for my casual clothes, they have been sent to Mallorca where I shall be spending most of my time, my life. What remains here is a working wardrobe, whatever that's supposed to mean. My wardrobe has never earned a penny. It's a slob. It just dispenses clothes everyday and taunts me when I can't find a vital part of an outfit. I swear it hides belts and shoes, or maybe, as in *The Lion, the Witch and the Wardrobe*, a secret world lies beyond. I push my arm through the bulk of suits and hit a wall on the other side. There are definitely no trees. I feel a pang of disappointment and potter off to the phone. I dial 123. A synthetic male voice announces frigidly, 'At the third stroke the time, sponsored by Accurist, will be 2.08 and 40 seconds.' I'm annoyed. Why does everything have to be sponsored these days? We never used to have any of that nonsense. I'm sounding like my Irish grandmother.

Perhaps I should try to sleep. I pace up and down the room, aware of the soft wool carpet contracting beneath my feet. A restless lion in a fur-lined cage. It's a strange, lonely sort of time to be awake in the city. There's a dull hum of traffic in the distance and I can just about hear rain dripping methodically from the gutter above the window. I peer under the blind and through the iron bars up to the starless sky and then to the sodden patio. Leaves have clogged up the drain and a discarded, empty packet of cigarettes is rotating in the scum and water. Some drunk or yob must have thrown it down. It happens every day. A large pile of rubble, like a tired old man, sits dejectedly in a corner, the remnants of a neighbour's crumbling wall that was never repaired. Here I am in my own private prison, protected from an invisible enemy. I slump back on the bed, longing to pick up the phone and speak to a human voice, and wondering what I'm doing here in this cramped flat, more like a lock-up, stifled with the trappings of city life which now seem so alien to me. I'm missing a soft sky pregnant with stars, chanting cicadas and the smell of jasmine floating on the breeze. And above all, I miss space and peace. Suddenly I want to be back home, curled up next to the homely Scot in our simple, white walled room with its gnarled beams and shutters, with the balmy, fragrant mountain air seeping through the bedroom shutters and fluttering about the sheets. For the first time ever, I'm even missing Alan's habitual snoring although I'd never admit it. God forbid! I begin to yearn for my bedtime story reading with Ollie, those secret moments of communication alone with my son, as the clicking cicadas and frogs croon outside his window. My family now feels like it belongs there, back on Mallorca, and tonight in London I feel like a lone tourist in search of some guidebook to help me make sense of my life here again.

A coach whooshes by in the distance and then there's a wail of sirens as two speeding police cars pelt up a nearby street, their tyres squealing in the rain as they spin round a corner. Then silence. I sip at a glass of water, forcibly make myself switch off the television, hurl everything from the bed and extinguish the light. I'm exhausted. Time to go home.

THREE

DOWNING TOOLS

This is what I hate about flying. You're given a departure time on your ticket but in truth it's just nonsense. What actually happens is that you merely board the plane at that time, taking off at the airport's leisure. Then again I'm on a no frills airline for which delay is a hallmark. Still, I'm en route back to Mallorca so things could be worse. I've brought *The Fearless Flier's Handbook* with me but immediately regret that I didn't think to wrap it in a false cover. Come on, to flaunt the title, rather like sporting an 'I love Cliff Richard' T-shirt on board, would be begging for ridicule from passengers and crew alike. I pull the book furtively out of my bag, turning the front cover back on itself. The man by the window appears to have dozed off. I hate him already. I am sitting in an aisle seat, row two to be exact, with an uninterrupted view of the air hostess's jump seat. Given that there is no allocation of seats on these budget airlines, this is some achievement. It took a serious amount of artifice and grievous bodily harm inflicted on my fellow passengers to end up here. As soon as they started calling us to the plane, I had leapt up, elbowed and kicked the early birds out of the way, and hobbled dramatically to the desk.

'Your ticket number is 98. That means you have to wait,' snapped a male attendant.

I groaned and writhed horribly.

'What's wrong?'

'I've had an operation.' Then in a whisper, 'It's a little personal and embarrassing.'

He reddened. 'Oh, er, well you'd better go ahead.'

Once out of view, I had walked briskly onto the plane and bagged my favourite seat. Was it necessary to lie or to abuse other passengers? Yes. Look, when you're a nervous flier, you will do anything to ease your inner hysteria. Like superstitious actors who carry their favourite amulets to the theatre, we fractious fliers take comfort from sitting in certain seats on flights, particularly if they are near exits, cabin crew, flight deck or drinks trolley.

The air hostess has returned to her seat and is fastening her belt. We've had the seat belt check which I presume is to stop maniacs like me from leaping for the exit just before take off, and then there's the demonstration about what to do when landing on water. We drown, don't we? Still, even in death's claws, we are strongly advised to remove high heel shoes and to secure our own oxygen mask before helping others with theirs. You bet, buddy. The plane is crawling towards the runway like a hearse and small lights are glinting in the dusk on the vast expanse of tarmac. In the dimmed cabin I can still read my watch face. It's nearly nine o'clock and the man next to me is snoring, his head and shoulders lolling over the vacant seat between us. I'm tempted to shake his arm and say, 'For heaven's sake, what the hell do you think you're doing? Do you realise, bonehead, that this is probably your last moment of consciousness?'

Instead, I turn my head away, intently scrutinising the face of the ever-so-young air hostess sitting ahead of me by the exit. How old can she be? No more than 20, I'd guess, and how on earth would she cope in an emergency? Badly, that's how. I close my eyes for a split second. BING! What's that? I bob my head out into the aisle to study her face. The features are foggy in the half-light but she remains seated and calm or is she just frozen in terror? There's a huge roaring sound and the plane is going faster and faster, racing out of control up, up and now practically vertical, and my mouth turns dry. Suddenly there's a strange creaking sound and a low humming. The ground below has become a huge chessboard listing from side to side. I strain to see the face of the air hostess which now looks like wax in the moonlight, her hands lying flat on her lap, her body pert and prim as if she's attending a church service. Maybe she's praying.

BONG! BONG! That's it! We're done for. Perhaps we're losing cabin pressure? I can hear an ominous hiss like air being released from a punctured beach ball and again another BING! She's up this time, unlocking her belt and grabbing the internal phone. Who is she calling? Is it the captain or a colleague at the back of the plane? Is she suggesting dispersal of life jackets or a communal mass? The cabin lights up, people yawn and my sleeping partner continues to grunt. We're still alive.

It's past midnight and I'm in a taxi coursing along dark country lanes, gulping in balmy and fragrant air from the open window while the driver hums softly, tapping the fingers of his right hand against the wheel. The car's headlights burrow into the blackness, briefly exposing scurrying rats, hedgehogs, rabbits and topaz-eyed bats in its glare. We reach the long and stony track that leads to the house. It is barely wide enough for a vehicle and my driver slows down, opening the door to inspect the significant drop on one side.

'It's only an orchard down there,' I say mischievously in faltering Spanish.

He whistles and clucks at me, '*Madre mia!*'

A few minutes later I'm in the courtyard watching him carefully reverse around large scattered obstacles left by the builders. The taxi rumbles slowly back down the track, laboriously picking its way over the stones like a giant beetle in a rockery. Soon the lights are no more than tiny white dots, fireflies in the obscurity, and the sound of the engine disappears into the night. Silence. I stand with my case at my feet, listening. There is a sudden hooting high above and an owl swoops over the trees. A hawk scuds by screeching wildly. To the side of me the rhythmic purring of the cicadas begins and a weird quack, not quite that of a duck, breaks out in the pond. Something plops in the water, and then a small leaping silhouette crash-lands soundlessly on to a terracotta tile balanced on the pond's edge. My eyes adjust to the darkness around me and there, surveying me impassively, is a large bullfrog – or is it a toad? He turns his head for a second and emits a strange crackly sound, not a croak. It is startling and I crunch back on the gravel at the sound. He dive-bombs into the pond with a tremendous splash. It's not only the geckos that have a weight problem around here.

As I bend to lift my case, two bats rustle overhead and suddenly I am aware of a fine gossamer sky, light pewter in hue and sprinkled with what seems like thousands of miniscule shards of shiny white glass. Mesmerised, I sink to the ground and lie face up to the sky. These stars are so dazzling that everything around me seems flooded with light as if the darkness is just a figment of my own limited imagination. With a stab of regret I realise that until moving to Mallorca, I rarely stopped to reflect on the infinite beauty of nature. Come to think of it, I rarely stopped to reflect full stop. A gecko darts up a stone pillar close by, unnerved perhaps by this dotty English woman stretched out on the ground in the early hours of the morning. The very thought has me giggling to myself. I put a hand to my mouth to silence any release of laughter. The sharp stones and gravel dig into my back. A door bursts open and the porch light flashes on. Alan, unkempt and clad in cotton pyjama bottoms, is straining to see in the gloom. He calls out my name anxiously but before I can rise, he has glimpsed me lying like a corpse on the ground and rushes down the steps.

'My God! Are you all right? Speak to me?'

I roll over paralytic with laughter, incapable of speech.

I'm sitting against the wall on the half-built *terrassa*, staring out over small heaps of rubble at the hills beyond. The builders have left for the weekend but semi-full bottles of water and unfinished packets of biscuits wedged beneath rocks are sure signs that they'll be back on Monday. I'm longing for a juice from oranges freshly collected from our own trees but it will have to wait for a while. First I must make an effort to don my running gear and tackle a few well-trodden Mallorcan tracks on foot. I only have myself to blame. In a moment of hubris back in London I foolishly agreed to run the London Marathon for The Scientific Exploration Society, a charity close to my heart. Even though friends warned me that it was a serious slog, I didn't believe them until, after my first two-mile run in Hyde Park, I returned home like a cartoon dog, with tongue lolling and my uncoordinated legs skating in all directions.

The temperature is already more than 30°C as I amble lazily along the track in shorts and T-shirt. I feel an irresistible urge to slope back to the garden to curl up in the haphazardly erected hammock under the olive tree but know that would be a real cop out. Thirty minutes later, with a face the colour of ketchup, I limp back, my skin seeping sweat from every pore. I hear a shout and a man, mid-thirties, appears from a house near the mouth of our track. He is munching on a fresh fig and beaming at me. 'Ah! *Una corredora!*'

He switches from local dialect to English. 'Runner, you say in English, *si?*'

Runner? The man's a diplomat. I feel like a doughnut that's been left to fry in the sun.

'How did you know I was English?'

'News travels fast here.' He smiles cordially, ruffling his dark mane of curls with a bronzed hand. Then he bounds over to a nearby fig tree and plucks me off a fruit. 'Here, *un regal*, a little gift. *Benvinguts!* That means, "Welcome!"'

A very nice welcome indeed. I lift up the succulent fruit with its heady aroma and brush its downy skin against my cheek. Can it be true that I've discovered a friendly, welcoming neighbour so soon? This definitely isn't London.

'You like to run? I am runner too. We go together. I am Rafael.'

I'm winded and still contemplating the purchase of a respirator for the rest of my training, so this invitation hits me like a tram.

'Thanks, but I'm really not very good. I need lots of practice. I don't think you and I…'

'*Poc a poc,*' he says, slamming a muscular arm on my back. That's the other lethal Mallorcan expression, like '*No problema*', that I'm getting to dread. Little by little. What that really, really means is that you haven't got a hope in hell of achieving whatever it is your aiming for. In fact, you'll probably go quietly mad first. In between gasps for breath, I tell him my name and attempt an introduction.

'So we're living here, but I'm commuting to England each month.'

He chews on this nugget thoughtfully. 'You like to travel, me too. This is good, but why you move in hottest month? You crazy English!'

'Well, our son has to start his new school in September or there won't be a place. We had to move here now.'

He looks confused. '*Home!* He can go to my son's school! There are many schools. Is not so important.'

Home literally means 'man' in Mallorcan, and is used, I quickly discover, as a general exclamation.

I take a sharp intake of breath. 'Oh well, it's a British school, you know. Not many places.'

'What? You going to drive to Palma every day? *Estas boja?!*'

I agree wholeheartedly with him. Yes, madness is a family trait.

'So now we are friends,' he says brightly.

I sincerely hope so. Besides, he is incredibly cheerful and welcoming, a tad manic and also, I discover, owns the main *pastisseria*, the cake shop, in the town. An irresistible combination of factors.

'You must come up for a drink,' I encourage. 'Meet the family.'

He nods enthusiastically. One day soon, yes, he will visit us. We too must meet Cristian, his nine-year-old son who, he tells me, is in the park walking his boxer, Franco. There's no sign of a wife. He also promises to give me details of a half marathon race which is coming up in Palma soon. It will be such fun and we can compete together, he insists. As I stagger back down the track I ponder on this curious trick of fate that finds my nearest neighbour, in the middle of nowhere, a fervent disciple of running.

We have been here barely a month and yet despite the on-going adversity, I have already grown accustomed to the scene of pine-clad mountains from my window at the top of the house. In no time at all I have exchanged a view of grubby concrete blocks and an unremitting grey London sky for one of breathtaking beauty. And yet chaos reigns around us. From dawn till dusk we share our home with a pack of swarthy, tool wielding strangers yelling good naturedly and interminably in a foreign tongue who clomp around the house and grounds in boots which exude enough sand and grit to fill a new Kalahari Desert. In every room yawning sockets disgorge tufts of gaudy wires, concrete floors remain un-tiled, walls unpainted, plaster crumbles, flatulent bathroom taps expel nothing but hot air, and ants and lizards run rampant throughout the house, but do I care? Somehow one glimpse of the verdant paradise unfurling from my office window makes it all seem OK. I can cope with the sawing and gnawing, the banging and clanging, the plaster disasters, and lack of furniture and amenities. One day, I tell myself, we will look back on this period and laugh. Maybe we'll be straight-jacketed at the time and in the high security psychiatric wing of a mountain hospital, but we'll be laughing.

Sitting at my desk each morning, gazing over the valley in wonder, I sometimes have to pinch myself to believe it's real. Beneath the high ridges and soaring peaks, a chain of brawny, squat hills, like small plump Buddhas, curl around our small market town in a firm, and one hopes, everlasting embrace. The sunlight moves mysteriously along the peaks and by mid morning a white film envelops the higher ridges and clouds settle on the lower plains like candy floss. By early evening, streaks of rich vermilion light spread across the entire Tramuntana range so that its face is suffused with a rosy hue like a happy imbiber of good red wine.

It's already sizzling hot as I sit in an old white T-shirt and shorts, tapping slowly on the computer keys. I take childish glee in not having to wear a suit, make-up, jewellery or even shoes and wonder what on earth my clients in London would make of my dishevelled state. More to the point, am I really bothered? The sense of personal freedom is palpable. The builders, clad in faded shorts and battered trainers, are singing outside in the courtyard, not pop songs but ballads in their native Mallorcan tongue. Everyday this small contingent of workmen arrives at the house to tile a bathroom, fix a door, lay some paving or repair a wall. These are not just cosmetic challenges; some are structural and we will have to grit our teeth and live in a certain amount of turmoil until the *finca* is truly completed.

Although it was five years ago that we acquired the *finca*, it had lain abandoned for half that time awaiting the completion of architectural drawings, planning consent from the local council and permission to upgrade its utilities. Having been recommended a talented local architect through our estate agent – albeit one who didn't speak English – we tried to straddle Mallorca and London, taking it in turn every month to visit him on the island in order to move the project forward. We didn't speak any Spanish or the local dialect so communication involved spirited charades, enthusiastic nodding and *si si's*, and hand-drawn diagrams. The *finca* had no running water and the electricity ran weakly to 115 volts so on our architect's advice we applied to go on mains water which would involve running pipes underground from the village to our house, and upping the electricity supply to 230 volts. This was no mean feat and in order to get things moving we enlisted the help of a builder-cum-supervisor named Senyor Coll. This wealthy builder from Palma advertised in a local newspaper and, bewitched by his impressive client list and chummy and solicitous ways, we had entrusted him with the task of reforming our ruin. As it transpired, Senyor Coll was a man so devoid of principles as to make my client Greedy George seem like Gandhi. Within a year it had become abundantly clear that he was nothing more than a wily con artist when, having drained us of funds, he abandoned the project halfway through, leaving us to pick up the pieces with an honest and hardworking local builder named Stefan. Did we bear a grudge? Yes, until, that is, we came to accept that there are prowling wolves even in Utopia.

So with a new roof, wooden beams, staircase, bathrooms, doors and windows we have at last been able to move in to our new home. Shutters have been fitted, mains water now brought up to the house and we have a decent electricity supply. The kitchen is without work surfaces, cupboards or tiles on the floor but at least we have a plumbed-in washing machine, and working hob, fridge and sink. When the newly installed plumbing isn't playing up, we even get some hot water in the guest bathroom although the other two still aren't usable and taps lie dust laden in their wrappers aloft heaps of tiles waiting to be attached to walls. The once gloomy *botega*, cellar, has been transformed into a guest en suite and the ancient stone walls of the *finca* have been re-pointed and made secure. There is still a long way to go and a huge amount of structural work to be done outside such as terracing, creating walls and the laying of paths. We have also set aside an area beyond the kitchen for a swimming pool but, given the cost, we shan't be able to make that a reality for some time. As they say in Mallorca, '*Poc a poc…*'

Having arrived half an hour ago, our workmen will sweat it out until nine and then stop for their breakfast, a fat *entrepà*, a crusty white roll, filled with Serrano ham or chorizo sausage and tomato. I've got into the habit of following their routine, pottering downstairs when they down tools to make some tea. Alan likes to greet them on arrival, standing with crossed arms in the front doorway, his tall frame blocking out the sun, until he hears the pop pop of the *motos* as they gnaw up the lane. Then with a huge beam on his face, he strides into the sunny courtyard and in his rich Scottish brogue exchanges hearty '*Holas*' with them as they gather under our porch. But my greatest entertainment is listening to Alan attempting to converse with them in Spanish. He's a master of the weighty '*Si*'. No matter what the topic, Alan can find a way to deliver the simple, delicious monosyllable. Sometimes he manages an '*Ah si*' with huge gusto and enthusiasm, usually when discussing the performance of the Real Mallorca football club. At other times, if conversation moves to summer water shortages, he looks thoughtful, nods his head sagely and mutters '*Si, si si*' with sad conviction. Then there's the questioning '*Si?*' when he furrows his brow as some revelatory information is imparted to him, and exclaims '*Si?*' as in 'Really?' This male bonding of an Anglo-Mallorcan kind can carry on fruitfully for half an hour or so with the builders hanging on Alan's every '*Si*', clapping him on the back and offering him broad smiles of encouragement. It can only be a matter of time before he conquers '*Non*' and then there's no knowing where the conversation may lead.

My office door swings open and Alan strides into the room with a satisfied air.

'Do you know,' he says cheerily, 'I can't quite believe it, but I think I've developed quite an ear for Spanish.'

'Really? What about Mallorcan?'

'Oh come on! I'm just trying to get to grips with Castilian Spanish first.'

This is often the dilemma facing the foreigner moving to Mallorca. Do you learn mainland Castilian Spanish first, or the local Mallorcan dialect? We have opted for Castilian lessons to begin with and hope to pick up the local lingo as we go along. However most of the building vocabulary we have learnt is in Mallorcan because that is what our builders converse in most of the time.

'So, tell me about your Spanish ear.'

'Well, I've just had a great conversation with Stefan and the boys. You would have been impressed. Maybe I should think about jacking in those language classes?'

Like an intransigent child, Alan has resisted all efforts by Paula, his seventy-year-old Spanish teacher, to get to grips with the language. Each week he returns dejectedly from her tiny flat in the town square with sheets of grammar exercises which he examines with glazed eyes out on the patio late at night, glass of malt whisky in one hand and the inevitable *puro*, a fat cigar, in the other.

I try not to smile. 'Since you're becoming so fluent, maybe you should increase your lessons with Paula. You know, move on to the subjunctive and more complex grammatical issues?'

He pushes a fretful hand through his greying locks. 'Hm. Actually I can't help thinking Paula's a bit past it.'

'Past what exactly?'

He draws up a swivel chair from the other side of the desk and sinks heavily into it. I notice that his tattered old shorts and brown legs are streaked with mud from the garden.

'I mean she's nice enough but not exactly exciting to be with.'

'I'm not sure if you're supposed to get excited about your Spanish teacher, are you?'

He gives me a naughty grin. 'Well, if she was forty years younger, and forty pounds lighter, I might.'

I give him a look of mock disapproval.

'Anyway,' he argues, 'When are you going to start lessons?'

'Look I'd love to,' I say a tad insincerely, 'But when I answered Paula's advert in the *Majorca Daily Bulletin* she only had one slot left. Anyway, your need is greater than mine.'

'I can't think why,' Alan grumbles. 'You've only listened to a few Spanish tapes yourself.'

'Well, at least I've progressed beyond *si*.'

'I take it you mean sea as in *el mar*?' He gives me a wink, stands up and peers out of the window. 'I'm a bit worried about the new irrigation channel Stefan's set up for me. The water's very slow. What do you think?'

Stefan has spent hours with Alan running water irrigation pipes around the orange and lemon trees in our field. Like small boys, they smacked palms triumphantly when the first drops came through. They work well together despite the language barrier, Stefan in the role of project manager coordinating the works while Alan acts as general overseer.

'Is there enough water in the *safareig*?'

He registers that I'm cockily using a Mallorcan word to fox him, but is not to be outwitted. He gives me a derisory look. 'Well of course there is. I'd be a pretty poor gardener if I didn't think to check the water tank.'

'Well then, I've no idea. You'll have to confer with Stefan.'

'Indeed,' he sighs and plods off downstairs.

The temperature has now risen to 40°C. I have several e-mails waiting to be sent which is a good enough excuse to vacate my seat and brave popping into town to investigate HiBit, the local computer shop which has Internet access, and to buy some vegetables from the market. The ADSL installation, which we need for e-mailing, will take time and, according to Stefan, will involve serious excavation of the nearby roads, but he ominously insists there will be no problem which is enough to make my heart sink. *No problema*, indeed. Miraculously we now have a phone line in operation but it is temperamental and given to seizures in the middle of calls. I can only imagine it takes umbrage at certain topics of conversation and cuts us off mid flow. I get up and walk over to the window that overlooks the field. Aha! Caught him. Small intermittent puffs, like smoke signals, are rising from the doorway of Alan's den, down in the field. I call this his *abajo*, which strictly speaking means 'down below'. Naively he thinks his daily *puro* smoking goes undetected, his lair being shielded by a conifer and two lemon trees.

I potter down into the garden where Ollie, clad in shorts and a floppy brimmed hat, is pounding a battalion of ants with his small fists. Like most small boys he has an unsettling fascination with all things in the soil of a hairy, swift of limb, creepy-crawly kind.

'Do you want to come into town?'

He squints up at me from the grass. 'What on earth are you wearing?'

This time, unlike my first and only ill-equipped attempt at walking along the track, I'm taking no chances. Today I'm kitted out like a proper walker, wearing sensible loafers and shorts. Sartorial elegance is not a priority.

'What's wrong with it?' I ask a touch defensively.

He shrugs his shoulders. 'Well, you look scruffy. In London you wear suits.'

'Yes, well, I'd look pretty ridiculous wearing a suit in this heat. Besides I'd stick out like a sore thumb.'

He sighs deeply. 'I hate this hat. I look like a girl.'

'Don't be silly. It'll stop the sun burning you. So, do you want to come with me?'

'I'm rather busy killing these ants.'

'I'll buy you an ice cream.'

He pauses and rises on his haunches. 'Are you driving there?'

'Heavens, no. It's a lovely day for a walk.'

He shakes his head. 'I'm not walking anywhere. I'll stay here with daddy.'

'OK suit yourself.'

He gives me a cryptic little smile. 'You're not scared to go all by yourself, are you?'

'Scared? What on earth of?'

He mumbles something and shakes his head dismissively, his interest diverted by the ant carnage around him. Maybe he knows something I don't.

Alan is puffing on a beefy brown cigar as I appear silently round the door of his *abajo* and shriek, 'Caught you!'

He nearly jumps out of his skin and vainly tries to dispel the clouds of acrid smoke with his arms.

'Don't bother. You're only making it worse.'

'My first one of the day,' he says lamely, choking on the fumes.

'Hm... and what about the other four cigar stubs in that ashtray?' I point to the overflowing terracotta saucer by his computer.

He knits his brows. 'Those are just old ones. I hope you don't think I've smoked them today?' He gives me a wounded look.

'Actually I think you're a lousy liar but I'm in a hurry so haven't got time to prolong the discussion.'

He seems relieved. 'Ah, you're off to HiBit. Can you remember to ask Antonia, the owner, about Ollie joining the local football club? Stefan says her brother, Felipe, is the chap in charge.'

'Will do.'

On my way out of the house, I pause to grab a handmade straw pannier from the kitchen, a new purchase from one of the mountain villages. Foolishly I imagine it might give me some kudos with the market stallholders who so far have found my linguistic combination of poor Spanish, mime and semaphore hugely entertaining.

Walking down our rocky lane without heels but with laptop and pannier in tow is verging on the enjoyable were it not for the intense heat. On one side of me is a lofty but misshapen stone wall, distended in the centre by ancient bulging rocks, which give it the wry appearance of an old *paisano,* a country dweller, with a pot belly. On the other, there's a steep drop into a veritable Eden of neighbours' orchards, densely packed with fruit trees of every kind – orange, lemon, fig, pomegranate, plum, pear, apricot, peach and cherry. I pause to contemplate the sheer abundance and richness of colour of the ripening figs and pomegranates, fruit which in London I might fleetingly glimpse, pale and cellophane wrapped, and exorbitantly priced in some drab supermarket. The fruit's pungent, sweet aroma hangs in the warm air and I suddenly feel giddy and so alive it is as if my every pore has been awakened. Like an ecstatic and entranced Eve on a voyage of discovery, I peer up above the porch of my neighbour Rafael's house, overcome with an inexplicable joy when I see clumps of maturing avocados and fat ruby grapes ripe for the picking.

We have four neighbours in the vicinity of our property but so far I have only met Rafael and had a friendly wave from the German owner next door. However, when we viewed our property for the very first time, an agitated, elderly senyora had hobbled from the chalet at the mouth of the track and blocked our path, waving her arms frantically and shaking her head. Toni, our agent, had spoken to her in local dialect and then explained to us with a nonchalant shrug that she had mistaken us for lost tourists. Although she stepped aside, like a border control guard she continued to gaze unsmilingly and suspiciously at our car as it heaved its way over the rocky terrain and up to our *finca*. Now as I reach the corner, I glance nervously at her porch, expecting the same small, bespectacled and matronly form to rush out like the troll under the bridge to challenge me. No one's about. I take a left and head for the town and the local computer shop. It is just off the main *plaça* with its gaudy Gaudiesque church and bustling outdoor cafés jam-packed with vociferous locals and small children squirming on their mothers laps as they try to grab at the tails of sly feral cats prowling beneath the tables. I decide to polish off my e-mails quickly, visit the market and hopefully have enough time to sneak a delicious iced coffee at Café Paris, my new favourite bar, on the way home.

The heart of our local market beats in a modest, unprepossessing white building in the town centre and yet its arteries extend far into an adjacent car park and spill still further on to a broad terrace where the sellers of livestock – birds, hens and rabbits – vie for space on a Saturday morning. During the week, the vast interior of the building is awash with fresh fruit, luscious vegetables, flowers and plants and the smell of sweet, damp earth fills the air. From behind mounds of lettuces, cucumbers, plump tomatoes and oranges, the heads of stallholders bob up and down like expectant geese as they search out potential purchasers and old friends. Lining the walls of the hall are permanent stands and kiosks selling dried beans and nuts, meats, grains and fat red sausages, chorizo and huge rounds of milky white *manchego* cheese. A side hall betrays its briny contents from the street as the strong whiff of fish seeps out from under the market's swing doors and fills the front porch. At the weekend, the whole place is seething with sharp-eyed housewives, keen for bargains and the best, most delicious produce. Queuing at stalls is a lengthy and, at times, dispiriting experience if you are an *estranger*, a foreigner. The town's women enjoy a loud and raucous gossip with the various stallholders and as a matter of course jostle and forcefully elbow their way to the top of the queue ahead of timorous newcomers. Forging their way to the front, they arm themselves with anything green, voluminous, and preferably spiky with which to make a final assault on those who fail to scuttle out of their path. To stomp off in ill humour in order to offer your custom elsewhere will serve no purpose whatsoever as each stall will already be mobbed with another baying crowd and should word get round that you're not a team player you might never get served at all.

I enter the fray and head for my favourite stallholder, Teresa, she who bellows the loudest and has the largest circle of admirers and observers. She watches me approach rather like a canny spider studying a small and gormless fly.

'Ah! There you are, senyora!' she yells in Spanish. 'Where have you been the last week? Living on tinned vegetables? Shame on you!'

I explain that I've been busy with work and had to resort to the nearby *supermercat* but no, I haven't been eating tinned vegetables.

'Did you hear that?' she calls out to anyone who will listen. 'She has so much to do she can't find time to spend five minutes in the market!'

A small cluster of elderly, buxom matrons suck their teeth and view me with disapproving eyes. I give a feeble shrug and try to explain in faltering Spanish that I'm very busy. Teresa wafts a dismissive hand in my direction. 'Does she know what hard work is?'

Raucous laughter from her chorus of old fans.

'So, now you're here, what can we do for you?'

She hurls me some small plastic bags which in a fluster I begin to fill rapidly with the various voluptuous offerings on her counter.

She settles her hands on her ample hips and smiles mischievously.

'What are you doing?' she yells with incredulity. 'Throw all that junk out and start again.'

I have to admit I'm confused. 'Er... what do you mean, Teresa?'

She sighs and shakes her head, as do all the other spectators, and grabbing an avocado, thrusts it under my nose. 'Smell it, feel it.'

Obediently I give the fruit a gentle tweak and sniff the surface. More titters and tuts.

'No, not like that! Watch.' Teresa snatches up another, gently feeling and prodding it rather like a doctor might do when examining a patient for mumps. Then she closes her eyes, presses her nose to the dark green skin and inhales deeply. Perhaps this is the locals' answer to glue sniffing.

'Now do you see?' She is greeted by approving smiles.

'Sort of, but how is it supposed to feel and smell?'

Teresa pats me on the cheek. 'Ah senyora, you've a lot to learn. Let's start with the peaches.'

My pannier brimming with fruit, vegetables, a baguette and a bunch of lilies, I stagger in the simmering heat out of the town, away from the bustle and eventually along our dusty track. As I pass Rafael's silent house with its muted green shutters, his boxer, Franco, barks loudly from the outside run. I dump the pannier on the ground and squeeze my fingers through the wooden railings to stroke the dog's ears. He wags his stunted tail and licks me, his warm baggy snout snuffling against my skin. At that moment, a ball comes thundering up the track from nowhere and hits me on the head. Bullseye! I pick it up and squint accusingly into the sun. Fast little feet pad towards me in a hail of dust. It's Ollie, red faced and panting. 'Ah. You've got it! Can I have it back? We're playing football.'

'We?' I ask irritably.

'Me and Helge.'

'Helge and I,' I sniff primly. 'And who is Helge?'

'She's German and lives next door. Bye.'

And off he trots with his football, leaving me nursing a bruised head and still none the wiser. I notice that he's abandoned the floppy hat. Picking up my bag, I slowly approach the house nearest to ours, a well-worn stone *finca* whose pergola overflows with crimson bougainvillea that hangs down in a dense fringe over the cobbled terrace. A stunning woman with glossy dark hair, clad in a slinky silk dress, emerges from a side gate which leads to the garden. She is holding Ollie's hand.

'What a gorgeous little boy you have!' she says sweetly in broken Spanish. I notice she's slightly out of breath from running. 'I'm Helge. I think you've met my husband, Wolfgang.'

I'm momentarily distracted by her apparent ability to wear silk and run without perspiring. What's her trick? I proffer a hand and explain that her husband and I have merely exchanged hand waves. She beams at me.

'You know we are so happy to have you as neighbours. Ollie says you speak some Spanish which is good because I don't speak English.'

She tells me that she and her husband live in Berlin but visit Mallorca during the summer. They'll be away from September but have a local family keeping an eye on their house. Ollie kicks the ball towards her and she scrambles after it energetically and somehow elegantly. Maybe some people are just born svelte.

'Listen,' I burble, 'If Ollie is being a nuisance...'

'No, no,' she smiles. 'He saw me on my terrace and invited me to play football. He was so sweet, how could I resist?'

I narrow my eyes at my devious little darling. 'Hm, I manage well enough. Now Ollie, I think it's time for your bath.'

He pulls a face. 'But I want to stay with Helge.'

I give him a warning grimace and he quickly drops his hand from Helge's clasp. 'Can I see you tomorrow?'

'Of course, *liebchen!*' she cries, giving him a hug. 'It's so nice to have a little boy around again. I remember when my son, Tomas, was small. Listen, why don't you all come and have drinks with us tomorrow night? It would be good to get to know one another.'

Given Helge's instant star rating with my son, he'll probably bring adoption papers round for them to sign. I thank her heartily and with Ollie shuffling behind me, make my way through the courtyard and into the house where I drop the bulging pannier on the concrete floor and collapse onto a flimsy beach chair. I try not to fix my eyes on the boxes of unpacked kitchen utensils and crockery around me. What I'd give to have fitted cupboards and a decent dining table and chairs, but I'm just going to have to wait.

'Had a fun time?' enquires Alan, striding into the kitchen with a pair of secateurs in his hand. Sometimes I think they're welded to him.

'I need a cup of tea before I expire.'

He steps over the assortment of vegetables that have spilled out of the pannier and cheerfully fills up the kettle. I notice Ollie skips over the same heap en route to the biscuit tin.

'Well, I got the e-mails done and met Antonia and Albert who own HiBit. She's Mallorcan and he's American and so I didn't have to use my awful Spanish.'

'What a cop out!' growls Alan. 'Were they any help on Ollie joining the local football team?'

'Yes. Antonia says there'll be no problem with him joining. She's going to speak with Felipe.'

'When can I start?' Ollie pipes up.

'I think the new season starts in September so very soon.'

His face brightens. 'Good and Helge's agreed to play with me until they leave.'

'Who's Helge?' asks Alan, slapping a mug of green tea in front of me.

'Our glamorous next-door neighbour. She's invited us round tomorrow night for drinks.' I give him a leading smile.

'A glamorous German,' he muses. 'I wonder if she likes gardening.'

'Yes', she does,' says Ollie enthusiastically. 'And football.'

'Sounds just like my sort of girl,' replies Alan roguishly.

It was one of those spontaneous decisions that are easy to make here. The sky was blue and the air still and warm so Alan and I decided to call it a day and go for an early evening walk in the mountains. And why not? Ollie, aimless around the house until able to start his new school, had been invited by our builder, Stefan, to spend the evening round at the house of Catalina, his older sister, and her husband Ramon, both of whom we are yet to meet. The promise of a large plate of *macarrones*, delicious pasta tubes with Bolognese sauce, the staple diet of children up here in the mountains, and a rumbustious game of football with Catalina's two tomboyish young daughters had proved irresistible. We agreed to collect him from Stefan's mountain village later in the evening.

So, having made a two-hour climb, here we are alone on the summit of one of the mountains in the Tramuntana range that offers a spectacular view over the whole valley. Alan is scrabbling around the rocks shovelling herb specimens into a polythene sandwich bag while I sit on a tree stump revelling in the peace. That's when Judas rings. The name Patterson flashes up on the screen.

'Honey, how are you?' a voice bellows as clear and loud as a bell.

'Oh, on top of the world, Bryan. Is everything OK?'

'OK? Are you kidding? You got me the best media coverage in town. That party was a triumph! We lurve you, sugar. You're the Queen of Aphrodite. No, that's me,' he quips smoothly. 'You can play Goddess, Aphrodite herself.' False laughter.

Bryan's party to launch Aphrodite beauty products on the London stage seems a million light years away but barely a week has passed since I was in the thick of it. As parties go in media land, it was a raving success. It was held at a private Soho club and two statuesque black bouncers called Randy and Baz stood on either side of the front door throwing mean glances at anyone who dared to walk up the red carpet without first fluttering a gilt-edged invitation in their direction. Guests were practically frisked before gaining entry and a few chancers were unceremoniously hurled back on the pavement. Bryan, grey haired and suave in a petrol blue velvet smoking jacket, matching trousers and monogrammed, tasselled Savile Row slippers, received his visitors cordially in the hallway with his white pet rabbit, Tootsie, in his arms. This adored and over-indulged pet sleeps on his bed, roams his Upper East Side apartment when he's at work and shares his popcorn while watching movies with him late into the night. At six every morning she wakes up and munches on a carrot while Bryan enjoys his first espresso of the day. He brings her to every Aphrodite launch, he tells me, for luck and I can only imagine that he's used his considerable power and resources to get round the quarantine laws to allow her on his private jet. Quite simply, I have acquired another deranged but fascinating client.

Alan is arranging sprigs of rosemary in my hair and doing a rather good impression of Bryan in mime. I try not to giggle, waving him away with my hand. Bryan is still gushing. 'The British press is so marvellous and the *Telegraph* interview hit just the right tone. I simply can't wait to see the party shots in *Tatler*.'

I try stifling a yawn. A rabbit pops up in front of me and then disappears down a hole. I wish I could join it.

'Oh and by the way, sweetie, no big deal but when your staff drop me a line, remind them that it's Bryan with a "y" and not with an "i".'

'Like Anne with an "e" who doesn't drink tea?'

'If you say so! Big hugs now. Tootsie sends a kiss. Love to London!'

There's a click and he's gone. Poor Bryan with a 'y', all the money and influence in the world and only a floppy bunny for company.

A passing bee hovers excitedly over a small bush of white flowers, before descending cautiously into its depths. I turn my head and see Alan some way off, poking a stick in among some rocks. Sinking back against a cushion of long bleached grass, I stare upwards but the sun glares down with such force that I scrunch my eyes shut. A golden glow, the colour of egg yolk, is playing in front of my closed lids. I remain still, blind, suppressing thought, suspended in a void where only the olfactory sense functions. Blankness. I drift off into a world of light and dark shades. Some time later, I prise open my eyes, squinting at the hot sun, and find Alan standing over me, smiling. 'What are you thinking about?'

'Nothing. Nothing at all.' After years of exhaustive and failed attempts, I have finally managed to hammer a spoke into the hamster wheel of unrelenting thought. I have learned how to eliminate thought itself.

He nods meditatively and then squats at my feet, rustling his small plastic bag of specimens. 'Guess what I've just found?'

'A pot of gold?'

'Of a kind. *Artemisia arborescens*.'

I'm used to these horticultural riddles. 'Which is?'

'Shrubby wormwood,' he says. 'The local nursery charges four euros a plant and here we've got it for free.'

I hold the gold and white flower in my hand. It's good to know that a saving of a few euros is sufficient to warm the cockles of a Scotsman's heart.

I slip downstairs, bare-footed to the *entrada*, our lofty hallway. The flat, cream, marble slabs feel sleek and cool underfoot. I open the front door. It isn't locked. It's unheard of to lock up your house at night around here. Alan and Ollie are asleep upstairs, unperturbed by the intense heat. I step outside on to the porch. The frogs appear to be partying, quacking and rasping at the tops of their voices like an amphibian boy band. Carefully I pick my way through the builders' rubble and rocks and up the steps to the pond. The singing stops, followed by a series of small plops. I'm the original party pooper. Water gurgles quietly from a small bubbling fountain, its spout obscured by a fine green stubble of moss. Come on boys! Don't ice me out. I draw my bare legs up in front of me and sit on the wide stone ledge. Still no sign of life. Then suddenly there's a sound like a small cough. I peer into the water and then on to the terracotta tile on the pool's edge. In the dull light of the moon I see the silhouette of a fat bullfrog. He's filling out his chest and fixing his bulging eyes on me. For a minute I'm carried back to Miami, where on a three day business trip I ended up with a group of Cubans at a crazy American diner where outside a gigantic electronic frog, or maybe it was a toad, wise-cracked clients as they entered the restaurant. I never discovered whether there was a real person hidden inside but the frog left a lasting impression on me. Insanely I fantasise that he's with me now.

'What are you looking at?'

I start back. 'Who spoke?'

'Who'd you think? Are you blind?'

'I'm sorry, I never knew frogs could speak.'

He eyes me coolly. 'They can't, to the best of my knowledge. Anyway, I'm a toad.'

I'm slightly abashed. 'Do all toads speak?' Can I really be asking this question?

'Not many,' he drawls. 'So, how d'you like it here?'

'It'll take time to adjust. You can't just up sticks from one place to another without feeling a bit disconnected.'

He quacks loudly, a sort of hollow laugh. 'Pah! I do it all the time. I've lived in more ponds than you can shake a lily pad at. The trouble with your kind is that you carry too much baggage. Jeez, all those trucks you had up here full of I don't know what. You don't exactly travel light.'

'It's stuff we can't live without.'

He shrugs sceptically. 'If you say so, but what's with the clothes and shoes? When are you gonna wear all that gear up here? People round here will think you're nuts.'

'Well I evidently am, since I'm talking to you.'

'What's wrong with talking to a toad? We always get a bad press. Look in a dictionary and it's all the same discriminatory frogspawn. Toads are ugly. Toads are slimy. Go on touch me, do I feel slimy?'

I touch his skin. It's bone dry and tough as leather.

He rants on. 'All that human fairytale bunkum about the princess kissing a frog and ending up with a handsome prince. Makes me want to throw up. He'd be gay, or even some kinda psycho, mark my words. Fairytales don't exist, honey. You gotta take the rough with the smooth, warts and all.'

He puffs up his cheeks. 'Hey and listen, don't come sneaking around at night when we're doing our vocals. Me and the boys are working on some new numbers. So long, kid.' He slides inelegantly into the ink-black water.

I get up slowly and make my way back to the house. Alan is standing sleepily in the *entrada*, having fetched a glass of water from the kitchen.

'What were you doing out there?' he yawns.

'Just cooling off.'

He's at the top of the stairs when he calls back dreamily, not expecting an answer, 'Well as long as you're feeling OK.'

Hardly. I'm hallucinating that I'm talking with an American toad and it's the best conversation I've had all year.

FOUR

DONKEY WORK

Ollie is scowling at me and scuffing one of his new black shoes against a wall. I don't bother to chastise him. Around us are children of all ages tearing about, screaming, laughing, babbling in various languages and playing with balls. Sun-kissed parents in shorts and T-shirts appear to be cheerfully exchanging news. I don't spy any designer labels and there are few nannies, for that matter. The noise is intense. A tall, smiling woman in a red jacket whom I recognise as the headmistress is standing surrounded by teenage girls, all of them vying to kiss her cheeks. I'm mesmerised, imagining that this must be some sort of new term ritual. Several gangly youths are slouching along towards a similar group some way off. Maybe two rival gangs? But no, now they're all laughing, calling out and falling on each other with bear hugs and hand shakes. A school where it's cool to hug?

'So will anyone speak English?' hisses Ollie, hoisting up his oversized grey school shorts. His skinny legs are covered in bruises and scratches, the spoils of football and treacherous ant hunts. I make reassuring clucking noises. His wavy blond hair is tousled and kissing the tip of his nose so I vainly attempt to smooth it back with my hand. He flinches, mortified, his blue eyes flashing angrily at me. 'What on earth are you doing? Someone might see!' He peers round furtively.

'Well, you look like a Komodo dragon. I should have got your hair cut.'

'Komodo dragons don't have hair,' he sniffs disdainfully.

My son may only be six but he has a great way of putting me in my box.

A small boy about his age runs up to him.

'Do you like football?'

Does a Scotsman like whisky?

Ollie nods.

'Do you speak Mallorcan?'

'Maybe,' he says. Enigmatic as ever.

'I'm Sebastià. See you at break.'

Ollie nods gravely and Sebastià trots off.

A school bell sounds and there's bedlam. Everyone's running to take his or her place in line. They seem to know the procedure. We don't. Suddenly I feel a little hand in mine as Ollie looks up at me pleadingly.

'Where do I go, Mummy? Where? Quick!'

I turn round to make sense of what's happening but the headmistress is already bearing down on us, beaming like a jolly Butlins Red Coat, enveloping my son in a huge embrace. She grasps his free hand and gives me a reassuring wink.

'Come with me, poppet. Mummy will be back later.'

He throws me an inscrutable look and walks with her to the back of a line of small children. I stand transfixed. Will he be OK? Should I accompany him? As if reading my mind, he looks back at me and shakes his head, indicating with his eyes that I should go.

I think back to his previous sanitised existence at St George's in Pimlico run by the ghastly Priscilla Eggerton-Smith. On one of the last days of the school term, I had deposited him as usual on the front steps where all the other little boy bugs were collecting in their stripy green shirts, grey woollen shorts and caps. The hideous Eggerton-Smith, with rotund white chignon sitting squat on her head like an albino toad, bent towards him frostily. 'Good Morning, Jamie! Remember polite boys shake hands in the morning.' She proffered a plump, ring-smothered hand, the nails blood-red.

'My name isn't Jamie,' he said in quiet fury.

'Hand please?'

'No!'

'No? Well then you'll stay on the steps until you remember your manners. Stand aside please.'

Brushing us impatiently away with her hand as if we were a pair of tiresome gnats, she theatrically carried on shaking the hands of her cowed pupils. I remonstrated angrily with her but she fixed me with a cold stare and snapped, 'Manners are key at St George's. No exceptions to the rule.'

The bell finally sounded, the last straggler had gone inside and still my small son stood resolutely on the doorstep, glowering at her, tears in his eyes and with utter defiance stamped on his little chin. I was frantic to get to a meeting.

'Oh for heaven's sake, he's only five…' I began.

'Very well, Jamie. No break today,' she barked angrily, ushering him roughly up the steps. I sprang after him and caught his arm tenderly.

'It's all right, Mummy,' he whispered, 'I won.'

But it wasn't all right. It was a travesty and had I been carrying a pair of scissors, I might just have disabled her albino toad of a hair bun and lain it to waste in the road, waiting to see it flattened by a speeding car. The parents at the school were no better: anorexic mothers in Armani dresses with full make-up and five-inch Jimmy Choo heels who swished up the steps, nannies in tow, wafting Coco Chanel and boredom. And their husbands? A rare sighting but occasionally a frazzled banker would roll up in a limo, instruct his driver to deposit a child on the steps as it were a bag of refuse, and then drive away.

One anxious, toothpick-thin American mother called Cecily Withers constantly tried to ensnare me with invitations to infant parties and coffee gatherings. I politely declined but on the fifth attempt, I took her aside and explained that I worked. She winced and the edges of her mouth drooped. 'Oh my God, really? You poor thing.'

'No actually, I like to work.'

She stared at me in awkward silence for a second. 'That's just fine then. Well, I'd best be going. Have a great day.' She never spoke to me again.

Then there was Joan Hedges whose child, Edward, spent every evening at some private crammer class or other, be it swimming, chess, piano, flute, Egyptology or Serbo-Croat. She insisted on taking my Mallorca address when I walked home from school for the very last time. Reluctantly I fished out an old bus ticket from my handbag and scrawled down our details on the back. After all, she'd never really get in touch, would she?

I drive back to the mountains from Ollie's school in Palma and coax the car up the mouth of the track, wondering whether Pere our plumber has managed to fix a bad leak in the bathroom. Alan was disappointed not to be with Ollie on his first day at school but Pere could only visit early in the morning and since water was gushing everywhere, he had no choice but to stay at home and wait for him. As I level with the first house there's a sharp knock at my window and there on the other side of the glass, squinting at me, is the troll on the bridge. She's wearing a stern expression again and her gnarled fingers grip a stick, which is raised in the air. I slam on the brake and roll down the window in trepidation. She talks breathily in local dialect and when I look baffled, wanders off returning with a small bunch of hand picked flowers which she thrusts at me through the open window. 'Senyora Sampol,' she says, indicating herself. Then as an after thought, '*Margalida. Benvinguts.*'

I tell her my name and thank her. To my relief she drops the local dialect so that we can at least converse in Castilian Spanish, the language that is spoken across much of the mainland. She tells me her eyesight is terrible, so bad that she can barely see her own hands. This, she says, is bad when you are an eighty-six-year-old widow. She is happy we have moved here and hopes we'll be good neighbours. As I rev up the car to go she peers foggily into my face.

'How old are you, senyora? Maybe twenty-five?'

Senyora Sampol's eyesight is definitely far worse than I'd thought.

Catalina is scrubbing the concrete floor in the kitchen to the accompaniment of the Gypsy Kings. The older sister of Stefan, our builder, she has been working here at the house for a month now, popping in for a few hours each day to help me set up my office and share the cleaning as well as babysitting Ollie. However, Catalina does far more than this. She is the eyes and ears of the valley, a local intelligence bugle arriving with a mountain of news and gossip each day to keep us au fait with neighbourhood affairs. Having spent some years in London and California as an au pair she speaks English fluently and is relied upon hugely by the local English speaking community in her village. Walking with Catalina through the town can be a lengthy business as she is stopped and greeted enthusiastically by locals and foreigners alike at every step.

Perhaps her greatest claim to fame is that she is a superb cook, spending many a patient hour showing me how to prepare local dishes such as paella, delicious meatballs known as *albondigas*, and *croquetas* filled with meat and vegetables. Like a nurse with a drug addict, she has gradually weaned me off thoughts of Tesco on-line and pre-packaged hummus from Marks & Spencer. As part of her therapy we have spent afternoons together hunting for hidden delicacies on our own land such as edible fungi, wild asparagus that grows in the hedgerows and *bleda*, Swiss chard. But there's a strange metamorphosis taking place because I'm actually having fun, getting covered in mud and grime, and loving it. A few months back whoever would have believed this is how I'd be getting my kicks?

I dawdle in the kitchen over a cup of mint tea, the leaves freshly picked from the garden, and the local British newspaper, the *Majorca Daily Bulletin*. Ollie is safely ensconced in school. Never have I seen him so happy and carefree. For the first time that I can remember, he actually nagged me to get him to school early so that he could play with his new friends before line-up. Catalina rises and stretches her back before sloshing the dirty water from her pail out into the backyard. Then she begins washing a large pile of chard in the sink, its leaves and stalks covered in tiny white snails and mud. She plucks them off quickly, engulfs the greens in water to rid them of silt, giving me a wry grin when I pull a face.

'You scared they going to bite you?'

'Give me time. It's not quite like M&S pre-packed, that's all.'

She throws her head back and laughs. 'Come on girl, the poor snails are more scared of you. I find all these leaves in your own garden. Soon you won't need to go to market, eh?'

'Yes, but I like going to the market, Catalina. How else can I practise my terrible Spanish and what on earth would Teresa and the other stallholders do for laughs?'

She giggles. 'You think speaking Spanish is hard. Just wait till you start learning the Catalan-Mallorcan dialect.'

Yes, that little challenge is yet to come. Still, despite my reservations I've heard that the local town council is offering free Catalan lessons for foreigners and I'm feeling strangely tempted to sign up. I look through the French windows and see the tall shadow of Alan struggling with a pair of bushy young cypresses behind a wall. It's like watching a bizarre shadow play. Catalina steps away from the sink where squeaky clean green leaves are now ready for the pot, and follows my gaze. She shakes her head and tuts.

'What's The Moro doing? Planting more of his trees? *Home!* Soon you'll have forest, not garden.'

I laugh. *Moro*, a term of endearment and a throwback to tempestuous times in Mallorca's history when Moorish pirates made many violent assaults on the island. Catalina and her family use moro to describe Alan because his skin effortlessly absorbs the sun like litmus paper so that he appears browner than the locals themselves. Catalina gets back to her cleaning then pushes back her long dark hair with hands covered in soapsuds and looks up at me disapprovingly.

'Remember I say Rachel rings from office in London? She want you to call her.'

Rachel rang an hour ago but it's unlikely to be urgent so she can wait.

'You go to the town for shopping today?' Catalina persists like a mother chiding a loafing teenager.

'Probably,' I mutter, reading the small ads with mock interest. We have bought this local British newspaper every day since we came here and now I have met Jason Moore, the editor, and agreed to write him a weekly column. It will be largely about London news and gossip. My monthly forays back and forth to England should provide plenty of copy.

'Don't forget you take Ollie to football tonight. At the pitch Antonia's brother, Felipe, will give you *inscripció*, OK?'

How could I possibly forget my son's admission or should I say *inscripció* to the local football club? It will be the highlight of his and Alan's day.

'Another thing,' says Catalina, tapping me on the arm. 'Remember tomorrow is bull running in my village. You come have breakfast with Ramon and me afterwards.'

'That's if you're still alive.'

'I strong woman, you know. I can run faster than a bull.'

'I sincerely hope so. Don't count on me to come and save you.'

She whips me lightly with a tea towel, waggles her finger in the air and pronounces, 'Next year you'll be running with me.'

'*Ni muerta!*' I mutter. In other words, over my dead body!

I turn over the page of my newspaper. I really should call the office, I suppose, but I'm enjoying this feeling of indolence too much. Do I feel guilty? Strangely not. After years of pushing myself to the edge of reason, I am basking in having time out so I shall sit here a little longer being idle and contemplating nothing in particular. Everything can wait. A gecko darts up the wall in front of me and hides behind a painting, its emerald face peeping out absurdly at the corner. I half expect it to start nodding and emitting a fragrance with Eastern promise. Catalina gives me a nudge.

'You want a turkey?'

I wonder if I've heard right. 'A turkey? What for?'

'Christmas, of course! Ramon bought some turkey chicks long time ago in Sineu market which he's been feeding up for Christmas.'

'But it's only September.'

'You think a turkey grow in five minutes? *Per favor!* It takes many months.'

I say we'd love one of her home reared turkeys and thank her profusely although I'm already worrying about the execution scene come Christmas. I hope I can duck out of that one.

'Hey, you help me fold the sheets now. Lazy woman!'

I yawn and slowly rise to my feet, trotting meekly after Catalina out of the kitchen and up the sunny garden path to the washing line where dazzling white sheets cavort in the breeze.

She pulls off the pegs and together we stretch and fold the crisp sheets ready for ironing. She stops suddenly and peruses the nearby mountains.

'It's a beautiful day, isn't it? Look at the sky, as blue as your eyes, no?'

I laugh and peer up above me. There's not a streak of a cloud in the sky, just an uninterrupted baby blue blanket of warm air and a dazzling sun. What more could a girl want?

The town's football pitch is only a 15-minute walk from our *finca* but Ollie insists that we drive there, given that walking is still a new concept to him. *Poc a poc.* Having parked the car in a nearby street, we cross over a small stone bridge adjacent to the entrance. At this time of the year the *torrent*, the river, is usually dried up but after a stormy night water gushes downstream from the craggy mountains and the wild ducks quack and splash about in the cold foam, like a gaggle of giggly girls. On one side of the fast flowing river is a narrow road leading to several mountain villages beyond and on the other, a strip of orchards and gardens where rabbits and hens cautiously peep out between the long grass and trees when they think no one's looking. We enter the football ground, and take in the scene. There's a modest bar to the left, heaving with locals, children with *gelats*, ice creams, old men sucking on *puros*, mothers gossiping over *café amb llet*, milky coffee, and local builders propping up the bar. In front of the bar is the pitch itself which somehow seems enormous to my untrained eye but then this is the first time I've ever seen one up close, never having been a fan of the game in London. The towering Tramuntana mountains form an impressive backdrop behind it and to the sides there are distant villages where wisps of smoke can be seen rising from the chimneys of seigneurial stone *fincas*. It's still sizzling hot even though it's late afternoon so heavens know why the home fires are burning up in the hills. It must be the wood stoves often used for cooking. Children of all ages in polyester green and white football strips are milling about, pushing past and looking us up and down as if three Martians have landed in their midst.

'Why are they staring at us?' whispers Ollie.

'Well, it's pretty obvious we're the only foreigners here and also that we don't have a clue what we're doing.'

As usual I have the patience of a bee in a jam jar and abandon the boys in search of someone in authority. Eventually I glimpse an official looking man in shorts and T-shirt with a whistle so stalk on to the pitch and ask whether he can direct us to Felipe, the club manager. He gives a friendly smile.

'I'm Felipe.'

'Fantastic! I wonder whether your sister Antonia might have mentioned me?'

He lapses into perfect English. 'Yes, don't worry. I was expecting you. Welcome. Your son can start in the under sevens today. Come with me to the office and fill in his application.'

Alan and Ollie amble across the pitch towards us and I make some hasty introductions.

'You speak excellent English,' says Alan.

'Well, I teach at an international school in Palma so I should.'

He turns to Ollie. 'You speak Mallorcan dialect?'

'*Un poc*,' replies Ollie softly, his eyes downcast. 'We're learning Mallorcan and Castiliano at school.'

Felipe puts an arm round his shoulder. 'Then surely you know how to say run and goal in Mallorcan?'

'Of course!' he replies a little heatedly.

'*Molt bé!* You'll be fine then,' says Felipe displaying a dazzling set of Persil white teeth, and leads us off to his office where we complete the form and pay Ollie's joining fee.

'When will I get my strip?'

'We have a special ceremony next month. You'll get it then.'

Ollie is flushed with excitement. I try to comprehend how the promise of lime green and white polyester shorts can induce such delight, and give up. Alan is beaming with pride at the thought of a mini Ronaldo in the family. A whistle is sounded and boys stream on to the pitch and take up position with their various teams. We are led to the under seven group where Felipe introduces us to Fernando, the cheerful coach. Sixteen boys of varying heights and weights eye Ollie warily. Alan and I beat a hasty retreat to the spectator area and take our seats.

'I hope he understands what to do,' Alan frets.

'Look, he only has to kick a ball about,' I say dismissively.

'You really haven't got a clue about football, have you?'

'Well, I'm sure I'll get the hang of it if I come here enough.'

Alan turns to watch the various trainers on the field instructing their teams. Groups of boys begin running about the pitch in their designated areas, kicking balls enthusiastically and responding to shrill whistles. After a brief team talk, Ollie and his polyester clad accomplices break up and begin to play in earnest. I try to follow the game but at that moment am distracted by a waft of strong tobacco coming from behind my seat. I spin round to face my tormentor, a bronzed, rather laid-back individual with flowing grey locks and moustache, dressed in a pale blue polo shirt and beige chinos. He puffs on an enormous *puro* and fixes his merry grey-blue eyes on me.

'Forgive me, am I blowing smoke on you?' he says in perfect English laced with a rich Spanish accent.

'Well, actually you are. I can move, don't worry.'

'Certainly not!' he cries. 'It's my fault. Here, I'll come down to your row.'

Before I can say anything he descends one level into our row of seats.

'I am Pep Ramis,' he says with a radiant smile. 'You are British, of course.'

Alan jumps up to greet him, delighted to meet another *puro* addict. We make introductions and sit down together. He places himself between us.

'Your son is a good player,' drawls Pep, blowing his smoke in Alan's direction. 'Mine is ten years old. He is playing over there.'

With his cigar, he indicates a tall, dark, lanky boy mid-tackle.

'Well, Ollie's not been playing long. He's tackling well but it's going to be a tough learning curve.'

Pep nods sombrely as if he and Alan are discussing the challenges facing a new recruit at NASA.

'Oh for heaven's sake! It's just a game,' I say impatiently.

Pep's eyes nearly pop out of their sockets. 'Just a game? How can you say that?'

Alan lights up a *puro*. 'Women just don't understand.'

Pep calms down and gives a hoarse cough. 'My wife, Juana, is as bad. So you are living here?' He turns to me.

'We are now. Just off Calle Alcover, down the small track past the church.'

'Ah! *Fantàstic!* We live just a short walk from you.' He fumbles in his trouser pocket. 'Here's my card.'

'I'm afraid I don't have one on me,' says Alan, who, since moving here, has found it hard to admit to not carrying cards anymore.

'I have.' I pull an English business card from a leather holder in my handbag and scrawl our Spanish telephone number on the back.

Pep studies it carefully. 'You have your own company? *Una dona?* A woman?'

I feel my hackles rise and then notice an evil grin on his face. 'I'm only teasing you. We Mallorcans are supposed to be sexist, aren't we?'

'And are you?' I retort.

'No, we are happy to let women work, then we can watch football and smoke all day.'

'Is that what you do?'

'More or less,' he replies, staring into the distant hills.

Alan gives him an admiring look. 'Well, you must come and visit us. The house is still a bit of a mess but…'

'No. First you must visit us,' says Pep graciously. 'And we can go to a match some time if you like? I always go to see Real Mallorca when they're playing at home in Palma.'

'Great,' smiles Alan, pleased as punch.

I hear some jubilant shouting and see that Ollie has just kicked a ball into the goal.

'*Molt bé!*' shouts Pep. 'That means very good in Mallorcan.'

'Even I can understand that one,' I say a little curtly.

'I beg your pardon,' he says in a parody of an aristocratic English accent. 'I shall take more care in the future.'

'Where did you learn to speak English so well?' I ask suspiciously.

He gives a slow, enigmatic smile. 'Ah, that's a long story.'

I'm like a dog on the scent. 'I take it you've lived in England?'

'I have lived in many places,' he says gravely.

Grinding some ash beneath his foot, he focuses his gaze on the field. I await further pearls but none are forthcoming so decide to end the questioning there for today. Somehow I feel there's a lot more to our new friend, Pep.

The hour flies by and I find myself gripped. Can I really have enjoyed watching a game of football? This is a revelation. Ollie has scored two goals for his side and is given a hero's pat on the back by several boys in his team. He basks in the moment then jogs over to us, red faced and panting. Pep leans forward to congratulate him on the game. 'I am Pep. You must meet my son, Angel, soon. He can practise with you.'

Ollie smiles shyly and turns to greet several team mates who've caught up with him. They acknowledge Pep with friendly nods and there's an exchange of banter. He takes a ten euro note from his pocket and gives it to them after a brief mock tousle. The boys pull Ollie by the arm and together they head off for the bar.

'They seem very friendly.'

Pep smiles at me. 'I have known most of them since they were babies. I tell them all to buy ice creams.'

'Well, that's very good of you,' says Alan. 'Do you fancy a beer?'

'Yes, but Angel and I must be off home or his mother will complain. I will call you.'

He shakes Alan's hand, kisses me on both cheeks and exhaling a long puff of smoke, saunters off towards the pitch, in search of his son.

The build up to Festa del Bou has been immense, and now we are jostling for position in a heaving crowd awaiting the release of a young black bull which once unleashed will run amok around

Catalina's local village. Five hundred or so wags, mostly young men who have spent the previous night imbibing heavily, will run in advance of the bull in a mad scramble, hoping to stay the course without being mauled. It is a kind of adrenaline rush which happens annually and Catalina and her village are proud that animal activists have so far been unable to ban the event. It is a matter of honour. This is the last village on the island able to hold such a fiesta because of its historical significance, and the regional government is twitchy about village insurgences, so chooses to turn a blind eye. Spectators and runners come from all over the island, many arriving the night before for some macho revelry. Evidence of a recent corybantic affair can be seen in the *plaça* where a line of tipsy black bin bags, bulging with empty wine and spirit bottles, prop each other up against a wall like a bunch of debauched and snoozing old soaks. Small groups of disorientated, haggard youths yawning and clutching beer cans drift around the streets mutely like sleepwalkers.

Alan and I stand in the crush next to Ramon, Catalina's husband, who has popped Ollie effortlessly up on to his rock-like shoulders for a better view. Being a stonemason in the mountains means that Ramon works on tough terrain outdoors and is subsequently bronzed all year round and has the muscular physique of Popeye. He's also a good football player, keeps hens in his garden, and drinks copious amounts of chocolate Nesquik and Pepsi every day, all major brownie points when it comes to coolness rating with Ollie. Catalina and Ramon's young daughters are at nursery school so Ollie is delighted to have his new hero's full attention. Ramon observes the excited runners with a nonchalant air and raises a cynical eyebrow when among them; he sees his wife yelling joyously at him. He throws me a slightly bewildered glance. 'She is crazy. Do you see other wives doing this?'

Ramon is one of Mallorca's natural philosophers, a man well beyond his years in wisdom, who tolerates the antics of his exuberant and tomboyish wife because he knows that he can never change her and in his heart he would never want to. He was born and raised in another village, and has the advantage of being able to revert to outsider mode whenever he chooses. No event in the valley passes by without Catalina's presence and sense of fun and Ramon is aware of this. It makes him proud although he would never show it. I catch her eye and give a thumbs up sign. She throws us all a dazzling smile and blows kisses, before gathering up her thick dark hair and scrunching it into a ponytail. Despite her cavalier attitude, I wonder if she might be just a tiny bit nervous.

A gun is fired five times to announce the arrival of the bull. Everyone calls out and claps, full of anticipation. From where we are standing, the creature's head can just be seen jutting out from the back of the truck. A huge cheer goes up when an official releases the catch to its cage and a stumbling dark form emerges, raises its head, pauses for an instant, then careers down the ramp of the van, sensing the chase is about to begin. And now at the sound of another gunshot, the bull is off, racing down the steep hill on the village's outskirts towards the *plaça*. Members of the *Guardia Civil* are pushing people back out of the roads and blowing whistles at the stragglers. At first, as if in a daze, the participants marvel at the animal's thunderous descent until snapping into action as it gains momentum and is nearly upon them. There's a scramble as they scream and fly in all directions, over walls, up trees, and squeezed against doors as it pounds down the cobbled streets. Catalina, her sturdy frame clad in T-shirt, shorts and blue sneakers is running fast amid the throng. Red-faced and exuberant, she hops gamely on to a pavement and, sensing the bull hot on her heels, leaps deftly through an open door of a house in the nick of time. She waves triumphantly at us from across the street. I feel my own heart beating fast. Alan shouts '*Bravo!*' in her direction and nudges Ramon. 'My God, you've got a plucky wife.'

Ramon shakes his head and laughs. 'Mad, you mean.'

One man slips on the stones and there's a sharp intake of breath from the hundreds of spectators lining the pavements and cobbled steps winding up from the *plaça*. Will he be trampled? Can he crawl away in time? The man is grabbed out of the way by a friend and the bull crashes past. There's a sigh of relief from the masses.

Ramon gives me a grim smile. 'Well, he will live to see another day.'

'I hope they all will,' I reply.

'Everyone makes their own choices,' he says enigmatically.

Although a part of me is caught up in the exhilaration of the event, I'm wondering what will happen to the bull when the event is over. In London, an all-night vigil and a 'Save the Bull' rally would already have been underway. Ollie, as if reading my mind, leans down and asks the question. Alan puckers his brow and gives an awkward cough indicating that he'll leave me to find a choice response.

'He'll go back to his field to play,' I reply as chirpily as I can.

When his attention is diverted I ask Ramon in Spanish what will become of the bull.

He is pragmatic. 'When it finishes running, it will be taken to the abattoir and killed. Then everyone in the village receives a piece of the meat. It is the tradition.'

There's a roar from the crowd as about fifteen strong local men, stripped to the waist, swoop on the bull and attempt, with three thick ropes looped around its neck, to lead it into the small *plaça* where it is to be crowned with a garland of wild flowers. A mass of villagers scream and shout as the men, jostled by the crowds, pull this way and that against the bulk of the creature which lashes out at them, snorting and baying indignantly. The men bob up and down, a small flotilla of fragile vessels dancing about in a wild sea. Rearing back, the bull bucks and thrashes against the ropes, writhing up in the air and lowering its horns in rage and fear. Some of the men, weakened and trembling with the strain of gripping the ropes, fall to the ground, others jumping backwards as the bull lunges forward, its horns homing in on them like a missile. With difficulty it is finally coaxed to the fountain where it immerses its shaggy head in cold water, then rises, shaking the drops from its hide and surveying the noisy, bustling scene with uncomprehending eyes. The leaves shiver on the bowed, ancient plane tree in the square, gently brushing the animal's hide and a cheer rises as a ring of gaudy flowers is placed brutally on the creature's dampened crown. I feel a rush of sorrow. The chase is over and the little black bull will soon be led away to meet its fate.

Ramon taps my sleeve. 'That's that. Now comes the really big event.' He pulls Ollie off his shoulders and begins tickling him. Ollie writhes mirthfully at his feet, yelling out loudly.

'Which is?' Alan asks expectantly above Ollie's squeals.

'Breakfast, of course.' Then to Ollie conspiratorially, 'For you and me that means chocolate croissants, Nesquik, Pepsi and biscuits…'

Ollie nods and gives him a cheeky smile. Then clapping his hands together loudly, Ramon leads us jauntily through the crowd towards his and Catalina's house.

The computer shop is in darkness, the metal barrier snapped shut like a heavy metal eyelid over the window. I look at my watch and frown. It is past five o'clock and siesta is over, so where is everyone? I wander up the street a little and discover that few shops are yet open. The menu in the window of a cosy little restaurant named Can Gata, catches my eye. It is offering a scrumptious sounding three course lunch with wine for about a fiver. I convert the euros to pounds in my head. That would just about buy me a coffee and a muffin in London. A *moto*, one of the small noisy motorbikes beloved by Mallorcans, screeches past me emitting a waft of acrid grey smoke. I fan the still air with my hand and walk slowly back down the quaint cobbled street past the colourful shop windows to the lively *plaça* where I spy Antonia's petite form huddled over a glass at a bar. She sees me and beckons.

'Oh it's so hot!' she complains, her face beaded with sweat, 'I'm having an iced tea. Here take the key. Help yourself. I'll be there in a minute.'

I'm a little thrown by her faith in me as I reach for the key to the shop but we've become friends and she's shrewd enough to see that I'm hardly robber material. For the last four years, she and her interminably unflappable American husband, Albert, who used to serve in the American armed forces, have run HiBit, the leading computer shop in the valley and therefore a Mecca for loping, geeky teenagers, computerate locals and neurotic, tech-obsessed expats. HiBit is of course much more than just a computer shop. It is a meeting place for computer illiterates in need of advice, people who just want a chat or those whose spirits and businesses have been all but broken by the incompetence or dilatory service of the local telephone provider. Antonia, in perfect English but with a pronounced Mallorcan twang, offers humour, sympathy and vengeful solutions where appropriate, while Albert, the ghost of a smirk on his face, listens quietly while fiddling with the plethora of coloured wires and metal screws of a computer he's just built. Then he'll blink, his pale blue eyes wandering towards the ceiling as though seeking divine inspiration and say, 'Well, I guess I can fix that if you can leave it in overnight.'

Even when a computer problem is terminal he'll manage a 'Well it could be worse' or 'Do you want the good news or the bad news?'

DONKEY WORK

Albert is one of those reassuring rocks that surfaces once or twice in town life. He's a friend to all souls given that he speaks the local Mallorcan dialect and Spanish fluently and subscribes to that staple school of thought that teaches that no problem is insurmountable.

Pottering back up the street and through the throng of shoppers, I attempt to open the door. A grim thought strikes me: say one of the neighbouring shopkeepers gets suspicious and thinks I am a *lladre*, a thief? As I struggle with the padlock for some minutes, a large man, cigar butt balanced on his lower lip, approaches me, puts down his shopping bags, turns the rusty key and brutally wrenches the door open. He nods and walks off without a word. A trusting soul. I turn on the lights, drop the key on the glass-panelled desk by the till and cross the showroom. It is small and functional with white walls and tiled floor but still manages to display a significant number of shiny computers against one wall and a selection of technical accessories against the other. By the bottom stone step leading up to the offices, I notice that new stock has arrived. Cardboard boxes are piled there, some already torn open with their contents, cellophane-wrapped Game Boys and diskettes spilling all over the floor. I climb slowly up the stairs to a narrow room where a row of computers is set up for locals and ex-pats alike who need access to e-mail and Internet and who, like me, are probably waiting for their own to be connected at home. *Poc a poc.* I switch on the overhead fan and plug in my own laptop. As soon as it connects it begins to flash wildly as if it's receiving a blood transfusion, whirring and purring, its lights flickering green and amber. Then like a clucking hen laying eggs, it bleeps excitedly as it downloads my e-mails. They appear on the screen in quick succession, as if by magic. The front door slams and a voice yells '*Hola!*' I pop my head over the banister. A shy young man with anxious grey eyes and thick chestnut hair swept back in a ponytail is staring up at me. He's wearing hippy-chic clothes, a nose stud and seems to want to buy a computer. Where's Antonia when you need her? I tell him to come back in five minutes. He shrugs and gives me a confused little smile, mystified that I don't want his business, then leaves. I return to my e-mails, noting with relief that none of them are particularly urgent.

The door bangs downstairs and another customer calls up to me from below. She is middle aged, bespectacled and wearing the sort of shapeless, flowery print cotton dress found only in local markets and Russian maternity wear shops. She speaks rapidly in fits and starts like the rat-a-tat-tat of a round of machine gun fire. At least she's speaking in Castilian Spanish. From what I can grasp, she needs some technical advice. I skip downstairs and start to demonstrate the workings of an infrared mouse to her as best I can. She looks startled and shakes her head sternly. She did say *raton*, didn't she? Antonia arrives in the nick of time and has a fit of giggles. Apparently the woman is a neighbour and has just popped by for a chat, to while away some time, *pasar el rato*.

'Is an easy mistake,' comforts Antonia, sporting an enormous grin. '*Rato, raton*, they sound so similar.'

God knows how I got the wrong end of that stick. It seems I'm going to have to work a little harder at my Spanish. Which reminds me that tonight I have my first lesson with Fransisca at the local language school. She's about half the age of Alan's teacher, Paula, and sounds a lot more fun.

Back upstairs I send off some e-mails and wade through those crying for attention in my in-box. The office in London has sent a steady stream of press release drafts and client proposals for approval along with the minutes of several meetings for checking. An important hotel client has had a major crisis, so I need to pen a carefully worded holding statement for the British media. There's never a dull moment in this job. I stare out of the window. It's nearly six o'clock. The shops are still open and people, their bags full of wares, are ambling along the little cobbled street below me, stopping occasionally for impromptu chats with friends and neighbours. Just a few doors from HiBit, I've discovered an enchanting little shop called Finca Gourmet which sells local food delicacies – home cured *sobrassada* sausage, honey, olive tapenade and seriously scrumptious wines. Then there's Colmado La Luna, our town's mini Fortnum & Mason, which sells heavenly cold meats and cheeses. It's a treat to go and chat with its showman of an owner Xavier, and Carmen, his dry humoured and no nonsense assistant. I'm sorely tempted to pop down and make some purchases but then remember I've already got my computer to carry home. Maybe tomorrow. I see our immaculately groomed deputy bank manager, Tolo, sauntering along, greeting passers-by with a nod of the head or handshake. I knock on the glass pane and he looks up and gives me a huge smile and a wave. He begins mouthing something so I pull open the window. '*Como?*'

'It's the party next month. You and Alan will come?'

'Of course! Wouldn't miss it for the world.'

He nods his head, satisfied that at least one of his customers will be there to witness the cutting of the ribbon. That's if they have such quaint customs in Mallorca. I close the window and observe the other shoppers. No one appears to be in a hurry, as if they have all the time in the world. This is in sharp contrast to London life where we abuse and bully time to mould around our increasingly frantic existences. As I peer dreamily into the street I dwell on how I constantly used to be running to catch up, breathlessly trying to cram as much into the working day as possible. Why? What has to be done today that we can't fruitfully put off until tomorrow? I close down my computer, and watch with satisfaction as the screen goes blank. Antonia plods up the stairs, her wavy blond hair pushed back behind her ears, and pulls out the swivel chair next to my desk. She's holding an unlit cigarette in her hand. 'I need a fag,' she declares and with that, takes some matches from her pocket and lights up.

'You finished already?' she asks quizzically.

'Yep. I fancy a coffee and a quick run before my Spanish class. Work can wait.'

'That a girl! Hey, I could do with a quick espresso too. I'll join you.'

Like a pair of naughty children we shut up shop and head for Café Paris in the *plaça*. It happens that there's a folk dancing demonstration going on in the square. It's the beginning of another fiesta and therefore another bona fide excuse for perfecting the art of doing absolutely nothing.

Rafael's son, Cristian, is sitting next to Ollie in the back of the car, a Game Boy balanced on his plump thighs. He is muttering in Mallorcan and then switching to Spanish and firing questions at me about donkeys. It's a dull day and the clouds are racing across the mountains. I groan at the thought of my marathon training which is scheduled again for tonight.

'What's he saying?' asks Ollie impatiently.

'He wants to know how many donkeys we're buying.'

Ollie looks hopeful. 'Are we going to, then?'

The fact is that I'm not sure why we're here. Rafael's father breeds donkeys and in a rash moment I mentioned to him that they were my favourite animals. The next day we were summoned to his father's field for, I presume, a lesson in donkey maintenance. Ollie and Cristian have become good friends despite a three-year age difference and so they have decided to accompany me on the trip. At least Cristian can converse with his grandfather in Mallorcan if my language skills give out. Alan has conveniently been invited to discuss a business proposition in the town square by Pep, our new friend from the football pitch, so has managed to wheedle out of this dubious excursion.

Old man Bernat, Rafael's father, is leaning on a stick as we walk across his massive pasture which backs on to sharply peaked mountains. At his side is a tiny shivery dog, a *ca rater*, a popular Mallorcan breed. Donkeys eye us cautiously as we approach a barred wooden hut in the corner of the field. Cristian stops still and shouts at his grandfather who shrugs nonchalantly and pulls at the bolts.

'What's in there?' I ask weakly as Cristian scales a fence and grins horribly at us. Ollie instinctively starts to wrap himself around my legs like a baby monkey. It's just a donkey, Old Man Bernat informs me, but apparently he is an angry, evil brute which presumably is why he remains locked up. He says he needs a home. What kind, I wonder – psychiatric? I step back gingerly, sizing up which tree to run for.

The door creaks open and a sinewy and grumpy Eeyore rushes out with the ferocity of an angry bull. Cristian's grandfather wards him off with his stick while Ollie and I cower by an olive tree. He doesn't seem interested in either of us but circles the field with a menacing look on his face before head-butting two docile females grazing nearby. They whinny and gallop away forming a huddle with the rest of the herd. This fiery bundle of fur has got one serious attitude problem. Cristian's grandfather is now yelling at him, tapping his flanks with his stick like a zealous circus trainer. I lift Ollie over the fence and am on the point of hiking myself up too when the mobile rings. It's Michael Roselock. He sounds hysterical.

'This is a bit of a bad time, Michael. Can I call you back in a minute?'

No. It's urgent, he has to speak to me now. Am I in Mallorca? Yes, I am. Well in that case, he says, we might get cut off so he has to speak with me while he has the chance.

'It's disastrous,' he's mewling. 'What are we going to do? The bank is foreclosing. I'm finished.'

When Michael calls like this, his chief intention is to reduce the recipient to a similar state of blind panic. It's a swift transaction, a transfer of terror in the form of WE. What are WE going to do? Like Alice in Wonderland chasing the rabbit down, deep in its burrow, the Michaels of this world succumb to their worst fears, allowing themselves to be gobbled up in a vortex of mayhem and chaos. I don't have a problem with chasing rabbits as long as it's into the sun.

'Hello? Are you listening? Prudence is besides herself. It's curtains.'

There's a loud, angry braying from the Rocky of the donkey world. He's showing me the whites of his teeth. Where's Old Man Bernat gone?

'What the hell is that noise?' snarls Michael.

'Just a motorbike, Carry on.'

Cristian and Ollie are laughing hysterically as the donkey waggles its long ears at me. I try to give it a friendly smile. It glowers back. Michael is telling me that bailiffs have been in, real thugs, who made him feel like a criminal. He says he has to get hold of money, any money, urgently or the shop will be taken. I know that any knee-jerk plan to save the business will, quite frankly, fail. Roselock Fine Jewellery has had its day. It's been well and truly snubbed by the new bovver boys of retailing on the Bond Street block. It's over.

'How would you feel about losing the premises?' I ask as calmly as I can with a donkey savaging my sleeve.

'How? I don't want to think about it!'

Brusquely I release my jumper from Rocky's jaws and head quickly for a nearby tree.

'Michael, it isn't the end. There are other things you can do.' Oh yes, such as? Retrain as a donkey breeder? Come on girl, get a grip.

92

'What?' he spits at me furiously. 'It's easy for you to say that out in the sun, having a life.'

The irony is that Michael could easily be doing the same, commuting between two destinations, having a life out in the sun. But he never would. Money isn't the issue. It's a fear of change, of facing the unknown, and starting afresh, be it in England or elsewhere.

'Michael? There are other things you can do. You're sixty-two. Isn't it time to let go?'

He's sighing heavily now. 'I don't know what to do or where to turn.'

An ambitious thought, a potentially life-saving scheme bursts into my head. Impossible, insane, unworkable and yet... 'I have an idea,' I say hastily as I butt Rocky with my left elbow. 'When I'm back in London, let's talk.'

Michael pulls himself together. 'I'm so sorry. Forgive me.'

I manage a few words of solace and a hurried farewell before dropping the phone and yanking myself up over the fence. Old Man Bernat puffs up to the tree, first bending down to pick up the mobile. He spits copiously on it, before wiping it against his sleeve and passing it back to me. He juts out his bottom lip and swears angrily at Rocky. The donkey does a U-turn and meekly returns to his shed.

'He wasn't happy today,' he says without a whiff of irony. No indeed. There's nowhere to keep a donkey in our unfinished dwelling at present but I wonder if one day in the future, with a little love, attention and a good shrink, I might possibly bring him to heel?

Alan potters into the kitchen with a large smirk on his face.

'Have a good time with your donkeys?'

'Actually, it was more like an SAS training session.'

'Really?' he replies absentmindedly as he flips through a pile of books and newspapers on the table. 'I'm just on my way out to see gorgeous Paula. Can't seem to lay my hands on the Spanish grammar book though.'

'I saw it in the garden yesterday on top of your wormery, of all things.'

He knits his eyebrows in bewilderment. 'Why on earth would it be there?'

'Search me.'

He frowns then shakes his head. 'I must have been distracted and put it down there.'

'Or perhaps you thought it would make excellent fodder for your worms?'

He tuts. 'Paula would be appalled at such a suggestion. I'd better go and retrieve it.'

'Not so fast. I want to hear about your meeting with our chum, Pep.'

He averts his gaze. 'Ah, very good. We met for a coffee at Café Paris in the *plaça*. He's an interesting chap.'

'So what did he want to talk to you about?'

'A little business scheme.'

'Such as?' I can tell he's being deliberately evasive.

'It's quite complex. Anyway, we're going to a football match in Palma in a few weeks so I'll probably learn more then.'

He wanders outside before I can interrogate him further, then reappears with his Spanish book. 'Well, best be off. We're studying the preterite tense today.'

'Lucky you!' I say sadistically.

'Aren't I just?' he replies and sets off through the *entrada* to his car.

I'm intrigued to learn more about Alan's tête-à-tête with Pep and the exact nature of our Mallorcan friend's complex business idea. If it's the opening of a specialist *puro* shop, heaven help me.

FIVE

WATERING HOLES

The shutters have crashed with such force against the windows that I can hear wood splintering on the glass. I sit upright in bed. The sky is dark and moody like a petulant Heathcliff and thunder rumbles ominously and loudly across the sky. Ollie wanders into the bedroom, his tiny frame caught in a Polaroid flash of lightning. He shivers in his pyjamas and climbs on to our bed.

'What's happening? It's pinch black,' he says endearingly, with a gulp.

Alan blinks and turns on the light. 'What's up?'

There's a thud as a tree tears away from the earth.

'JESUS!' The Scotsman is wide awake now and leaping out of bed. The lights flicker and then darkness. The electricity's gone. Alan curses and thrashes his way in the dark like a sightless Gloucester in *King Lear*.

'Let's batten down the hatches.'

I follow his lumbering form out on to the landing and down the stairs, Ollie gripping my nightshirt from behind. It's suddenly icy cold and the wind wails outside, incandescent with rage that it can't penetrate the glass panes. We reach the *entrada* and head for the kitchen and candles. Lightning snaps and frizzles overhead like popcorn in a pan as we feel our way to a drawer, reach inside and pull out some candles. Sightlessly I fumble with a box of matches, startled by the brilliant light as one ignites. Once lit, we steady the candles in melted wax around the kitchen, the eerie light forming weird and monstrous shadows on the walls. Rain starts to hiss on the panes then grows louder and heavier as it gathers momentum. It's now torrential as we yank open windows around the house to pull in the outside shutters. Like fighting an invisible force, we grab at the wooden slats as the shutters dance in Bacchic frenzy in the wind, slimy with rain and stubborn as mules. An hour later the house is secure but the storm rages outside like an incensed ogre, thumping our walls, and spinning tiles off the roof. We hear them tinkle as they crash to the ground. Huddling upstairs in the dark and shuddering with the chill, we finally fall wearily back to sleep.

The room is still and airless when we awaken. The closed shutters have sealed us in a tomb of darkness. I push open a window and a needle of bright light pierces the room. The wind is still strong and clouds scud across the sky with the speed of a racing pulse. We stumble around sleepily, try light switches and taps but nothing works. Blearily looking out into the field, I do a double take. It resembles a watery bog with orange trees floating strangely on its scum. Water has seeped into the cellar and our shutters, casualties of an all night battle, are battered and blasted, some with broken slats. The gardens are strewn with bruised lemons, broken trees and upturned pots, and building materials have blown away in the night, heaven knows where.

As we survey the damage outside, a car makes its way up the waterlogged track, its wheels skidding dangerously towards the edge. We watch as it parks in the courtyard. Out jump Ramon and Catalina.

'Everything OK?' she yells above the wind.

We walk stiffly towards the car.

'Could be worse,' says Alan breezily.

Oh yes? How much, I wonder? We've got no phone, water or electricity and our *terrain* has rapidly transformed into a moat. Everything is just fine and dandy. Ramon explains that no one has electricity in our part of the valley given that it was knocked out in the night. He looks up at the straggling, makeshift telephone line dangling forlornly from a metal telegraph pole and whistles disconcertingly.

'Your line's been hit by lightning. It's come loose from the wall.'

'That'll put paid to the phone for some time then,' Alan says flatly.

'Ah well,' Ramon rejoins brightly, 'at least you'll have some peace and quiet.'

'And I won't have to go to school,' Ollie squeaks excitedly. 'I can watch DVDs all day long.'

'Not without electricity,' quips Catalina. 'But I can give you Catalan homework instead.'

Ollie puffs out his bottom lip. 'Don't you dare!'

Catalina ruffles his hair. 'Well it all depends on how good you are...'

She laughs and then chases him round the courtyard to his shrieks of delight.

Rather more critical than a defunct telephone is the fact that we have no running water as it is driven by an electrical pump. With a modicum of cheer I contemplate not having to wash up in our half-finished kitchen for a while, and eating out at local joints until it's fixed. That's before it dawns on me that we can't wash or use the, er, facilities. 'We'll call Pere,' says Ramon reassuringly. 'Perhaps he can help.'

Pere, our handsome plumber, is always good value, being infinitely patient and full of good humour even when dealing with the grimmest of watery tasks. However, with the best will in the world he won't be able to do much given that it's the electricity that drives the water pump. In time, we may need to consider buying an additional generator for emergencies like this. We enter the dusty kitchen and sit in aluminium beach chairs around the rickety old picnic table, discussing the storm. I dream of having a seigneurial, solid oak dining table big enough to seat at least eight guests and buttermilk wooden furniture around the hob area with gleaming granite work surfaces and, a fantasy too far, a dishwasher! This won't happen for a few more months as the floor tiling is yet to be done, the walls still need painting and we simply don't have the budget. For now we'll have to cope with the bare essentials. In Girl Guide mode, I pour half a bottle of mineral water into a saucepan and place it on the butane-gas hob. At least we can have a hearty cup of coffee. I place a plate of chocolate biscuits on the table and watch Catalina's eyes light up. Like me, she is an inveterate chocoholic.

'You wouldn't believe it,' she says, mid-munch. 'The whole port is flooded so everyone there is completely marooned. All the shops are closed. Heavens know what they'll do for bread.'

Fetching fresh bread daily from the local *forn*, the baker's, is an essential part of Mallorcan life. For a Mallorcan to survive a day without it doesn't bear thinking of. Catalina reaches for another biscuit.

'Hey,' growls her husband. '*Poc a poc* with those.'

She wafts the second biscuit tauntingly above his head. 'It's not fair,' she moans. 'Look at him, the skinny dog, not a tiny bit of fat and he eats chocolate all day long.'

'Yes, but you're much more cuddly,' says Alan giving her arm a squeeze. 'Who'd want to have muscles like Ramon anyway?' he says, winking at her.

'Me!' Ollie looks up adoringly at his hero.

'*Molt bé!*' Ramon gives him a little punch on the arm. Then he looks thoughtful. 'I'd stay put if I were you. The river has burst its banks and is gushing along the main road to Palma. You won't be able to drive beyond your track.'

Many of the roads are apparently impassable, strewn with trees, huge boulders and rocks.

'They're saying the government might declare a state of emergency up here,' says Catalina glumly.

This just gets better and better. Much as he enjoys his new school, Ollie is euphoric at the thought of using the inflatable dingy to set out on an Indiana Jones-style adventure down in the water-logged field rather than settling down to lessons. There really is no way we can drive to his school in this weather. Alan has a certain glimmer in his eye.

'What a nuisance. I'll have to miss my Spanish lesson with Paula.'

'You can always walk,' I say robustly.

'Don't be ridiculous! It would be a nightmare walking in all this rain. No, I'll have to postpone it – sadly.' He manages to look dismayed. I hadn't realised he was such a thespian.

'Well, the phone isn't working so you'd better use the mobile.'

He sighs deeply and gets up. 'I'll go and call her now.'

'When things calm down a bit, why not come up to the house for a shower and dinner?' says Catalina with largesse. 'We can always put you up for a few nights if things get desperate.'

I say we'll wait to see what happens. Perhaps the electricity will return soon and the skies will clear. She and Ramon look dubiously at one another. I should know better. Things have a habit of taking forever to put right here.

Before they leave, Ramon unloads a pile of sandbags which implies we really are under siege, and does a tour of the perimeter of the field and gardens. He discovers that a huge rock terrace has collapsed and our newly fitted drains are disgorging their contents all over the paths. He and Alan patch things up as best they can in the howling wind. Rain has started to fall again and Ramon and Catalina make a dash for the car. They are soaked to the skin. She kisses me on the cheek, bellowing above the din from the skies. 'When the rain stops, come up to the village. We can at least open some wine and laugh.'

When they've gone we do an inventory of our supplies. We have two small glass-covered oil lights with wicks and curved handles like props used for a period drama, three sturdy new paraffin lamps, unopened, and a big bundle of candles. It's a start.

There's a thumping at the front door. It is Rafael wrapped in a moleskin and dripping with water. We usher him into the *entrada* where he shakes his curly brown mop and flops on a chair by the cold hearth. He is still full of smiles. Doesn't anything get this man down?

'*Amics!* Well, look at this! Now you see the real Mallorca! It rain now for many days, yes. You have candles, food? Everything OK?'

Such astonishing selflessness from a neighbour is in danger of making me mawkish. I think of my London flat in a building where, by contrast, nobody connects. Like laboratory rats in isolated cages, we coexist blindly under the same roof in such close proximity that, but for an intervening wall, or separating floor, at night our heads might touch, or fingers interlace. Yet it is as if we live on different planes, not floors, with neighbourly civility strictly confined to snatched greetings in the communal hallway when by hazard any of us should collide there unexpectedly. It's not anybody's fault, just one of the afflictions of urban life.

'We have *festa*, eh?' Rafael, the comic turn, is laughing manically. 'We get good wine and do what you say, rain dance?' He raises his arms, claps and wiggles his hips, shuffling around the *entrada* singing, with his backside upturned like a bumbling Baloo the bear. Ollie covers his hands over his mouth, shaking with laughter.

'Eh *amic!* You laugh at me?' he says, pouncing on him and tickling him until he yells for mercy amid explosions of giggles. Rafael then pokes around the cellar, looks at the rain seeping in and blocks the doors with our sandbags. He shows us how to ignite the paraffin light safely and promises to bring us some of his well water.

'Rafael, do you think the old lady at the end of the track will be OK?' I think of her alone in her bungalow and wonder if I should bring her some soup. Our German neighbours have already returned back home to Berlin, luckily avoiding the storms here.

'You mean Margalida Sampol? *Segur*,' he says, nodding his head. 'Her daughter lives just on other side of the track. *No problema*.'

I forget what a close-knit community it is up here. Happily, meals on wheels are surplus to requirement.

'Come up for a drink later,' says Alan with gusto. 'At least we've got wine in the cellar and we can unfreeze some soup.'

'*Molt bé, mi amic!* Tonight I bring bread and cake from house and we have party. I bring Cristian down to play with Ollie, yes? He no go to school today and I can't take him to his mother's house in this weather.'

Cristian, at nine, lives a happy coexistence between his divorced parents' homes although I always suspect he leads a more laddish life over at his father's, putting homework on a backburner in place of football, walking the dog, riding on the back of Rafael's motorbike and dining out a lot.

As he sets off up the track whistling heartily, I wonder momentarily what Greedy George would make of him and decide that they would be soulmates.

'Good egg, that Rafael,' he'd say, 'Life and arsehole of the party.'

Yes, a jolly good egg indeed.

The house is forlorn when Rafael leaves and the day passes slowly while the rain just gets heavier. Cristian and Ollie tire after some hours sailing our dingy around the field and so decide to dry off and help Alan to get a roaring fire going in the hearth, which raises our spirits considerably. We eat some oatcakes and cheese for lunch and attempt washing up in boiled mineral water. In the past I wouldn't have questioned such waste but now it almost hurts. In London it never crossed my mind to conserve or recycle because I always deemed it another of those infuriatingly politically correct things to do like not making jokes about Irishmen or buying *The Big Issue* but shamefully binning it as soon as the vendor had turned his back. When we arrived here and unpacked, a wooden crate was emptied and thrown by the packers on to the rubbish heap. Later that day one of the builders wrestled it into his van. When I asked Stefan about it, he said the man was going to make a kennel from it for his dog. I recall how I used to think nothing of hurling a pair of jeans into the nearest dustbin when they had a tear particularly because as a lousy needlewoman, I had no desire to attempt a home repair job. Now, I wouldn't dream of it but then again, I do have the best of both worlds, given that all our frayed, ripped and hole ridden garments are carted off by Catalina to her ninety-year-old grandmother who lovingly and industriously restores them to near perfection.

The other thing I used to throw away without a thought were egg boxes. That is until one day here I happened upon a chapel in the mountains. It was hewn out of simple stone and the inner walls were white and uncluttered by religious memorabilia. A simple cross stood at the nave faced by ten wooden pews but the thing that fascinated me most was the far wall. Unlike the others, it was textured and seemed to ripple. I had to touch it. When I got closer, I realised to my amazement that it had been entirely fashioned out of hundreds of egg boxes which were painted metallic silver. A small sign nearby revealed that the children of the mountain community had created it under the direction of a local Mallorcan artist. Now I'm nauseatingly evangelical and recycle all my egg boxes. In fact, *Blue Peter* should embrace me as a new disciple, given that Ollie uses them for painting and models, although the majority go to a friend who rears her own hens and is always in desperate need of them. Any spares I take grovellingly to the market each week, hoping to ingratiate myself with the friendly but stern Theresa. It seldom cuts any ice with her but begrudgingly she takes them just the same.

The thunder rolls overhead and a tongue of lightning illuminates a pine tree that writhes and thrashes about with the wild abandon of a tribal dancer. The sky has grown so dark that we check our watches for fear that we have somehow jumped to the middle of the night by some numinous artifice. Neighbours' dogs are barking loudly as the wind outside gathers speed. I suddenly think of Franco, the ebullient bulldog owned by Rafael, shivering outside in his fenced run, pitifully alone and afraid. Mallorcans living in the rural areas like to keep pets but most have a brisk, unemotional view of them. Animals should live outside the home, not be indulged and should, where possible, serve a useful purpose. Despite my Francis of Assisi leanings, I am an inexpert animal handler, not having possessed a pet since my childhood and having been forbidden to keep animals in the London flat by the building's officious management committee. I hunt through the fridge and discover some old lamb chops and the remains of a hunk of gammon. Wrapping them in a plastic bag, I go down to the cellar, find an old tartan blanket once used for packing, and set off down the boggy track to Rafael's house. Foolishly I have left without informing Alan but imagine even on a murky night like this, little harm can come to me along a short track. I call out Franco's name in a hoarse whisper, not wanting to alert Rafael to my presence. How could I possibly explain to my neighbour why I feel the need to feed his dog in the midst of a storm? In the darkness, I hear the sound of doggy breath at the fence. Franco licks my fingers through the bars of wood and barks with excitement.

'Shhhhh...' With the spare key to the dog's run, given to me some weeks ago by Rafael, I attempt with trembling, numb fingers to insert it in the lock. It's stuck. What is it with me and keys in this country? The rain and wind are unrelenting and I'm practically blown across Rafael's yard and into his chicken shed like an ungainly Mary Poppins. I can see the *Majorca Daily Bulletin* headline news:

Storms claim life of English Woman

Storms which have rocked the island for two days have tragically taken the life of an English woman found swept by gale force winds into the wall of a chicken shed in the early hours of this morning. Rafael Sastre, owner of the property, said he was devastated at the find. 'She was lying wrapped in a blanket gripping a bag of old meat. We don't know why. She was good neighbour. I very sad.' Family of the deceased are too distressed to comment at this stage.

Franco is howling. 'All right. For heaven's sake, shut up! I'm trying my best.' I listen anxiously in case Rafael might have decided to investigate what's going on outside but his front door remains tight-lipped. For once a spot of luck.

With cold fingers I hook the blanket over one of the fence posts and rattle the key, which this time budges, and the gate swings open wildly in the wind. The dog rushes at me in the dark, his huge bulk sending me flying into the sea of cold, muddy water on the track. So much for doing a good deed. I get up with difficulty and grab at the gate, my feet sliding in the mud. Franco is pawing me roughly and licking my face. The rain lashes down and my scarf is swept away in a gust of wind. With chagrin I see it float off high above an orchard, heading for the local church roof. I squelch up the steps to Franco's run, my clothes clinging to my body, and try to fend him off while tipping the food in his bowl. Miraculously the blanket is still dry so I haul it into his basket and lift them both up on to a dry sheltered ledge and quickly slam the gate shut. Franco falls on the meat like a savage. Back at the house I attempt to wash with a litre of cold mineral water before throwing on some dry clothes and pouring myself a stiff drink.

We sit in the kitchen reading books by candlelight and finally, in desperation, pull out an old Monopoly board to amuse Ollie. Cristian returned to his father's house some time back and we are expecting them at any moment for dinner. I haven't played a board game in years but needs must. However, by eight-thirty, we are all hungry and Alan and I are totally broke. I have been bankrupted and forced to sell my stations, and the Scotsman is stuck with a duff set of properties and has no money, so we decide, in a state of stalemate, to risk the car and head for Es Turo Restaurant where Catalina will hopefully be on shift.

'What about Rafael and Cristian?' I ask.

'Maybe they've forgotten,' Ollie pipes up.

Alan rubs the glass pane of the front door and peers into the gloom. 'Well, we can always knock on his door and see if he wants to join us.'

At that very moment, there's the sound of crunching gravel and a singing Rafael arrives, Cristian tripping along in his wake.

'I bring wine, cake and bread but I can't find no women!'

Like a one-man hurricane he whisks through the *entrada* and warms his hands by the fire, laughing raucously. Alan thumps him on the shoulder.

'To hell with it, we've decided to go out. Come on, let's find some good women and wine up in the village.'

'Why not?' yells Rafael. 'Come, let's go party!'

Despite the near impenetrable roads, we finally arrive and cram into the warm interior of Es Turo. We exchange kisses with Xisca, the cheerful owner, and visit Catalina at the back in the kitchen. She gives a big grin.

'Ah, you smelled my meatballs down in the valley, eh?'

We sit down with a warming bottle of red wine, bread, *aioli*, the local garlic mayonnaise, and olives, and soon a steaming plateful of delicious meatballs arrive, drenched in Catalina's home-made tomato sauce. We are lucky to have found a table since the place is heaving and several groups of woebegone locals who've turned up in search of a plateful of hot food and cheer have had to be turned away. Rafael scans the room, and seeing a group of friends, excuses himself and rushes over for a gossip. Xisca makes her way to our table.

'Listen,' she says, 'Catalina has told me about your problems. You can come over to our house. We have gas heaters and hot water.'

Once more, the kindness of relative strangers leaves me speechless. We thank her but explain that we must learn to brave the elements. There may be times when we have no choice but to go it alone. Replete and happy, with Rafael's jokes ringing in our ears, we return home to our dark and icy house, still naively believing the worst must surely be over.

There's a loud tooting, so loud that it permeates my dreams and has me stumbling out of bed, disorientated yet alert. I'm still fairly exhausted. It was only yesterday, after three further days of blinding rain and storms, that we finally had our electricity and water reconnected. Alan is still cocooned beneath the duvet, oblivious to the noise. Opening the window I look down into the front courtyard and see Lorenç, the wood man, beaming up at me.

'Open the door, you lazy woman! It's eight o'clock!'

I yawn and give him a half-hearted wave and nod of the head. It suddenly dawns on me that it's Saturday. What on earth is he doing delivering wood today? Catalina told me he was coming on Monday. I plod downstairs, open the heavy wooden doors and wince as cold light streams in. Lorenç, full of good cheer in his warm logging jacket and gloves, leaps forward to kiss me on both cheeks.

'I thought you were coming next week?'

He shrugs. 'But I come today.'

There's no point in pushing the point. Spontaneity is the name of the game around here and quite frankly you'd have to be crazy to turn away wood, even at the weekend, given that it's your main source of warmth during the chilly Mallorcan winter. Lorenç begins piling wood from the back of his grubby and battered white truck on to our front porch. I shiver with the cold.

'Get a jumper on, woman, or you'll freeze and get the sleeping senyor to come and give me a hand.'

Alan is already halfway down the staircase as I stomp back up. He rubs his hands together. 'Ah, wood. What a wonderful sight!'

'Your back won't be saying that tonight.'

He grimaces. 'Well, the promise of a relaxing massage later…'

'In your dreams!' I give him a prod in the direction of the front door and watch as Lorenç comes over to greet him. Upstairs, I quickly change into my running gear and give my face a quick splash. Given that I've been forced to rise early, I might as well get my run over with before the day gets going. Ollie is still in a deep slumber when I pop my head round the door of his room. I'm impressed that he can sleep through the din of crashing and splintering wood as Alan and Lorenç hurl logs, one on top of the other, in a giant heap on the front porch. I watch them from the doorway.

'You still got no water and light?' quizzes Lorenç.

'It came on last night,' says Alan. 'Four days of living like moles and the phone won't be fixed for a week.'

'You saved on some bills though?'

'No way! It cost us a fortune. We had to eat out all the time.'

Lorenç stands erect and gives a philosophical shrug. 'You want to live in rural Mallorca. Now you see what it's like.'

Alan swings a log at the pile. 'Yep, no surprises any more.'

I slip out on to the steps and do my warm up exercises in the courtyard, much to Lorenç's glee.

'Ah look, the professional at work,' he taunts. 'You going to win the London Marathon, *si?*'

'Well, I'm expecting her to do it in under two hours,' Alan says with a wink.

'You reckon it'll take me that long?' I scoff, joining in the banter.

Lorenç laughs. 'Well it would take me about a month.'

'And me about a year,' rejoins Alan, 'but I'd never be mad enough to do it.'

I bid them farewell and jog off up the track, nearly colliding with Margalida Sampol outside her house. She squints at me and begins muttering in Mallorcan.

'Look at you! Uncovered arms on a day like this! You'll get the *grip*.' Mallorcans are always predicting colds.

'I'm fine, Margalida. Once I start running, I get really hot.'

'You'll be running a fever more like,' she tuts.

I try to smother a guffaw.

'Young people never listen to good advice. You should be wearing a coat at this hour.'

I thank her as sincerely as possible for her pearls of wisdom and excuse myself before I really do come down with a *grip*, standing around in the cold. I don't even want to try contemplating what it might be like running in a heavy winter coat.

As I set off along the main road for the port, a car honks from behind. I slow down and turn round to see Pep, Alan's new accomplice, leaning out of the window, *puro* in hand. He stops the car abruptly, seemingly oblivious to the truck tooting behind him which is forced to overtake. He pushes his wavy grey hair back behind his ears and leans his head out of the car window.

'Hey you want a *churro*? It will give you energy.'

He delves into a bag on the passenger seat and produces some *churros*, the sugary doughnuts savoured throughout Spain. I smell their rich aroma.

'Are they still warm?'

'*Segur*, of course, I have just come from the town. They're fresh from the bread shop.' A tanned arm juts out from the car door, at the end of which he is dangling a fat, sugar and oil drenched *churro*.

I'm almost tempted to accept which just goes to show how dedicated a runner I really am. 'Pep, my mother told me never to take sweets from strange men in cars.'

'Good advice, but I'm not so strange really and even your mother would have succumbed to a *churro*.'

I give an exasperated sigh. 'Put them away! I'm trying to get in training for heaven's sake.'

He sniffs disdainfully. 'Oh well, if you insist. I'd better let you go but remember we all have dinner tonight? We'll feed the boys early so they can go and play in peace. You won't forget?'

'How could I? It will be the highlight of my day.'

He gives me a curious smile and takes a long drag on his cigar. The engine rattles and with a languid wave from the window, he drives on.

We are sitting at the spacious mahogany dining table in Pep's parlour, replete after huge helpings of *arroz brut*, literally meaning 'dirty rice' in Mallorcan, a mountain delicacy which is rich and flavoursome and anything but dirty, except maybe in colour. It's the nearest you might come to a soupy rice stew – a hearty fusion of vegetables, rabbit, pork, *caracoles* (snails) and when in season, *tords* (thrushes). I am thankful that no *tords* are in evidence.

'You know,' drawls Pep, 'Now is the beginning of the hunting season because the birds are migrating from Europe to Africa.'

'Presumably thrushes need to take cover?' asks Alan.

'To be sure. The *tords* are a great Mallorcan speciality and are hunted until the end of October. '

'Do you hunt them?' I ask pointedly.

'When I was young, *si*, but now I can't be bothered. My father and grandfather used to fix up the *filats*, big nets that stretched between bamboo poles which we put in the fields. The stupid birds would fly straight into them and get trapped.'

I can't bear the idea of thrushes being killed by the bushel in such a seemingly heartless way. Alan chews on a piece of bread thoughtfully, not wanting to pass comment on an ancient Mallorcan custom. Pep leans back in his chair and observes us coolly.

'You British think we're barbaric, no? We kill little bulls, we eat thrushes, and you British are so proper.'

Alan frowns, trying to make light of it all. 'I have to admit, I'm not a great one for game hunting of any kind, but I'll eat it just the same. I just don't see the necessity to kill small birds.'

'Yes, what's the point when there are so many other things to eat?' I ask.

'Well you can apply that to anything,' grunts Pep.

Juana, Pep's sturdy Mallorcan wife who is bustling about the kitchen preparing coffee, wipes her hands on her pinny and shakes her head. 'You can debate all night on the subject but at the end of the day, we eat them because they taste good and it's a tradition, although it's not so popular now. As they say, when in Rome…'

'Absolutely,' says Alan, with some relief. 'We've moved here to be part of Mallorcan life, and that means embracing all the traditions.'

'Good,' says Pep, mischievously. 'Then I'll pick you up for a spot of *tord* shooting in the morning.'

Alan's face expresses momentary discomfort before he registers that his leg is being well and truly pulled.

'Very funny,' he says, narrowing his eyes.

Juana gives a husky chuckle and places a tray of cheeses and bread on the table and sits down. A pot of coffee simmers on the stove.

'Ah, there's nothing like good Mallorcan *yeso*,' says Alan eyeing the cheeses with satisfaction.

Pep and Juana share a smile at this while Alan looks on helplessly.

'Be careful,' says Pep, unable to control his facial muscles. 'If you go into restaurants asking for *yeso*, you might get more than you bargained for. *Yeso*, means plaster. I think you meant *queso*, cheese.'

Juana and I are already giggling inanely as Alan fights to maintain a little dignity. 'Well, it's damned similar,' he protests. 'Sometimes I think I'm too old in the tooth for learning a new language.'

'Not at all,' says Pep kindly. 'You do admirably well. Think of all the lazy English living for years in Mallorca who don't bother to learn a word. You should be proud of yourself, *mi amic*.'

He jumps up and rumbles about in an old cupboard. There's a clinking of bottles and he returns to the table with cognac and Herbes, the local Mallorcan liqueur.

'Let's drink to new friends!' he says heartily. 'Juana! Go and get the glasses.'

She obediently ambles over to a wooden sideboard and fishes out four small tumblers which she dumps on the table. Then, before sitting down, she unceremoniously whacks Pep round the ear with a tea towel. He yelps in shock. 'Next time, remember to ask nicely,' she says with a warning smile.

Alan's eyebrows rise a slither as he catches my eye. Pep may be a cool customer but he certainly met his match when he married Juana.

Our local Banca March is throbbing with people as we push against the glass front doors and enter the throng. The new look bank is now open plan with a light marble floor, shiny polished wooden counters and gleaming white paintwork. The manager still retains his own office but in the refurbishment, one wall has been fitted with a large glass panel so that he is now exposed to the customer. Alan seems to disapprove of this.

'The poor chap won't have much privacy, will he?' he says above the din as we squeeze towards the drinks table.

'You mean he can't sneak a quick cigar if he wants one,' I reply crisply.

'Exactly,' he says.

Someone touches my arm and there is Tolo, the deputy bank manager, bearing two glasses of chilled cava.

'Here,' he beams. 'I am so happy you have come to toast our new refurbishment. What do you think?'

'Jolly nice. It's very open.'

'*Si, si,* it's much more friendly and bright. Come, let me introduce you to some clients.' He leads us towards a group of suited men quaffing drinks and apparently sharing a private joke. They halt their huddling and turn politely to greet us.

'This is Senyor Rivas, *el Batle,* the mayor, and Senyor Marco Arbono, one of his councillors, and finally Senyor…'

The senyor in question is Xavier, owner of Colmado La Luna, my favourite local grocery store.

'*Hola guapa!*' he says, kissing me on both cheeks and shaking Alan's hand warmly. The mayor and the others relax, pleased that we are known to at least one of them.

'This senyora is one of my best customers,' Xavier says in Spanish.

The mayor smiles. 'So you are helping the town's economy?'

'Single-handedly,' I say.

Alan leans over to Tolo and says dryly. 'Maybe now is the time to freeze our account?'

'If she runs your account into the ground, we'd be happy to give you a loan,' replies Tolo with a broad smile.

Alan punches him on the arm. 'No doubt.'

We pass a few pleasantries with *el Batle* and decide to take our leave.

'Wait,' says Tolo. 'I want you to meet Victoria Duvall, she's a local celebrity – a film director.'

We dutifully trail behind him until we come face to face with a tall, striking woman, who is hastily bidding farewell to another guest.

'Senyora Duvall,' says Tolo with gravitas. 'May I present…'

Impatiently she whips out a card from her handbag and places it firmly in my hand. 'Nice to meet you, but I really must be off. Call me some time.'

And with that she glides through the crowds and disappears into the street. I peer at the thick cream card which has the words, 'Victoria Duvall, Film Director' embossed on its surface in rich, black ink.

Tolo shrugs his shoulders. 'I apologise. She is a busy woman but at least now she knows who you are.'

Hardly. She didn't even wait to be introduced. Nevertheless, I have her card and also a strange feeling that we shall be meeting the elusive Victoria Duvall again before too long.

The alarm clock bellows in my ear. It's seven o'clock. I turn to awaken Alan but he's not there. The pillow is plumped up which indicates that he hasn't been to bed at all. The previous night he and Pep had agreed to meet in the town's *plaça* to discuss their secret business scheme, and I had been warned by Alan that it could be a late night. Late indeed. I hope nothing untoward has happened to him but have a vague memory of hearing the front door slam at some stage in the night. Maybe he never made it as far as the staircase.

I wake Ollie and get him washed and dressed before pottering into the kitchen for my morning cup of tea. An intriguing sight greets me. Alan is slumped in a chair, his head resting heavily on his crossed arms on the kitchen table. He snores loudly and contentedly, blissfully unaware that I have entered the room.

It's only then that I notice the debris littered on the table – an assortment of empty and half drained bottles of specialist whiskies together with empty cigar boxes, a gasping ashtray and two small grubby tumblers.

Ollie walks in and stares calmly at his father as if he's examining a laboratory rat. 'What's he doing?' he asks as he places a chocolate croissant on a plate and sits down at the table.

'Sleeping,' I say while filling the kettle.

'I can see that,' he replies disdainfully. 'Can I wake him up?'

'Sure.'

He strides over to Alan and pounces on him like a rather zealous cat with a gecko, and then begins shaking him violently. Alan gives a deep groan and raises his head, his eyes blearily scanning the room.

'What am I doing down here?'

'Good question.' I am savouring the moment.

'Looks like you've had lots of naughty drinks and *puros*,' says Ollie helpfully.

Sadistically I place a cup of black coffee in front of him. 'It seems to me that you and Pep had quite a long business meeting.'

He surveys the bottles and winces. 'Well, Pep wanted to try some of my rare Scottish malts so we came back and had a few drams.'

'So I see. And then what?'

'Well, Pep walked home…'

'Staggered more like.'

He glares at me. 'We were doing some important research for our business scheme actually.'

'Really? And what might that be?'

He looks defeated. 'I suppose I might as well tell you. We're thinking of opening a specialist whisky shop.'

It's difficult to suppress an urge to snort out loud.

'Don't tell me, it will also sell rare *puros*?'

He brightens a little and regards me with admiration. 'Well funny you should say that. We were just thinking along those lines.'

I leave him nursing a sore head, shower, dress and rush Ollie out of the door ready for school. As I jump in the car, engine humming, Catalina drives into the courtyard. She beams from behind her window, parks and comes over. I lower my window.

'Hey,' she says with a huge grin. 'A little bird tell me two bad men were out on the town last night. They were drinking in Café Paris until very late.'

I tap her on the arm. 'Your little bird was correct but what you don't know is that the two revellers carried on back at the *casa* until the wee hours.'

Catalina shakes with mirth. 'And where are they now?'

'The Scotsman is a fragile wreck in the kitchen and I hate to think what Juana said when Pep crawled home.'

'I look after Alan,' she says compassionately. 'Maybe I cook him nice eggs and some *jamon serrano*?'

'Lovely,' I say, imagining Alan's green aspect at the very suggestion of fried eggs and smoked ham. 'Oh and do remind him that he has his Spanish lesson with the luscious Paula at ten o'clock.'

She gives an enthusiastic and complicit nod of the head and disappears into the house.

SIX

LONDON: OCTOBER

Thursday 6 p.m., Caffè Nero

Ed is gorging on a chocolate muffin and eyeing the door of the café warily. In order to maintain his vigil, he fretfully pushes back his dishevelled mop of hair, which falls in front of his owlish spectacles like a dense black veil. I give him a kick under the table. He shoots me a frightened chicken look.

'What on earth is the matter with you today?'

He touches the rim of his MEK for reassurance like Linus with his blanket, and scrapes some crumbs from his lip with his hand.

'It's just that I've got a little nervous about terrorist extremists, Scatters. It's the idea of a bomb-laden nutter walking into the café and blowing us all up.' He gulps at his cappuccino.

'You mean terrorists against the evils of caffeine?' I ask naughtily.

'You may mock, but there are always shoot outs in fast food places in the States. All it needs is one stray lunatic to get the idea…'

'You don't think they'd choose a more obvious target? I mean why here, today?'

'Why when anywhere?' he sniffs deeply, taking a small yellow pill from the MEK and popping into his mouth. 'Look, you're a bit out of it where you are. I just think one should be vigilant.'

'Fine, Ed, but you did choose the location.'

He swallows some coffee. 'You're still annoyed because it's not Starbucks.'

'Ed, these days I really don't care where we go. At least they have real cups here.'

Now there's a thought: obsessional London coffee behaviour. In the mountains of Mallorca you simply order your coffee black, with milk, iced or as a *solo* – an espresso. But in London there are a hundred and one permutations and boy, how I used to care about mine. Sometimes it was a tall, triple-shot, cappuccino extra hot, or a short, double-shot caramel macchiato or a grande, decaf latte with extra froth or a hazelnut and vanilla iced mocha with cream. I mean, what was I on? Now I prefer to drink tea which has subsequently made me far less stressed and has saved me a fortune.

Ed's sucking noisily at the froth in his cup. 'So, what's happening back in wild Waltons' country?'

'Nothing much, really. We've just had the worst storms in the island's history. We had no electricity, heating or water for five days and no phone. The garden was completely flooded and is still in a total mess.'

Ed has dropped the last piece of his muffin. 'You're joking?'

'Sadly not.'

'God! What a nightmare! Why didn't you all fly back to civilisation, immediately?'

'And where would that be exactly?'

'Oh very funny.'

'Ed, remember we live there now. It's all one big adventure.'

'And what about Alan, does he view it all as a grand adventure?'

'Well, now he's met Pep, his new cigar smoking accomplice, he's very chipper.'

Ed knits his eyebrows. 'What does this chap do?'

'I don't know but he's trying to involve Alan in some insane business venture selling whisky and cigars. They have secret assignations.'

'What?' he almost chokes. 'He's not mafioso or anything is he? I hope he's not fronting some dodgy contraband outfit.'

'That would be rather exciting but I fear not. The contraband business dried up in our town some years back.'

Ed looks unconvinced. 'Just tell him to be careful.'

I try not to snigger.

'And how is my godson doing?'

'Oh he's very happy. He's taken up with an older woman, a glamorous German living next door who plays football. It's very racy where we are.'

He shakes his head. 'We might as well be living on different planets.'

I decide to switch subjects since he's getting maudlin.

'Anyway, tell me more about your Internet babe, Cotton-Georgia. I've been waiting for news with bated breath.'

He hangs his head sadly. 'Look if you're just going to laugh…'

I frown. 'Of course I'm not! I take your Internet fantasy girls terribly seriously. Remember Mary Lou from Wisconsin?'

He runs his fingers through his unkempt hair. I remind myself to nag him about getting it cut.

'Mary Lou was different. We had music in common. Emotionally she wasn't right for me. That's all.'

'Nothing to do with her being 18 stone and a Moonie?'

He shoots me a wounded glance. 'Anyway, Cotton-Georgia is my new soulmate which is why I'm distraught that she hasn't e-mailed since our row.'

Despite his traumatised state, I notice he's still been able to tuck into his giant muffin. He flips me an evil look.

'Before you say anything, I'm comfort eating.'

'Of course,' I nod without conviction. 'Anyway, what row? I thought you'd only just met her through one of those American Internet dating agencies.'

He sighs heavily. 'I've known her at least three weeks. Her father's some sort of lay preacher who can do snake handling and I made the mistake of saying he sounded a bit weird.'

'Can't you find anyone normal?

'She is normal!' he splutters. 'She has a degree in Social Psychology.'

'Oh, that's a surprise.'

Despite the barb, he carries on. 'She happens to be a talented cross-stitcher and even plays basketball against the odds.'

He takes a sip of coffee and tries not to catch my eye. I'm like a pig detecting a truffle.

'Against what odds, Ed?'

He stares intently out of the window and shakes his head. 'I shouldn't have said anything.'

'Ed???'

'OK, she's got a club-foot.'

I take a deep slurp of black tea. 'Ah! I see…'

Friday 8 a.m., St James's Park

Having spent a raucous evening over at the home of James and Sophie, some local friends, I wake up with a mild hangover, something I occasionally suffer from in London but never in Mallorca. Put it like this, in London we so often drink to forget, whereas in Mallorca we simply drink to enjoy. I enter Birdcage Walk and stroll into St James's Park. Streaks of sunlight are wriggling through the branches of the horse chestnut trees and ducks and haughty pelicans are calling from the bank of the lake. The sound reminds me of my raucous Mallorcan frogs. I'm sad to think that with the onset of cooler weather they'll soon leave our pond, hopefully to return in the spring. A young gardener, white breath coiling up like tobacco smoke and hands thrust into woolly green mitts, is planting bulbs, patting his trowel down on the earth as each one is bedded. He stands up briefly to examine his work and then squats to pluck out some weeds. I loll by a tree, coat collar turned up and watch him, absorbed and inspired by this scene of rural bliss happening right in the centre of London. Around us, the sound of heels clip-clopping furiously on the paths seems deafening as commuters, oblivious to their surroundings, march by in corporate combat gear. Unsmiling and on automatic pilot, they speed along, slicing up any straggler that crosses their path. I used to be one of them. I would take this route every day and did I ever stop for a second to observe the ducks and swans or witness the planting of bulbs? Are you kidding? I walk slowly up the path, yearning to stay in the park but for a while longer I must play the game – so off I stride in fitted suit, kitten heels and grown up's camel coat in the direction of Mayfair and my office.

Friday 1.30 p.m., Hatchards Bookshop

I'm scampering around the new titles section on the ground floor of Hatchards, my favourite London bookshop and haunt, which just so happens to be conveniently situated a stone's throw from Fortnum & Mason, the Queen's renowned grocer. Roger Katz, the store's famed sales manager and a good friend, pops out, lean and keen, from behind a bookcase and kisses me on the cheek.

'Aha! So you're back in town?'

'One of those flying visits, Roger. Any recommendations?'

His head tilts slightly to the left as he ponders the question, then he's off, a gleam in his eye as he scuttles over to the shelves, a child in his own sweetshop, talking ten to the dozen and pulling down books at an alarming rate. Ten minutes later I leave the shop with a groaning carrier bag stuffed to the brim with several signed novels, a horticultural wonder for the Scotsman and three *Horrible Histories* for Ollie. It seems that when I return to London I spend all my earnings on books, a phenomenon that Alan finds thoroughly frustrating and yet he waits avidly for a show of my book booty when I return to Mallorca.

I have to get to Roselock & Son. I examine my watch and decide that I can just squeeze in five minutes in the food department of Fortnum & Mason to satisfy my tea fixation and to buy gifts of truffles for my lovely stallholder Teresa and neighbour Margalida Sampol. I shall have to squirrel away all the receipts from Alan when I finally return home.

Friday 2.15 p.m., Roselock & Sons Fine Jewellery

The polished mahogany doors of Roselock Fine Jewellery feel silky and cool as I push past them and into the shop. A buzzer sounds immediately above the door and a young man with a sombre face, more suited to a funeral parlour, approaches me ingratiatingly.

'Can I help you, Madam?' His hands are clasped and his black short hair is smeared with gel which gleams like aspic. He must be a temporary recruit since most of the staff have left. I explain that I am meeting Michael Roselock and he looks apprehensively at his watch and then at a velvet curtain behind which I know to be Michael's office.

'It's all right. You won't find Polonius lurking there,' I say cheerfully. 'Michael is expecting me.'

His face is blank. The product of a Shakespeare-free education.

'He didn't say he was expecting anybody,' he whines.

I waltz by him and rap on the door behind the curtain. Michael peeps through, his watery blue eyes downcast, and ushers me in sadly. Sitting on a chair by his elegant desk in a voluminous mauve worsted suit is Prudence Braithwaite, her face carved with an expression of beatification.

'How lovely to see you dear,' she says in motherly tones. 'You do look well. Mallorca's obviously suiting you.'

'It's been quite a change.'

'No regrets, then?' says Michael with an attempt at a smile.

'None whatsoever.'

'I suppose you'll be thinking of winding up your PR business in the not too distant future to make your living over there?' Prudence chips in.

I'm not quite sure how to answer this. It has been on my mind for a while. 'We'll see, Prudence. Anyway, how have things been with you?'

'It's been hell. You've no idea,' Michael says almost inaudibly.

I have known Michael for six years and in that time have shared innumerable dramas with him and his company. He has resisted takeover bids by several industry giants and fought off the big international retail players who came like thugs with fists full of cash to squeeze out the little guys on the street and relieve them of their premises. For some time, Michael held out, like a lonely sheriff in a lawless town, holed up in his shop with his faithful deputy, Prudence. Then business took a turn for the worse, the nouveau customer moved into the area replacing the bluebloods and modest spenders, shunning Roselock's jewellery in favour of trendy brands with ugly baubles designed by quasi celebrities and spoilt It girls. Chic glossy magazines no longer featured talented names of the past but feted celebrity instead. The dawn of a new, fickle, personality-led era had begun and Michael Roselock and his ilk's days were numbered. Had he succumbed, invested in celebrity himself and embraced a new kind of customer perhaps he might have survived, but I doubt it. He was too set in his ways and too proud to admit defeat. When the rent reviews came, Roselock Fine Jewellery was, in effect, finished. The rents doubled and despite a pig-headed attempt to keep afloat, Michael spiralled into debt, laid off staff and saw the family business wither to nothing.

So, I have awaited this dirge for some time and in my heart feel a huge swell of pity for this dejected man who has been making the most exquisite jewellery for the great and the good for more than 40 years.

'You know,' he smiles stiffly, 'my father used to sit behind this very desk.'

Prudence is shaking her head sorrowfully and glancing with misty eyes at the grand leather chair into which Michael now sinks with utter weariness. His white hair is thin and wispy, and the left-hand parting is carved with military precision. When his jacket flaps back I notice a frayed Gieves & Hawkes label, but it's a tired, stuffy old suit, not like the flashy new ones that adorn the shop windows in Savile Row now. He shuffles papers on his desk distractedly, laboriously puts on his gilt-edged reading glasses and unfolds a piece of foolscap paper like a solicitor about to announce the contents of a will.

He clears his throat. 'I have put a few words together for a press statement. Would you look over it for me?'

'I don't think we should say anything to the press at the moment, Michael. When is everything hitting the fan?'

He gives a bitter little croak. 'Things have already hit the fan!'

'It's been awful, dear,' butts in Prudence. 'You'd be mortified.'

Prudence has an Essex twang that she proudly emphasises when imparting dramatic news.

'To think what this company has been! I've worked for Mr Roselock for 20 years and never in my life have I seen such goings on.' She stabs her fingers fretfully through her lacquered grey hair. 'I just said to him last week, "Enough is enough."'

'They've slit our throats and bled us dry,' Michael adds with asperity.

I make sympathetic clucks and then take a deep breath. Somehow since I've been in Mallorca, I have more clarity of vision. When I gaze over the Tramuntana mountain range, nothing seems insurmountable, and that includes Michael Roselock's problems.

'I think you've got to see this as a new era, Michael, and move on, just like I'm doing.'

I pass him and Prudence a document each. They look puzzled.

'What's this?' says Michael cagily.

'You know my client, Havana Leather?'

'What of it?' he grunts.

'I have an idea which might prove to be your salvation.'

Friday 10 p.m., en route to Mallorca

I am one hour into my flight and sitting in the aisle seat of row three with a Bloody Mary and a packet of Pringles. Someone beat me to the row in front but instead of kicking the usurper in the leg, I sat behind him, took several deep breaths and quickly unearthed *The Fearless Flier's Handbook* from my handbag. I am about to read when the air hostess stops by my seat. It's the same girl from last month's flight. 'Thought I recognised you,' she beams. 'Are you a regular commuter?'

'Trying to be,' I mutter.

'Well it's lovely and calm out there. The pilot hopes to make it in record time today,' she says cheerfully. I pray that our Speedy Gonzales pilot won't take risks in his desire for *Guinness World Records* fame.

So here I am on page 43. There is a sub-heading in bold letters:

Water Landings
The chance of an aircraft like the 747 or 767 ditching, or making a water landing in the ocean is so remote that one should count on a win at the lottery first.

And a little further on:

Once an Asia-based airline had a plane that overran terra firma during a takeoff in Hong Kong... the plane ended up competing with the ferries in Hong Kong Harbor!... Nobody was killed...

Nobody was killed. That's the point, isn't it? I imagine what must have been running through the minds of those poor passengers in the middle of take-off and then... Someone taps my shoulder. I look up and am momentarily thrown to see a familiar face peering down at me.

'Victoria Duvall,' she says briskly. 'We met at the Banca March party.'

I attempt to stand. After all she is the queen of film in our valley.

'No need to get up.'

I sit back down and introduce myself.

'I know all about you,' she says airily and without explanation, 'and I occasionally read your column in the *Majorca Daily Bulletin*. I know Jason Moore, the editor.'

'I see.'

'So, are you going to be a regular commuter? There's a whole bunch of us. We call it the easyJet Commuter Club, the ECC.'

'Is there a joining fee?'

She smiles. 'Well, the offer of a round of G&Ts to exclusive club members usually does the trick.'

'Then I'm your girl.'

She breaks into a deep throaty laugh. 'Is that seat taken?' She indicates the middle seat.

'No, I managed to keep it all to myself.'

She doesn't need an invitation. 'I'll join you for a while. Now, judging by your choice of reading matter, I take it you're a nervous flier?'

I feel like a child whose bed-wetting has just been discovered. I can feel my cheeks burn.

'I only ask because I used to find flying such a drag. First I tried hypnosis then acupuncture and all that twaddle until finally a friend bought me that book. It's marvellous.'

I eye her suspiciously. Maybe she has shares in the publishing house.

She chirrups on. 'After that, I went on a flying course for nervous passengers and now I love being in the air.'

I take a gulp of my Bloody Mary and offer her a crisp. She politely declines but presses the call button.

'That's encouraging,' I say. 'What's this course, then?'

'Oh they take you through everything to do with planes, you get to meet the captain and end up going on a flight with your trainer.'

That bit doesn't sound so appealing. The air hostess appears and Victoria orders a G&T.

'So aren't you scared any more?'

'Never.'

'What, even in storms?'

'Not really. I just read a film script or two and have a G&T.'

As if on cue, her drink arrives and I insist on paying for it. We chat for the duration of the flight and I am so absorbed with her film industry anecdotes that when the plane finally makes its descent, I have completely forgotten to grip the armrests of my seat in terror, as is customary. We land smoothly and I gather my belongings and wait patiently for my companion who has returned to her seat to retrieve her bags. Most of the passengers have left as she strolls languidly down the aisle, talking loudly with two men.

'Do you know James Grant?'

Why would I?

'No, I don't believe we've met.' I extend a hand which he shakes warmly. 'Not related to the whisky family, are you?' I ask.

'Sadly not,' he replies jokily. 'Anyway, welcome to the ECC.'

'He's a television producer,' Victoria rattles on. 'So you're both in the media business and this is young Spike. He's a travel courier.'

We shake hands and are diplomatically invited to leave the plane by the easyJet crew. I get the impression they know these characters pretty well.

In the arrivals hall we say our farewells and promise to catch up on another flight soon. Victoria, whom I've decided is a lot of fun, invites Alan, Ollie and me up for lunch.

'You must meet my husband, Charles and of course the donkeys…' In a flash she's disappeared. I gather my belongings and head off for the taxi rank. Oh to be back home. I could almost dance!

Suddenly Judas is ringing. Who on earth would call at this time of night? I wrestle it out of my handbag and hear Greedy George's booming voice.

'Back in Lalaland, eh, guv?'

'Just. Are you aware of the time?'

'Of course, but you career girls never sleep.'

Well this one has discovered the wonders of sleep since living here and has no intention of reverting. 'Where are you, anyway?'

'Bloody Milan. Looks like I'm going to be here another week. They can't get production right. Still I've found a great new all night bar.'

'I spoke to a journalist at *Condé Nast* magazine yesterday. They all seem to be cooing over the lounge lizards.'

There's a twang of coarse laughter. 'Yeh, well, those girls at *Condé Nast* get excited about anything if you bribe them enough.'

'Don't be mean.'

'Think of all that advertising I'm giving them this year.'

'You still haven't paid them for last year.'

He wheezes with pleasure. 'That's true! Every cloud's got a silver lining.'

The man really is incorrigible.

He gives a cough. 'By the way, when you're next over can you bring me some of that Spanish serrano ham?'

'Only if you behave.'

'Maybe. Anyway, I got your voice message. What's up?'

I brace myself. 'Well, you know my client, Michael Roselock?'

'That old fart, the jeweller?'

'The same. Well I've had an idea...'

SEVEN

PLUMBING NEW DEPTHS

The dreaded day of the Palma to Calvia half marathon has finally arrived. When my neighbour, Rafael, first mentioned the race very casually several weeks ago, I never thought he really expected me to enter. Wrong. In fact, Rafael had made it his unwavering ambition to toughen me up for the big event ever since I had foolishly let slip that I would be doing the London Marathon the following April. He had digested the news sombrely, pointing out that 44 kilometres was a very long way and that without adequate training with a half marathon or two in advance, I'd be sunk. So, under Rafael's tutelage, I began my training programme. Valiantly I would set off on a twenty-minute mountain jog, and then make my weary way back up our track. Hard as I tried to slip quietly past Rafael's front door each time, he would instinctively dart out from the house and on to his porch with the speed of a rattlesnake and point accusingly at his watch.

'You lazy woman! *Venga!* You joke, yes? Only twenty minutes? This is nothing! We must be strong for the race, yes?'

Then laughing manically, he'd lead me into his kitchen to swot up on a whole raft of potions and energy drinks needed for building stamina. One of his favourite pick-me-ups was carnitine, a protein supplement with a milky white hue which he bought in tiny glass phials from the chemist.

'You drink this with an espresso and you go off like a rocket.'

The thought of being turbo-fuelled, running like the possessed, frightened the life out of me, so I opted instead for mineral water and a spoonful of honey before each run.

Although I never liked to admit it, I began to enjoy the practice runs, particularly those in the early hours when the country lanes were bereft of cars and *motos* and the near edible fragrance of rosemary and lavender hung bewitchingly in the air. At that time of the morning I would happen upon all manner of early risers, hawks and eagles sweeping the blue-grey skies, mice, hedgehogs and rats peeping warily out from the undergrowth and most captivating of all, an abundance of rabbits hopping across the fields and pathways, their fur flame-coloured under the beams of the emerging sun. Sometimes a rabbit would hop out on the path and I would chase it as fast as I could until its little taupe body effortlessly outran me over the hill, its frame caught in a patch of sunlight. In time I began to recognise those locals who routinely walked the country paths early in the morning, mostly old *pagès* (country folk) and farmers with their *ca raters*. At first disconcerted to stumble upon a female runner, and a foreigner at that, they gradually succumbed to my cheery greetings and before long were on *'Bon Dia!'* terms, sharing smiles and waves. In fact, I was soon on first name terms with one or two early birds such as jolly Gaspar, the newspaper delivery man, who every morning chugged through the town and down to the port on his old *moto*, its frame wheezing under his hefty frame and the weight of the bulging newspaper bags strung across the handles. One of Gaspar's favourite games was to allow me to overtake him along the pavement before gathering speed and passing me on the road with a flourish of kisses, shouts and honking. It worried me that such frivolous distraction might one day make him veer off the busy port road and into the *torrent*, the fast flowing river.

In just a month my twenty-minute forays were doubled and before long I was managing regular eight-mile runs without too much trouble. Old Margalida Sampol would wave her stick in disapproval and chastise me as I ran by but Rafael would look on approvingly as I tore up the track having completed what he termed a real run. However, 13 miles is a long way and the Palma to Calvia race, which is one of the high points in Mallorca's running calendar, is run in the intense heat of the day.

So, the big day has finally arrived and there's seemingly no going back. I can hear Rafael's heavy stride crunching on the gravel outside and then he bangs on the glass door of the porch and bounds into the house.

'*Hola!* Come on now. *Vamos!* You still sleeping?'

His loud voice echoes around the *entrada*. I bob my head over the stair rail and notice that he is wearing a brand new designer running vest offset by red nylon shorts.

'Give me a break, Rafael. We've got ages.'

He raises his hands dramatically and examines his sports watch.

'*Home!* Are you mad? We must go now. Aha! I think you want to miss race, yes?' He gives me a crooked smile.

Goodness knows what has ever given him that impression. Alan and Ollie are fussing over a camera and attempting between them to fix a huge number 808 on my chest with the aid of two safety pins. I ponder on whether the number reflects in some way the ranking of the runner. We clamber into the car and at the mouth of the track stop to greet Margalida Sampol, our sentry guard, who is looking none too happy. I get out of the car to kiss her on both cheeks as is customary.

'You'll kill yourself with all this running,' she frets. 'It's bad for the heart. And fancy driving all the way to Palma in this heat!'

'*Déu meu!*' says Rafael with irritation. 'We'll be there in less than an hour. *Per favor!*'

'I'll pray for you.' She pats my hand, ignoring Rafael. We wave and set off along the mountain road to Palma.

As we enter Palma city, the roads are lined with *policía*, wearing their trademark dark shades and officiously blowing whistles and directing drivers away from the main traffic arteries that are closed off by barriers. We have thirty minutes to go before the race starts but already there is a huge swell of toned would-be Power Rangers in bibs strolling around, gossiping and limbering up against walls.

'How many people compete?' I ask Rafael nervously as we park the car some distance away and head for the start area on foot.

'Six hundred or more,' he says cheerfully. 'Is a lot but just think, next April you run with over thirty thousand people in the London Marathon.'

It's a sobering thought, as is the stark realisation that it will also be double the mileage of the race today.

'How many women are taking part in this race?'

'Maybe twenty.'

This gets better all the time. We poor, outnumbered women are going to look like a party of minnows in this sea of pure Mediterranean testosterone. Alan can see I'm wearing my burning martyr expression and tries to offer some comforting words. 'It'll be over before you know it and then we'll have a wonderful celebratory lunch up at Es Turo restaurant with Pep and Juana.'

'What about Angel?' asks Ollie anxiously, keen to meet up with his football playing buddy.

'Of course they'll bring him. You can keep each other out of mischief.' He turns to me. 'Come on, we'd better let you line up while we find a good vantage point.'

They administer good luck hugs and set off to find a place among the spectators.

'*Venga!*' says Rafael and pulls me into a swirling crowd of sweaty male armpits. There is a real camaraderie between these men as they laugh and joke together. They turn to look at me a tad sulkily like a bunch of little boys whose Superman game has been crashed by Barbie. And an English one at that.

Ollie is raised high on Alan's shoulders in a swarm of spectators, and is blowing me kisses. I look round for signs of other women and see a group of fit and toned girls chatting just behind the start line. Rafael was right, we are the minority and out of the twelve or so I have seen, I am by far the oldest. A moment later and a small man, corpulent and sleek like the Fat Controller, in a tight black suit, white socks and shiny shoes, raises his hands authoritatively and addresses the runners in Mallorcan from a high rostrum. I can't understand a word. The runners begin to whoop and clap and the crowds are jumping up and down with excitement. A moment later, he puts a whistle slowly to his lips and we're off!

A young woman in a shiny black lycra top and tiny shorts sprints ahead of me, her legs thin and brown like strands of toffee. The crowds are cheering wildly and the heat sears my skin like a branding iron. Groups of swarthy, tight-muscled men are bounding past me now, their elbows brushing my sides. There's a distinct whiff of rancid garlic in the air and I look round accusingly at my fellow runners. The smell dissipates and is replaced with sea brine as we head for the docks where a slight breeze lifts my spirits. Thirteen miles. Thirteen long, hot, sticky miles. Why am I doing this? The crowd starts to thin as the more athletic types leap past, leaving the laggers panting behind. On a lamp post by the side of a bridge, an electronic temperature monitor flashes up 30°C. My addled brain calculates that at about 90 °F. To the side of the road an official in a bright orange T-shirt is waving a flag and yelling, '*Venga! Venga!*'

Don't *venga* me, matey, not in ninety degrees.

We run on a seemingly interminable road that leads from the Port of Palma along the coast to the west. I look out over the calm azure sea and try to distract myself by counting the number of docked cruise liners and gin palaces forming a ring around the harbour. Nearly 30 minutes have passed and the sun is boring into a point in the middle of my back. Small clusters of spectators watch morosely from vantage points along the road. No one cheers. Since running doesn't figure much in the life of the average Mallorcan, I wonder if they are unsettled by such manic activity. Mallorcans rely on their vocal chords to do the walking, and running of any kind is out of the question.

I look at my watch and see that we've been running for 45 minutes and 40 seconds. The sweat is streaming into my eyes and there are still seven odd miles to go. For a second, in the blur of runners coursing along in the distance, I imagine that I see Rafael, but it is someone else. Rafael is an excellent sprinter and will reach the finishing line long before me. I pass a refreshment table on the pavement where male runners, like an angry swarm of bees, heckle the volunteers for water. Squeezing between their extended arms, I manage to snatch up two bottles, one in each hand. I feel like Rambo gripping a pair of hand grenades.

Slowly I clock up the miles, while my legs mechanically blunder on. It's hard to determine what's worse, the pain of running or the sensation of being barbecued slowly under a simmering sun. I have a vision of Greedy George suddenly appearing up ahead, his great bulk packed into tight lycra running gear. He lurches and staggers along, inhaling deeply on a fragrant leather lizard while cramming a sweat-smeared croissant into his mouth with the other hand, between heartfelt groans. I manage to suppress a snigger as the image fades. Eventually, the route curls up a steep hill and I watch the runners, like resolute ants, climbing to the summit then toppling and disappearing over the crest. I clamber on, my calves twitching with the effort. I'm now on a sharp descent and almost freewheeling down, down, very fast, until we come abruptly to another road, this one lined with cypresses, which afford no shade. Officials in luminous jackets are marking the route and urging us on with shouts and cries of *'Venga! Venga!'* Can these people think of nothing else to say?

I reach the final bend and discover that I have one mile further to go. My bottles are empty and my legs are buckling in the heat. We're in tourist heartland now by the south coast in Magaluf. Crowds of holidaymakers scorched red and packed together like sun-dried tomatoes, line the pavements. A resonant voice catches my ear. 'She's gotta be a Brit with that colour hair! Go on love, go for it!'

I glimpse a smiling couple just feet from me holding pints of lager and frantically waving Union Jack Flags. I'm feeling about as nationalistic as Guy Fawkes. I give them my best cheerleader smile and plough on. To my left the sea is glinting, flanked by a long blond beach smothered with sunbathers basted in suncreams and gently roasting in the sun. Momentarily distracted by this vision of heaven, I take a wrong turn and am pursued by a yapping official who steers me back on course like an attentive sheep dog.

I'm now on a wide tarmac road and from all sides officials are jumping out, screaming for me to hurry. Hey, what's the rush? I'm still moving. Isn't that enough for these sadists? There's a hand on my shoulder. It's Rafael who has gallantly run back from the finishing line to spur me on, having apparently completed the race some time before. He too is now yelling, the sweat running down his cheeks, telling me to run, run, run. I can see the bunting, and now an official ahead of me is frantically crying out, 'Si, Si!' If he'd dared to utter, *venga*, I might have just knocked him on the head with my empty water bottle.

Just a few paces to go and a woman is suddenly in hot pursuit, her breath on my neck and, as if in a pantomime, the crowds are jeering and with exaggerated hand gestures and facial expressions warning me that she's nearly upon me. I can't let that happen, not now. With one desperate leap my foot crosses the finishing line just ahead of her. She curses. It's over. I did it! Rafael is ecstatic. I almost detect tears in his eyes. Maybe it's laughter?

There are scores of hot and weary bodies flopping on the grass and as I look round I notice a gaggle of sweat-soaked female runners talking animatedly as they sip colas. They stare at me for a second and then, with broad smiles, raise their drink cans in a salute. I reciprocate the gesture. Girl power exists in Mallorca. There's the sound of panting and Ollie hurls himself at me. 'You didn't come last!'

I'm not sure if I'm supposed to take this as a compliment. Alan is his usual unflappable self and greets Rafael warmly. He tousles my hair. 'Knew you could do it. Now why not have a quick shower, and we'll be off to the mountains.'

'What about the award ceremony?' says Rafael, pointing at a large stage set up on the grass. 'Everyone comes, *el Batle*, all the local dignitaries and the press.'

'Well, we'll watch the beginning and then shoot off.'

Rafael shrugs his shoulders. '*No problema*. I stay here with my friends to celebrate. They'll drive me home tonight.'

I leave them and potter off to the makeshift shower area and am drying off when I think I hear my name called over the loudhailer. It can't be. Rafael bangs on the door. 'Quick! You win prize!'

I hurl on some shorts and a T-shirt and sweep the wet hair from my face. People turn round as Rafael and I make our way hurriedly to the stage where Alan and Ollie stand by the steps, their faces full of bewilderment. Rafael pushes me forward and in some confusion I accept kisses from the mayor and the sponsor, take my towering silver trophy and line up for photos. Two sporty women, probably fifteen years my junior stand in front; the victor and runner-up. I have come third out of the female runners. Armed with the trophy I walk jubilantly through the crowds with Alan and Ollie while Rafael strides in front. People are smiling and patting my arms and to my delight, Ollie actually looks rather proud of me. That's a first! In my brief moment of triumph, even the thought of running a full marathon no longer seems unattainable.

'They think you brave to run as a senyora,' Rafael says without a hint of malice. 'Normally is very young girls.'

Now there's a thing, to think that a female Brit, apparently past her sell-by date, can successfully challenge Mallorcan stereotyping. Never has the thought of a lunch in the mountains seemed so good.

I am struggling back from the market with two heavy shopping bags when I hear a loud 'Senyora!' from the mouth of the track. It is my elderly neighbour, Margalida. She is panting and waving her stick at me as if flagging down a passing car. When I reach her, she hooks one arm under mine and carries her stick with the other. I stop to re-adjust my load, at the same time asking her where she wants to go. There is only one other *finca* aside from Rafael's and ours at the end of the track. She points straight ahead with her stick and staggers on. As we walk she quizzes me on what I have been buying and looks satisfied that it is vegetables from Teresa, her old friend at the market, and nothing frivolous. Perhaps I have the makings of a good housewife yet. We walk slowly in silent intimacy. Margalida is so close that I can feel the warmth of her arm under mine. Her skin is translucent and forks of raised green veins run like rural map boundaries across her small, arthritic hands. She is vulnerable and bird-like, her small blue eyes squinting sightlessly behind thick lenses. I feel like Little Red Riding Hood but this is not my grandmother. A sorrow wells up in me remembering the grandmother I adored and my frail elderly aunt who now lives miles away back in England in a nursing home. Now I see her infrequently and my visits are punctuated with interruptions by care workers and communal meal times. Forever under public scrutiny, we are rarely permitted the freedom to speak together alone.

Margalida comes to a standstill outside the handsome stone *finca* with olive green gates and shutters whose occupants are still unknown to us.

'This is my daughter and son-in-law's house,' she says. 'I have lunch here every day.'

Lucky Margalida. If she were a pensioner in England, her family would probably have dispersed and she'd be in a care home or relying on meals on wheels. She bangs on the metal gate with her stick and calls out sharply, 'Sílvia! Sílvia!'

A grand, statuesque woman appears, wiping her hands on a tea towel. She is high cheek boned and buxom and her hair, the colour of sand, has been carefully set and lacquered. We make our introductions and she appears bemused that I am on such friendly terms with her aged mother.

She gives me a smile. 'My mother tells me you have become great friends. I'd love to know what language you two speak.'

So would I. It's certainly not Spanish, more a mix of sign language, telepathy and rudimentary Mallorcan.

'We have our own special language,' I reply.

She chuckles. 'Well, thank you for keeping her company. My husband, Pedro, and I are very happy you have moved here. It's nice to have the old *finca* occupied again.'

Once Margalida is in her daughter's care, I set off up the track. As I reach the *finca* I can hear Ollie screeching with delight. Something's up. I enter the house to find both he and Alan sharing secret smiles, and almost goading each other in to speech. They help carry my bags to the kitchen, suspicious in itself, and then Ollie blurts out.

'We've got a cat!'

I narrow my eyes. 'A cat?'

Alan interjects. 'We were up buying olive oil at Can Det, when Bartomeu presented Ollie with a kitten. We could hardly refuse.'

Catalina recently introduced us to Bartomeu whose family runs one of the last privately owned olive presses in Mallorca. There's a high-pitched mewling coming from a cardboard box and as I peep inside, a tiny face, oyster-hued, and with massive blue eyes looks up at me beseechingly. It appears to be part Siamese and has a ridiculous stunted tail which curls round like that of a monkey.

'What's wrong with its tail?' I ask.

'Born like that, apparently,' yawns Alan.

'I'm going to call it Inko,' says Ollie.

'But it's cream coloured?'

'Exactly,' he says gravely.

'And what do we do with it? I mean, what do cats eat? It's a terrible commitment.'

'Food?' proffers Alan helpfully.

Thankfully this scene is not happening in our London residence where Lord Jim Jam has been known to prowl the premises with his air rifle in search of contraband pets. Indeed, the pigeon population of our local square already fears for its life, after he took a pot shot from an upper window and instantly felled one in a tree. Although I dislike hunting, at least out here our mountain *caçadors*, the local huntsmen, eat the birds they shoot.

Alan languishes unconcernedly in the doorway tinkering with a screw and a broken hose nozzle.

'Inko will keep the mice away,' says Ollie eyeing his father.

They're in collusion.

'Fine. Then you two are in charge of it.'

They nudge each other and nod their heads but I know that the care of this new charge will inevitably be down to me.

It is a few years since I've driven. When my car was stolen outside the front door in London, involved in a collision and subsequently burned out, it seemed like a good idea to put my faith in public transport and invest in a pair of sensible walking shoes. However, where I live in Mallorca a car is a necessity, on the level of breathing, unless of course you have time on your hands and prefer to do it the hard way and choose to ride a *burro*, a donkey. Therefore, I decide that a few lessons on Mallorcan soil are called for and Catalina suggests a local driving instructor, Tomeu Borras. Together we visit his school, a modest set of offices in an old stone *finca* on the outskirts of the nearby port. Outside, the place is teeming with babbling students, all of whom barge through the front door en masse, excitedly clutching sheets of road symbols and Spanish highway code books. Catalina explains that Tomeu holds evening classes for them on the theory of driving. I bet that's fun. It seems that whole generations of families have trained with Tomeu and many aspiring youths in the area automatically gravitate to his school. Given the high number of prangs locally I reckon he's got a good deal to answer for.

Catalina waits until the students have dispersed and pushes open the large mahogany front door that gives on to a spacious reception area, its white walls cluttered with large area street maps and posters depicting coloured road symbols. To the right there is a large stone fireplace built into the wall, on either side of which are several forlorn, grey plastic chairs. It has the stale air of a doctor's waiting room. A table piled high with antiquated Spanish reading material sits squat in the middle of the room and in the far corner an *al.lota*, a young girl with Bambi eyes, sits behind a wooden reception desk laboriously copying names, presumably of students, from a sheet of paper into a large blue register. To the side of her runs a corridor lined with doors. She looks up brightly when we walk in. Rattling away in Mallorcan, Catalina explains that I need a refresher course. The girl nods and looks at her watch nervously, explaining that the driving instructor has just commenced a theory lesson with students and will probably not want to be disturbed. I wonder why she can't just book me an appointment herself. Finally she plucks up the courage to knock on one of the doors. There's silence, the sound of muffled footsteps and then a large man suddenly emerges from the room.

'What is it?' he asks irritably, striding into the reception, glaring all the while at Miss Bambi. He is tall and well built with a moustache the shape and size of a large arachnid, a forest of a beard and a shock of thick black hair. He views both of us with some disdain.

'She speaks Spanish?' he enquires brusquely without looking up from the open diary he has whisked up in his hand.

Catalina lies. 'Oh yes, she's fluent.'

'Can she drive?' That's debatable.

'*Déu Meu!*' says Catalina. 'She's driven all her life.'

'Well then, she's in the wrong place,' he says with a thin smile.

'But it's been some years.'

Tomeu grunts and scribbles in his appointment book. 'Five lessons, then. Starting from Monday. Don't be late.'

He drops the pen on to the desk and steams back to his class. Bambi throws me a nervous smile and writes out an appointment card. This is going to be a barrel of laughs.

And now it's the morning of the first lesson and I sidle up to the green Renault parked by the town square as pre-arranged. It is ten in the morning and the place is bustling with life. I see Tomeu at the wheel, his face serious and stern, and tap gently on his window. Impatiently he gesticulates that I should get in, indicating that it is best for me to take the passenger seat until we get on to a quiet road in the environs of the port. Good idea. Ten minutes later after a rather stilted, monosyllabic conversation, he drives to the edge of the port and parks in a small side street.

'OK,' he sighs, 'Get in the driving seat and I'll give you instructions.'

He rattles off a string of commands. I nod obediently although only understanding a fraction of what he's saying. Why hadn't I mugged up on Spanish driving jargon before the lesson? And what on earth was I thinking of hiring a male instructor in a macho place like Mallorca? More quickly than I had hoped for he has me turning on to the busy main road and heading towards the harbour area. The sea glistens temptingly on my left and to my right there are an assortment of souvenir shops and restaurants offering cheap menus *del dias*. At least I'm in motion. Surely he'll give me credit for that much? Apparently not.

'You're wobbling. Keep the car straight!' he bellows as I veer towards the middle of the road. The light from the sea catches my eye and beckons invitingly. It's a far cry from my days learning to drive in the cut and thrust of London with the sound of traffic pounding around me and buses and taxis bearing down on the car, their menacing frames looming large in the car mirror. I'm jolted back from my thoughts by a vehicle in front which stops abruptly and turns right without indicating. I hit the brake sharply and Tomeu's head lolls forward. He narrows his eyes and gives a deep threatening growl. 'Take the next right!'

I indicate and tear round the corner. The car screeches and I struggle to straighten it as it lists towards the pavement. Tomeu hits the dual control brake.

'Remind me when you last drove?' His grin is sardonic.

I decide that silence is the greater part of valour.

'OK now take the next left.'

On cue, a dog strolls out in the road and I am momentarily distracted, completely missing the turning. He tuts irritably and erupts with,

'*Per l'amor de déu!* Use your indicator. I said turn LEFT! *Loca!* Now where are you going?'

He really is calling me mad. When I was 17, my London driving instructor used to sit mutely beside me, as cool and unemotional as a gecko. He would certainly never have mustered up enough energy or passion to hurl abuse at me. Here, in Mallorca, however, everything is done with passion and that includes lambasting an inept English woman for her appalling road sense. I sniff defiantly and look in the mirror at the traffic building up behind me. Tomeu instructs me to take the following left turn; a small street lined with acacias which curves round and leads directly into the harbour area. I stop at the junction. He rubs his eyes and yawns.

'Go left, but remember this is a busy road.'

The road to the port is always packed with cars and local sporting machos who attempt elaborate manoeuvres in the middle of the main road and snarl up the traffic. There are a series of anguished and discordant blasts from horns when this occurs and then everyone starts theatrically yelling and flapping their arms out of the windows as everything comes to a grinding halt. A few minutes will pass and then this outstanding free entertainment is over as cars begin circulating again and tourists, riveted to the pavement by the spectacle, are broken from their spell. On this occasion I cause the hold-up because when I attempt to turn, I somehow stall.

'*Fre de mà! El fre!*' Tomeu is shrieking. Ah, the handbrake. Not a bad idea given that the car is sliding backwards. On both sides of the road hysterical drivers are tooting. A cyclist enters the fray and decides to cross in front of me, so I remain rigid. The road's log jammed. Tomeu is so incensed that he clutches wildly at the dashboard as if he might break it free and smash it over my head. Luckily he can't. He sniffs loudly, turns his head away and leans out of his window, mumbling darkly like a disgruntled sorcerer, in local dialect. The car suddenly roars and bucks as I turn the ignition and swerve round to the left narrowly missing two tourists with a death wish. We carry on in awkward silence. Small fishing boats bob up and down on a choppy sea on one side, and far off beyond the lighthouse I can see bulky vessels waiting to enter the port. Tomeu stonily tells me to continue until we reach a roundabout.

'*Gas! Gas!*' he bawls.

Heavens, this is like giving birth.

'Why are you stopping? Can you see a car?'

Well yes actually, I can. In England we stop when a car's got lane priority. I don't feel inclined to hurtle at top speed in front of a fast moving vehicle two feet from me. He holds his head in his hands. Some minutes later, as we tootle along the main road that leads back to his offices, we get to a give way sign. I stop.

'*El gas! El gas!*' Tomeu is practically hitting the dashboard with his head in frustration as I stubbornly wait until I am sure the road in front of me is devoid of traffic. We reach a crossroads with traffic lights.

'*El gas ! El gas!*' he hollers again.

I glare at him like an intransigent mule, frustrated that I don't have enough of the lingo to make some clever quip. The red light turns to green and I release the handbrake and cross over the road wearily.

'I'll see you tomorrow,' Tomeu says dryly as I park the car shakily outside his driving school. I groan inwardly at the thought. Can I survive another such session? More to the point, can he? Still, this lesson has served a useful purpose, enlightening me as to the guiding principles of Mallorcan driving, as follows:

1. Forget who has priority at roundabouts, screech out and get ahead. DON'T indicate and DON'T let other road users second-guess you.
2. Save time and fool other motorists by ignoring NO ENTRY signs. Make a principle of driving the wrong way down one-way streets.
3. Should you stop at give way signs? *Home!* Ever heard of Mallorcan pride?
4. A fast car is approaching on the opposite side. Do you overtake the car in front? Of course! The other driver can always use the hard shoulder or veer into a ditch.
6. Car mirrors serve no useful purpose other than for your girlfriend to touch up her make-up. Ignore them.

On my fifth and final lesson with Tomeu, he takes me up a winding mountain road at nightfall and then instructs me to drive back down again using my headlights in the dusk. I actually enjoy the challenge and find Tomeu no longer threatening but, dare I say it, endearing. Once he decides to stop yelling at me and begins to acknowledge that I'm not going to make him another dismal road statistic, we begin to talk. In fact, on that lonely last run, I'd almost go as far as to say we connected. We laugh and chat about work, travel, and politics and suddenly it dawns on me that I am being instructed by a hugely well-educated man who, on leaving university, opted to open a driving school rather than follow in the family accountancy business. As we arrive back at his driving school he shakes my hand, slaps me on the back, and with a broad smile says, 'You'll do, you'll do.'

It's a crisp November day and heavy white cloud is draped like a thick pearly mantle over the valley. Alan, clad in a heavy knit, twill trousers and green wellies, is manhandling a lavender plant on the terrace and replanting it in a perfunctory way in a nearby flowerbed. Defiantly he puffs on a *puro*, his brow furrowed and eyes downcast. I have no intention of remonstrating with him about his nicotine habit at this juncture. He is in ill humour because despite excuses, artifice and subterfuge on a Machiavellian scale, our house visitor has not been deterred and is still arriving tonight. Catalina has made up the basement guest room, previously our dank and creepy cellar, and cut fresh seasonal flowers which she arranges in a small glass vase on the dresser. The room is spotless, the terracotta floors scrubbed and polished to perfection, the white walls and ceilings cleared of any lurking cobwebs, ants, spiders, diminutive scorpions and moths. The bathroom is the only truly functioning one in the whole *finca*. The old four-poster bed is covered in simple white cotton sheets and duvet and a selection of reading material from *¡Hola!* to *The Economist* is piled neatly on a side table. Even Charlotte Jacobs, fashion and style guru for one of the broadsheets with her own TV spot to boot, won't be able to find fault with anything. On second thoughts… I walk into the kitchen where Catalina is brewing some savoury concoction on the stove. It smells heavenly.

'You busy in office, so I make you *albondigas*, tomato sauce and rice for dinner. Your friend like meatballs?'

Heaven only knows what she likes. Charlotte's fads change with the weather. Formerly a vegan in her chrysalis period she evolved into a vegetarian then a macrobiotic but last time we met she had switched from the Atkinson diet to the blood-group dietary plan. However the whole thing is a sham so there's no point in sharing this lunacy with Catalina.

Charlotte is a menopausal woman in her early fifties who can't accept that she is no longer the staggering beauty she once was. Divorced and childless, she now lavishes her money on three overfed Persians with whom she shares a luxury flat in St James's, a hair's breadth from the Ritz. She has a full time maid and a butler for weekends and dinner parties. Her lovers are wealthy, some married but most are divorcees who, rejoicing in their newfound bachelor freedom, are only ever interested in short-term affairs. Charlotte is a useful stopgap, a polished companion for sporty weekends hunting and fishing in the country, a valuable party ticket in London's media land, and a reasonable bit of crumpet for an indulgent, naughty weekend in Paris, Venice or Rome. Hailing from a modest family in Sussex, Charlotte – real name Katie – yearned as a young child to live like her picture book American heroine, Eloise, in a luxurious hotel with servants, nannies and the best things that life could offer.

So, from her early twenties she reinvented herself, developed a plummy accent, and claimed to have been educated not at the local grammar but at an exclusive finishing school in Switzerland. At twenty-three, she disappeared to Paris to study haute couture, returning two years later in a new guise. Katie, the *ingénue*, had departed and the sensational debutante,

Charlotte, had arrived. In a short while, she became grand, orgulous and imperious, hacking her way with ruthless ambition to the top of the fashion ladder working on the glossies and then the national press. Television was a natural progression and her thrice-weekly fashion spot on a breakfast show continues to secure her a healthy income. But Charlotte has a few dark secrets. She is clinically depressed, hopelessly insecure, lonely and neurotic and in daily decline. Ostensibly a health junkie, she is, in reality, a vodka slugging, pill popping, bulimic who needs extended siestas each day to sleep off her various addictions. Poor Charlotte thinks her secret is safe, but her brooding army of adversaries are watching and waiting for her to crumble and then the media machine will do everything in its power to drive her to the point of destruction and ultimately, extinction.

I met Charlotte some years ago at a magazine launch party at the Savoy. She was wearing a bronze silk evening dress with a sash at the waist and a slit that ran half way up the thigh. Her hair was swept up in a French pleat and fragile crystal baubles hung from her ears and neck. Provocatively and covetously she leant close to a powerful newspaper magnate, giggling and sharing small confidences with him. However, I observed her hand shaking as she raised a glass of champagne to her lips and in her other, a redundant jade coloured cocktail cigarette burned slowly. An editor friend noticed her too and crassly interrupted her intimate tête-à-tête to introduce me. Her cold eyes met mine for an instant and then with a look of ennui she asked condescendingly how I came to be at the party. I told her that I had managed to slip the doorman a fiver to gain entry, hadn't a clue who anyone was, but had brought my disposable camera in case I caught sight of a celebrity. She looked momentarily disconcerted and then suddenly rolled her head back and screeched with laughter. 'Are you always like this?'

'Always,' said our mutual friend and left us to chat.

There was something about Charlotte that intrigued and amused me. She was obnoxious, capricious and downright rude at the party but when a serious player crossed her path she became beguiling, coquettish and animated. Her behaviour was both appalling and fascinating.

After the event, I was about to step into a taxi outside the hotel when I heard quick footsteps behind me, and Charlotte, tearful and distraught, tersely demanded that she share the ride. I agreed to drop her off en route to my flat. Tipsily she fell on to our shared seat and stared morosely out of the window at the falling rain, tears staining her face. Awkwardly, I made a vain attempt to comfort her but she was as brittle as Brighton rock, indignant and vengeful, yet revealing nothing. Two days later she phoned me at the office and invited me to lunch at which she frostily advised me to forget the whole taxi episode. For some inexplicable reason we keep in touch. Like a member of a Greek chorus I observe her charade of a life from the sidelines with pity, powerless to influence, and wretchedly waiting for the whole sad denouement and tragic climax. For her part, she finds me unthreatening and an occasional emotional prop when things aren't going her way. She has been in Mallorca for a fashion shoot and found herself with a few days spare. Much as I created a million ingenious excuses as to why she couldn't stay, she haughtily brushed them all aside and finally and pathetically I caved in.

There's a commotion at the kitchen door. Three workmen are attempting to shift a small digger full of rocks which has broken down. They are here to repair the stone wall which runs the length of the garden and which was partially washed away in the recent storms. The engine suddenly bursts into life and there are cheers. Sluggishly it crawls forward over rubble and to my relief, away from the patio. Catalina turns to me.

'He is unhappy, *si*?' she inclines her head in Alan's direction on the far terrace.

'He doesn't like Charlotte very much. He thinks she's flaky.'

She frowns, registering the word flaky and rightly assuming it's not complimentary. 'But you said she's your friend. Why she comes if you don't like her?'

'That's because we're hypocritical cowards. She's not a real friend, just a contact, a leech really. There are lots of them about, but this one is particularly clinging.'

Catalina has already fumbled in her handbag and located leech in her pocket dictionary. 'A blood sucking annelid worm. Hm. It's good thing she stays only a few days.'

I'm on the mobile to Bryan Patterson in London when I hear the sound of feet crunching gravel in the garden. Alan has arrived back from Palma where he had gone to collect Charlotte from her luxury hotel. My stomach sinks like a botched soufflé. I muster up enough enthusiasm to leave the call on a high note, and am just saying goodbye when Bryan cuts in sweetly, 'Tootsie sends you a whiskery kiss.'

I ring off with a shudder. A vision in white floats towards me from the *entrada* with arms outstretched. I display a well-rehearsed smile of welcome. 'Charlotte! Great to see you.'

'You too, darling. Isn't it simply divine here although it's much colder than I expected.'

'Did you have a good flight here?'

'No. My penny-pinching paper flew me out on one of those ghastly budget airlines. I'm still recovering.'

'What about the shoot?'

'A disaster.'

Alan raises an eyebrow and stalks off to the kitchen, no doubt to embolden himself with a glass of whisky. I make small talk, and ascertain that Charlotte now only eats white meats, fish, and vegetables (no potatoes or carrots) but she will succumb to a little wild rice and polenta. I decide it's best to humour her.

'No one does caffeine, wheat or dairy now. It's very passé,' she says breezily. 'Oh where's your son? We're yet to meet.'

'Ollie's staying with his friend Angel in the village tonight. You'll meet him tomorrow.'

'Oh good,' she says without enthusiasm.

I settle her downstairs in the guest bedroom and rush off to the kitchen to organise supper. I'm half way through chopping at some beans when I hear a blood-curdling scream from her room. Alan has already bounded down the stairs ahead of me. Charlotte is standing in the bathroom where water gushes vertically from one of the taps whose top has blown off and lies broken in the basin.

'Do something!' she commands with vitriol, 'I'm soaked!'

Alan stems the flow with a hand towel which he winds round the body of the tap.

'Hold this,' he growls at her.

She doesn't move. Instead I grasp the towel, leaving him to sever the water supply to the bathroom. He fiddles under the basin, closes off the gauge and the torrent is halted. He gets up and wipes his face with a towel.

'You wrenched the tap the wrong way and snapped the valve.'

'Well it was awfully stiff.'

Alan stares at her with incredulity, shakes his head and plods back upstairs, muttering about calling Pere, the plumber. I gather up the wet towels, mop down the bathroom and attempt once again to make dinner. An hour later, Charlotte drifts upstairs in a flowing Moroccan style robe and observes me while I cook.

I offer her a drink. She declines, saying that she never touches alcohol now. I wonder why we have to play these games. Opening the fridge door, I charge my glass for a second time.

'It's very rustic here, isn't it?' A sugary smile lingers on her lips.

'Yes, the countryside usually is.'

'It must be simply ghastly here in the winter with no culture and no one stimulating to talk to. Thank God you can escape back to London each month.'

'Oh, it's not so bad. I've got an imaginary friend, actually a rather highbrow American toad, and there are macramé classes in the town during the cold months.'

'Don't jest.'

'Charlotte, we're not on a desert island. Of course there are things I miss, like theatre and oatcakes, but I make up for it when I return.'

She eyes me keenly. 'It's novelty value now, but you'll get bored with island life.'

I can feel my hackles rising, so quickly select a CD and engross myself in cooking.

'Still playing *Buddha Bar*?' she rolls her eyes.

'When I'm not dancing to Des O'Connor's greatest hits.'

She titters. 'Is that garlic you're using?'

'You don't like it?'

'Indeed, but I usually cut it Zen style, to release the energy flow.'

I ignore her and hurl the chopped pieces into the pan.

'Now listen, I don't want to put you out while I'm here. I'll just do my own thing. However in the mornings I'd appreciate a lift to the sea for an invigorating pre-breakfast swim. You must be up early for work anyway.'

'Charlotte, the water will be freezing. Are you mad?'

She looks fleetingly afraid, as if I've uncovered a hidden truth.

'Of course I'm not mad,' she says heatedly. 'Cold water's good for you.'

Wearily I explain that it will have to coincide with Ollie's morning school run to Palma and that we will have to leave her on the beach for an hour or so before picking her up on the return trip.

'But I can't possibly wait there until you've returned from the school. I just want a quick dip. Oh, I suppose you don't have such things as spas here, do you?'

'Amazingly, we country plods do!'

'Right, well I'd like a massage and a facial if you could arrange it but only with someone good.'

My friend Cristina runs the luxury Aimia Hotel in the port. I shall have to beg her sublime beautician, Anette, to take pity on Charlotte.

'I'll sort everything out for you.'

'Bless you,' she says sweetly.

I hear Alan's heavy tread in the *entrada* and serve out the food, thankful that we have only two days to endure.

There's an urgent rapping on the bedroom door. I wake up with a start. A voice is calling tremulously in the darkness.

'It's me. Charlotte. You must come. There's a bat in my room.'

Alan is snoring gently, blissfully unaware of the scene unfolding before me. Still capable of exorability, I groan and stagger out of bed and down the stairs with her to the basement. She is wearing a jacinth coloured silk kimono and kitten heeled, mink trimmed slippers which scrape on the marble steps. She appears bony and ornithoid in the half-light, her long chestnut hair scraped back from her face in to a loose plait. Without make-up she seems vulnerable and childlike. I step into her room. A small bat is circling the rafters unable to find an escape route.

'I was doing some Pilates on the floor with the French doors open and it just swooped in,' she sniffs.

I resist the desire to ask why on earth she is doing Pilates at this time of night. Some things are best left unsaid. Alan had told her to keep the shutters closed and the door open. I wonder why he bothered. I turn off the lights to a stifled cry of alarm from Charlotte.

'Shh! It will go, just give it a minute.'

In a moment it has glided out into the field. I stomp off upstairs and am just extinguishing the hall lights when Charlotte hisses at me from her basement door.

'Please don't turn out the lights.'

'Why ever not?'

'I'm afraid of ghosts.'

I'm hitting the bottle of cava earlier than I should do, but I'm in survival mode now. We've had a fraught day with Charlotte which began at 6 a.m. when she lay in the field on her duvet intoning vowel sounds and doing Buddhist chanting. The noise was so loud that both Alan and I woke up in synchronisation, convinced that a stray bull had entered our land. After driving her to the beach an hour later, we all waited in the car until she'd bathed, then deposited her back at the house, before racing off to Ollie's school. We needed the break. Most of the day she lay slumped on a lounger with a blanket, book and a half written fashion article that she never seemed to have the heart to finish. We fetched her iced water which, in the reflection of the kitchen window, I saw she topped up surreptitiously with a clear liquid from a bottle in her handbag. Her agent rang once or twice about her breakfast time slot on television in which she superciliously lectures the nation on its appalling lack of style and poise. Now and then she pounces on some poor viewer, a gormless housewife or overweight fashion victim and gives them a makeover. Invariably they come off worse, plastered in make-up, and their hair whisked up into the sort of disastrous pile-up you only ever see on motorways. She dresses them in cheap branded clothes, provided free by opportunistic PR people who welcome the publicity on a prime time show, and then parades them in front of the millions of silent viewers who mercifully remain invisible to her wretched guinea pigs. I imagine the majority must sit sniggering by their television sets. After lunch, Charlotte set off for a walk to the town and returned later with four pairs of shoes, a bikini and a bag of nectarines which she devoured in one go. For the last hour or more she has been having a siesta in her room.

Tonight Catalina and Ramon are joining us for dinner and with seared tuna, asparagus and wild rice on the menu, I feel all should go as planned. Ollie opted to eat earlier and after completing his homework went to bed with a good book. A few brief conversations with Charlotte convinced him that it was safer to stay out of her way. At eight o'clock when our guests arrive I'm feeling wonderfully mellow. Two glasses of cava and all is well with the universe. Dinner is on the point of being served but Charlotte fails to appear. Finally Alan knocks on her bedroom door and calls her name gruffly. She emerges, radiant and perfectly groomed in a purple dress suit, more suited to shopping in Bond Street than supper in a mountain *finca*. Ramon politely steps forward and shakes her hand before taking his seat at the table again. I begin serving the food while Alan lights the candles. Charlotte makes herself comfortable and examines the tuna carefully. 'Oh good, it's rare,' she says almost to herself. Ramon helps himself to a roll from the bread basket. He taps my arm.

'You want to know how your turkey's doing?'

'Ah, tell me. Is it going to be ready for Christmas?'

He shakes his head and titters before he and Catalina start laughing uncontrollably.

'What's so funny?' I seem to have missed the joke.

'The turkey is huge!' exclaims Catalina. 'Ramon is worried you won't fit him in oven.'

'What?' says Alan with alarm. 'How big is it?'

'Oh, thirty kilos, maybe?' says Catalina.

Alan drops his knife. 'Impossible! That's almost double the weight of Ollie!'

Ramon is now hooting. 'No, Catalina! Is only about twenty kilos.'

Alan throws me a look of panic. 'That's about three stone. There's no way that'll go in our oven. What have you been feeding it on, Ramon?'

'Well, he greedy. He eats more grain than others.'

'It must be obese!' yells Alan.

'It's OK,' says Catalina, wiping her eyes. 'We kill him early if he grow too big.'

'But we can't have it too early,' I say with a nervous giggle.

'We feed him less now and maybe he grow more slowly,' Catalina replies weakly.

With only a month or so to go until Christmas, I can't imagine this monster bird shrinking enough to fit in our oven. Charlotte has been sitting quietly until now, listening in confusion and growing horror.

'What are you all talking about?' she demands.

I explain that Ramon has been rearing a Christmas turkey for us.

'It sounds like a freak of nature to me. Besides, I could never eat an animal I've reared, it's too barbaric.'

Ramon gives a grunt. 'But you're happy to eat a turkey from butcher?'

'That's different.'

'How?' says Ramon.

'Because you haven't got to know it.'

Ramon doubles up while Alan tries to control a snort.

'Oh you're priceless, Charlotte,' he says.

She sips at her water and purses her nose. Catalina rushes to the rescue, complimenting Charlotte on her frock.

'You have so many wonderful clothes!' she exclaims.

Charlotte blushes with pleasure. 'Yes, I have.'

Ramon chews thoughtfully on his tuna. 'I have two shirts, two pairs of trousers, and two pairs of shoes. Why would I need more?'

Charlotte is momentarily unsettled. 'Yes, but Ramon, aren't you a builder? My job is a little different.'

He shrugs and shovels some rice in to his mouth. I notice that Charlotte is picking at her food.

'Is it OK?'

She sighs wistfully. 'I have to watch my weight. Life's a constant diet.'

'Pity the poor worms,' scoffs Catalina. 'When I die, at least they have a good fiesta, no?'

Charlotte's face crumples in disgust. Alan uncorks a bottle of red wine and sniffs the cork. 'Give me a curvy woman any day.'

'A shapely woman is best, for sure,' Ramon opines.

I throw Catalina a desperate look. She winks at me conspiratorially.

'You like your job, Carlotta ?' she questions politely, gratefully accepting at the same time a large glass of deep red wine from Alan.

'It's hugely stressful writing and performing everyday and of course I have streams of fan mail to answer from my television show and newspaper column. It's amazing I find time to view the new collections each season. I'm constantly on a plane.'

'If you don't like it,' says Ramon laconically, 'you could do something more worthwhile.'

There is a glacial tone to her reply. 'Oh, and what might that be?'

He sips at his Coca-Cola. 'You could be a cook or shopkeeper maybe, but you would need to train.'

Alan gives a snicker. 'Just think, one day we could be dining out at Ca'n Carlotta.'

Charlotte puckers her lips. 'Somehow, I think not.'

'And do you consider your job worthwhile, Ramon?' she asks waspishly.

'I build houses, like Stefan, the brother of Catalina. That's all. It's just a job. There are more important things to do.'

'Oh really, such as?'

He puts down his fork and fixes her with an iron stare. A ghost of a smile plays on his lips. 'To live, Carlotta. To live.'

There's a cool wind whipping at the edges of the porch and the gravel courtyard is swollen with rain from the night's storm as Charlotte, draped in a peach pashmina and white linen dress, wafts into the courtyard ready to depart. Pere the plumber has just arrived to fix the broken tap and gawps in genuine amazement at the apparition before him. The Jimmy Choo slingbacks seem to captivate him. Quite rightly he's wondering what in heaven's name this woman is doing wandering around in flimsy summer apparel on a wet, cloudy day in November. Charlotte wanders listlessly over to the small pond in the front garden and peers into the depths.

'Oh those damned frogs of yours!' she exclaims. 'They have kept me awake with their rasping every night. You'll have to get rid of them.'

I stalk over to the edge of the pond. 'No way, José! I couldn't live without my musical frogs. In fact, the big toad and I have a special understanding.'

She considers me carefully. 'You really are becoming more eccentric by the day. Try to spend more time in London, darling.'

Pere the plumber, easily one of the most handsome studs in the valley, saunters over with an immaculate Colgate smile. Charlotte surveys his bulging biceps with wonderment. He kisses me on the cheek and shakes her hand.

'My God! He's absolutely gorgeous,' she hisses at me. 'He can't be a plumber!'

'He sure is and very happily married so hands off.'

'What a waste!' she says sadly.

We walk to the car where Alan is trying to squeeze Charlotte's three Louis Vuitton cases into the back of the Renault.

'Alan, you really must get a decent car some time,' she fusses.

'Well, the Porsche is on order. Just trying to get the colour spec right,' he says wickedly.

'Oh very droll,' she snaps. Then air kissing me on the cheeks, she gets into the car. Pere disappears into the house with his toolkit, heading for Charlotte's vacated bathroom. Despite the cloudy day, I'm feeling elated that Charlotte is on her way.

Alan starts the engine and rolls down his window. 'I'll see you later.'

I wave as the car moves slowly out of the drive and down the stony track. Once it's disappeared, I nip over to the pond in search of my toad. He's nowhere to be seen. Catalina has warned me that the frogs will be gone very soon and won't be back until the spring. In fact, it's unusual that they're still hanging around and I half expect to find them gone any day. I sit on the edge of a rock and dip my fingers in the icy water. There's a loud plop and he suddenly appears, eyeing me intently. Is he still going to be my wise cracking Yankee friend today or should I make him more, let me think, Latino? No, a Latino toad just wouldn't work. I'm going to keep him to a fast talking American script. I let him go first.

'Jeez! Where d'you pick up that broad? She was a piece of work.'

I shrug philosophically. 'You mean Charlotte? Oh, she's OK, just a product of London.'

'Well, let's hope she stays there. Anyway, it's getting pretty cold around here so me and the boys are heading off soon.'

'Where will you go?'

'Here and there. Catch up on some relatives in other ponds, lie low until the warmer weather, I guess.'

I'm sad that there'll be no quacking and barking from them for some time.

'You'll be back in the spring?'

'Sure,' he says. 'We like it here although you gotta control that cat. She's already sniffing around, trying her luck.'

'OK, I'll have words with her.' I get up and watch as he dives clumsily into the water. Someone gives a diplomatic cough and there behind me is Pere wearing a curious expression on his face.

'*Lo siento!* I disturbed you?'

'Don't apologise, I was just day dreaming that I was chatting with a, how d'you say it in Mallorcan, er *calàpet?*' I say as chirpily as possible.

'*Un calàpet? Doncs, perquè no?*'

A toad? Well, why not? he says. I'm relieved that Pere is obviously unfazed by such things although I imagine that the tale of a mad English woman talking with toads will be half way around the town by tonight. I accompany him into the house and down to the bathroom where he has dismantled the taps and has spread out the contents of his toolkit. He clicks his teeth and shows me the snapped valve indicating that this isn't a straightforward job. It never is, after all plumbing is a serious business around here.

The sun is shining bravely in a cool blue sky as we arrive at the home of Pep and Juana. It is an important day in the calendar for a Mallorcan, being 11 November, the day of Sant Marti, when locals officially start celebrating Matances. As far as pigs are concerned, this date is about as favourable as 25 December is for turkeys and there can't be a pig in the land that isn't shaking in its trotters come this inauspicious day. Matances means 'pig slaying' and whole households are involved in killing, gutting and preparing different parts of a local pig around this time. It's a jolly affair – unless you're a pig and if you don't mind the sight of blood and guts – with everyone rolling up their sleeves and making mincemeat out of the poor little devil. These days Matances can happen anytime in the cold months from November through to February and is a way of keeping rural traditions alive. In the Middle Ages it served a critical purpose, supplying families with cured meat for a whole year. Later in the eighteenth century paprika arrived from America and suddenly Mallorcan *sobrassada* was born. The main product of the occasion is sausage and boy, don't the Mallorcans know how to make sausage! There are so many different varieties, *sobrassada* being king of them all, which is made of pork cured with paprika and salt, though honey and other ingredients are often added. There are *llonganisses*, narrow sausages for grilling, *botifarrons*, a blood pudding variety, *varia negra*, made from offal and *camaiot*, a plump black pork sausage which is stuffed into ham skin.

Pep is holding a *puro* and looking pleased with himself as he greets us in the spacious drive in front of his *finca*.

'Good timing,' he says. 'We are about to kill the pig. Do you want to watch?'

I pull a face. 'Hm. Think I might pass, if that's OK. Ollie?'

Ollie is curious but apparently not enough to see an animal killed. 'Er, I'll wait with Mummy.'

Pep punches my shoulder. 'I am disappointed in you. I thought nothing would faze you.'

'Apparently so,' I say flatly. 'Where are Angel and Juana?'

'In the garden with the pig, of course.'

He takes Alan's arm. 'Come, let's get the slaying over with and these two can join us in a few minutes.'

I notice that Alan appears none to eager to set off. He manages a smile. 'I thought it would all be over before we arrived.'

'No, we waited for you,' says Pep cheerfully. 'The local guy from the abattoir has come with the stun gun.'

'Great,' says Alan without conviction as he slowly follows Pep inside.

'Do they zap the pig with a gun?' asks Ollie when they've left.

'Yes, it's very quick and then the pig wakes up in animal heaven.'

He shakes his head. 'Give me a break. The poor pig just dies.'

'No, he goes to heaven.'

'How do you know?'

'Well, everyone knows flying pigs exist and so there must be angel pigs, in which case there has to be some kind of animal heaven.'

He frowns while he absorbs this nonsense. 'Maybe you're right.'

We sit on the grass in our heavy jackets and jeans until Pep saunters out to us with an encouraging grin.

'All over! Come and have some wine. Now the family is starting to clean and gut the pig.'

He gives me a glass of wine as we pass through the kitchen and out into the beautiful garden. Angel rushes over to meet Ollie and takes him off to inspect the pig gore. I see a pale-faced Alan talking to Juana as she hovers over the carcass, clutching a bloody knife. I come over and give her a kiss and am introduced to four other women, her two sisters, mother and grandmother. All of them are busily preparing the pig for sausages.

'Why is it black?' asks Ollie.

'Because it's a Mallorcan black pig,' says Pep. 'It's very special. One day I'll take you to see them in Sineu market.'

'Can we buy one?' asks Ollie eagerly.

'I'm sure your mother would like a black piglet around the house,' he chuckles, exhaling a cloud of smoke.

We spend the rest of the day eating and drinking. Once the gory business of sausage making is over, Pep chases Angel and Ollie around the garden with the pig's tail and teeth which he tells me, are the only inedible parts. The boys screech and run around before setting off into the field for a game of football. Alan is sitting in the kitchen, happily replete and talking in stilted Spanish to Juana's mother and sisters. They talk animatedly, laboriously describing the sausage making processes while Juana fusses round him with cognac and cheeses. I pull up my collar and walk into the garden for some fresh air. Pep joins me, *puro* in hand.

'Let me show you our vegetable patch,' he says.

'Now there's an invitation I can't refuse.'

We stroll along the gravel path and down into the adjoining field. The boys are running about at the far end.

'So, how's your business scheme coming on,' I ask Pep.

He shrugs his shoulders. 'OK but you know these things take time. Alan and I are off to see some retail outlets in Palma. It's all a question of viability.'

'Absolutely,' I say a tad sternly.

He sits on a stone bench to catch his breath and indicates for me to join him. 'So, how is your business going in London?'

'It's fine. I'm back and forth, as you know.'

'How much longer are you going to do that?' He fixes me with a long stare.

I'm rather taken aback. 'Well, we've got to earn money. I can't just give it up.'

He doesn't reply for a second, then he gives a long sigh. 'Why not just sell your business and the flat in London and do something more fun over here.'

'Like what?'

'You're a business woman. Think about it.'

Old Pep is a shrewd customer. He knows that I get stressed with my frequent trips back and forth to London and there's no point in my hiding it from him now.

'I suppose, selling the flat would clear the mortgage and then we could invest any money from the sale of the business in some new enterprise.'

He slaps me on the back. 'Now you're talking.'

I narrow my eyes. 'I hope you're not imagining for a second that I want any part of your whisky shop scheme.'

He rolls his head back and laughs. 'Of course not. I know that you're far too proper and English to consider such vulgarity. Alan being a Scotsman is different.'

It is suddenly chilly and the sky begins to darken. 'Come on,' he says, 'Let's visit the vegetables before it's too late.'

I get up and follow him down through the long grass and towards the plot. He shows me around the potatoes and sprouts and plucks up some cabbages which he thrusts in my arms. We make our way back up into the garden and are about to enter the house when he catches my arm. 'Remember, life's for living. Don't spend your life on a plane.'

The boys race up behind us before I have time to reply. He gives me a wink and steps into the warm and cosy kitchen.

EIGHT

UNEARTHING TREASURES

Christmas is nearly upon us but I have two more glorious, hermitic weeks of hiding out in the hills before I need to return to London for my last round of meetings before downing tools for the festive season.

There's a haze of ice on the office windows and a white sun, as smooth and round as a peppermint drop, is hovering above the trees, spreading sharp, cool light across the valley. Snow covers the tips of the grey Tramuntana mountains and cascades down from the peaks in soft waves as if the whole range has been dunked in hot white chocolate. It is nine in the morning and Alan is bustling about in the courtyard, chopping up firewood and clearing weeds from the pond. A car rumbles up the drive and a door slams. I peer out of the window, and see Miquel, our *siquier*, the Valley's professional irrigator, heading for the sluice gate in our field with Alan at his side. They descend into the orchard to examine the orange and lemon trees and to open the lid of our irrigation channel which delivers free water to the *safareig*, our water tank, from the mountains. This is a weekly ritual much prized by the Scotsman when he and

Miquel commune on horticultural matters. There's a great deal of head nodding, *si si*-ing and sighs, finger pointing and grunting, but few words pass their lips.

I skip down the stairs and join them outside. Miquel isn't much of a woman's man but he acknowledges me with a gruff *'Bon Dia!'* as he fumbles with the large wrought-iron key which opens the sluice gate. Once opened, he diverts the flowing water from a communal channel directly into our water tank. Although excluded from the action, I am permitted to observe their toings and froings from the sidelines, providing I don't interrupt. The concept of water rights is based on an ancient Arabic system adopted by the islanders hundreds of years ago when collective water was distributed to smallholders each week through a myriad of stone channels running across the rural landscape. Nowadays, a *siquier* tootles round in his car or on his bike opening the channels on private land, allowing the owners a preordained amount of free water to use for agricultural purposes. In times of drought, the system can be quite literally a lifesaver and in the summertime a *siquier* is in great demand. When we acquired the house, it stated in our *escriptura*, the title deeds, that we would be entitled to one hour of irrigation water each week and so Alan basks in this regular ritual of water play when Miquel arrives like a munificent priest administering *aigua*, water in Mallorcan, to the sick and dying of the plant world.

Today Miquel is frowning down into the channel of fast moving water and sucking his teeth with disapproval. He beckons both of us over. I peer in and espy the cause of his distress; a large, bloated, drowned rat that has become wedged across the channel. Its eyes, blinded by a milky white film, bulge horribly and its sharp incisors are clenched shut, although water manages to penetrate the side of its mouth, giving the impression that it is still twitching or making a stealthy wisecrack. Its pink paws appear to be clapping manically like those of a born-again preacher as the water speeds past, squeezing them together and then apart.

'What shall we do with it?' Miquel is staring into my face.

Why ask me? I suggest pulling it out and burying it in the field. Miquel dismisses me with a brusque shake of the head, saying it is far better just to leave it there. It will disintegrate in time. I wonder why he bothered to seek my opinion in the first place. He sneezes loudly and wipes his nose on the sleeve of his jacket and strides off in the direction of the orange trees. The first of our oranges are beginning to appear and he pinches one suspiciously, then sniffs the skin and walks on wordlessly. Alan, his silent shadow, does likewise. I trail along behind them. Suddenly aware of their irritation that I'm still in tow, I slope off back upstairs and sit down at the computer. It has taken several months of perseverance but finally I have ADSL installed in my office so the e-mails effortlessly flow in. Now I'm beginning to wish that I too had some sort of sluice gate device so that I am only able to receive an hour's worth per day.

Alan wanders up to my desk a little later clutching a dog-eared letter bearing an English stamp which he tells me the postman delivered yesterday. He plods off, deep in thought. It is rare to receive letters here because the postman seldom makes the effort to locate our *finca* in the labyrinth of mountain country lanes and paths and quite understandably gets confused by the lack of street names. Instead he deposits our mail at the town post office and our telepathic powers are supposed to divine when a letter has arrived. Therefore I am puzzled by the appearance of this renegade missive. I rip open the flimsy envelope – airmail weight – revealing a shaft of powder blue sheets covered in large rambling scrawl. I don't recognise the handwriting but suddenly stiffen when I decipher the name at the bottom of the third page. Joan Hedges. I remember back to my son's last day at St George's school and my foolish gesture of giving this mother my address in Mallorca, never expecting her to make contact. I skim read the letter which centres entirely on the heroic exploits of her six-year-old prodigy, Edward. According to our Joan, Edward is now learning Egyptology, advanced chess, the violin, the piano, flute, karate, drama, sailing, can count up to one hundred backwards in French, do the 12 times table and is a whiz in the kitchen. Naturally he has been advanced a year ahead of his age in school and is taking the leading role, Joseph, in the Christmas nativity play. She adds that Christmas will be spent in Russia where Edward will be tutored in chess, skating and Russian doll making. I am about to scrunch the pages into a ball for instant disposal when a juvenile thought occurs to me. I peel open the creased letter, note the address and rattle off a typed reply as follows:

Dear Joan,

It was a delightful surprise to receive your letter today and to hear all Edward's news. Our little cherub seems to be adapting well to life in Spain although at six, we are a little concerned that he has only reached A level standard Spanish despite several months' tuition here. Nevertheless, he appears to be enjoying Plato's *Republic* in the original Greek and Homer's *Odyssey* which is one of the reading for fun books, chosen for his year group. Last week he received a standing ovation for one of his solo piano performances at the Palma Auditorium but we are keen to see him progress beyond Mozart to something more substantial. As for hobbies, he's excelled in astronomy and advanced maths this summer and should be completing his aviation exams in the next few weeks. Well, must dash, got to pick him up from his tai chi grand masters class. Keep in touch.

I print it off, scrawl my signature with a flourish at the end and am about to throw it in the bin when the phone rings. It's Rachel.

'Busy?'

'Very.'

'We've got that perfume pitch in two weeks. Just wondered if I could run the proposal by you.'

'You mean Heaven Scent?'

'The same.'

'Have you suggested a complete re-naming and re-branding job?' I tease.

'Of course not. It's making twenty million dollars for the company each year so why should they care if the name's naff?'

Someone's shouting below my window. 'Gotta go, Rachel. Just e-mail it over.'

I open the window, feeling like a slovenly Rapunzel. Beaming up at me is Fransisca, my ebullient Spanish teacher, clutching a letter. This is thrilling. Two letters in one day. I mutter '*Un moment*,' and tear down the stairs. It appears that she and her German husband, Hans, are holding a pre-Christmas fiesta and we are invited. I open the invitation, lovingly written in gold ink and decorated by hand, and promise to attend. She hugs me goodbye and saunters cheerfully along the path, exhaling white breath into the icy air. Alan sidles up, his hands pushed into the pockets of his jacket.

'I'm off to plant *faves*. Wondered if you could give me a hand?'

How can I possibly resist? Planting broad beans has to be an experience on a cold wintry day and offers a wonderful diversion from answering e-mails. I go indoors, retrieve a warm jacket and join him in the field. There is a white frost on the soil which looks like fine mould and the grass along the hedgerows is soaked in dew. My wellies make a swishing noise as I plod through the weeds and dandelions to the centre of the terrain where Alan has dug a series of shallow trenches. He is fiddling with two bags of seeds.

'Can you start planting at that end?'

'Sure. How exactly do I plant?'

He shakes his head sorrowfully, patiently explaining how to complete this simplest of tasks. An hour later and the *faves* are happily bedded in the soil. Alan announces that he needs to post some letters so bounds towards the house to find the car keys while I pull off my muddy boots with red raw, ice-cold hands and head for the kitchen to put on the kettle. Catalina is busy sweeping the *entrada* and gives a wry smile when I appear before her with rosy cheeks.

'Has Alan gone for his Spanish lesson with Paula?' she quizzes.

'No, that's tonight,' I reply. 'The highlight of his day.'

'You are very naughty!' she says waggling a finger at me.

Shortly afterwards, I am back upstairs in my office when I hear a scream and a loud exclamation of '*SUSTO!*', the Spanish equivalent of, 'Oh my God!' I rush to the *entrada* to find Catalina gripping a broom at the bottom of the staircase leading to the cellar. The word *susto* always implies shock or fear so I know something is up. She is poking gingerly at the cellar door with the handle and muttering '*Susto*' under her breath.

'Are you alright?'

'No, there is mouse.'

'Where?'

'In cupboard.'

She bangs on the door and this time a small streak of fur whizzes up the staircase to the *entrada* and disappears into the fireplace. Catalina shrieks.

'*Déu!* There are TWO!!'

I have already, cravenly, alighted a chair and am watching her as she stands with broom upturned like Britannia with her trident.

'How do you know there are two?'

'The other one was different colour.'

How she has deduced what colour the speeding fur ball was, I have no idea, but I'm not going to argue the point.

'What are we going to do?' I ask lamely.

Catalina views me sternly and strides over to the fireplace, chases the small rodent from its hiding place and shoos it out of the French doors with the brush.

'There is still one in cupboard,' she says grimly. 'We need the cat.'

Inko is slumbering on a kitchen chair and isn't remotely interested in the drama unfolding around her until she is unceremoniously dumped in the cellar cupboard with the door closed behind her. We stand tensely outside. After a few minutes of silence, there is a frantic scratching and Inko's familiar mewing.

Catalina opens the door a fraction and the cat squeezes past and leaps up on to the chair next to me. It arches its back and whines pathetically.

'You feed too much the cat,' says Catalina, glaring at it. 'He is lazy.'

She is of course right. Inko is thoroughly spoilt and overfed and, although Catalina uses her he's and she's indiscriminately, is female and very manipulative. Courageously, Catalina enters the large walk-in cupboard and clatters around, poking the broom into plastic bags and wicker baskets, cardboard boxes full of cleaning materials and the toolbox. Nothing moves. After ten minutes of assault, she rests the broom against a wall and admits defeat. We decide to close the door but at that moment I spy a small terracotta air vent high up on the wall that leads directly out into the garden. Our interloper has, it seems, already made its escape to freedom.

The front door bangs and Alan appears, peering at us over the banister. He's holding a pile of mail collected from the post office.

'By the way, posted that letter for you,' he says cheerily.

'What letter?'

'The one on your desk. Put it in an envelope and addressed it.' He wafts out to the garden, glimpsing the contents of several opened envelopes as he goes. I scramble upstairs to check that my flight of fancy to Joan Hedges is still on my desk but it's gone. Too late. Somehow I suspect that this may be the last time I shall ever hear from her.

Fat Phillip is sitting on the bedroom floor of Ollie's room gurning about his lost Game Boy while his stressed mother, Susie, Silk Cut cigarette hanging from her lower lip, searches frantically for it in his rucksack. I pop my head round the door and suggest that he may have left it back at their hotel.

'Don't be stupid!' fizzes Phillip furiously.

His mother looks up and remonstrates with him. 'Darling! Don't be so rude. Apologise immediately.'

'No!' hollers the little beast.

I look at his large, podgy face, round and white like a ball of lard, and decide that he really is the most charm-less child I have ever had the misfortune to meet. Back in the days when he and Ollie attended St George's school, they had shared a passion for Digimon swap cards but that's about as far as the relationship ever developed. Of all the mothers at St George's, I had a genuine fondness for Susie Simpson because she was real. A single mother and freelance journalist forever on the edge of a nervous breakdown, she smoked like a dragon and drank wine with the gusto of a hydrophobic. Her lumbering son, Phillip, was the school misfit and a year older than the rest, who bullied the other kids, ripped up storybooks and ruined the school nativity play. Susie despaired, never seeming to realise that indulging his every whim, did nothing to curb his maladjusted behaviour. And here they both are, spending a long weekend at a bijoux hotel in the north of the island which she is reviewing for the travel pages of *The Times*. When Susie called, requesting to spend a day with us in the mountains, I could hardly refuse, and as Ollie would be celebrating his birthday, I thought it might be fun for him to see an old friend from London.

Alan treads heavily up the staircase and beckons to me. I skip down a few steps to join him.

'What's going on in there?' he whispers crossly.

'Phillip's lost his Game Boy.'

'His what?'

'Oh, never mind. Look, we'll set off on the treasure hunt as soon as the other kids arrive and hopefully he'll forget all about it.'

He shakes his head impatiently and plods back down again. I put on my best smile and enter Ollie's bedroom. Susie is leaning out of the open window gazing pensively across the orchard in a world of her own. She is scrawny and unkempt and her hair hangs lankly about her face. Distractedly, she draws deeply on a cigarette and shivers. It is wintry and fresh but the sun is shining, an ideal day for walking in the hills. The two children are now playing a game of snakes and ladders but Phillip is already growing restless and is gazing around the room, in search of something to destroy. I clap my hands together cheerfully.

'Right chaps, let's get our coats on because we're going on the treasure hunt shortly.'

Ollie leaps up in anticipation. Since moving to Mallorca, treasure hunts have become his passion. In the absence of television and electronic toys, we have created the treasure hunt as a ploy to get him walking in the mountains and away from the house bound pursuits of his erstwhile sedentary London life. Now, at weekends, we set off into the hills with a hand drawn map indicating treasure points along the way and Alan or I sneak off in advance to place booty in fairly easy to find spots. Each hunt is themed differently and treasure takes the form of coins, little toys, or coloured objects. Today we have devised a mammoth toy hunt for him and his two best friends and Phillip, which should take us on a six-mile circuit. Angel, Pep's son, has kindly offered to come along to help supervise the younger children. We have pre-prepared a lavish tea for our return and have invited Catalina, Ramon and their daughters together with Pep and Juana.

Phillip is wailing and has thrown himself on the floor in a fit of pique. His dishevelled fair hair splays out from his head on to the rug and his eyes blaze. Susie throws her cigarette stub on to the gravel outside, closes the window and comes over and kneels beside him.

'Please, darling, don't do this. Not now.'

'I HATE WALKING! I don't want to go on some stupid treasure hunt with stupid children. I'm staying here.' He's blubbering hysterically now.

Ollie steps over him dispassionately and runs down the stairs when he hears a car roll up outside. The others, Ignacío and Gunter, have arrived and Angel is waiting in the courtyard, kicking a football about in the gravel. I suggest to Susie that Phillip will be fine when we get going.

'No, you don't know him,' she says bitterly. 'He'll be a monster. I'd better stay with him. He'll ruin everything for everyone else.'

I notice that she has tears in her eyes. Exhausted and at the end of her tether, her hands are shaking badly. A voice bellows from downstairs. It's Alan.

'Come on!' he roars, 'We'll find your Play Boy thingy later, Phillip. Hurry up or we'll go without you.'

Desperate measures are called for. I shoo Susie out of the room and tell her to go downstairs and wait for us. She agrees hesitantly but assures me that I'm wasting my time trying to reason with her son. As soon as she's left, I sit on the floor next to the sobbing child. He is unnerved that his mother has gone.

'It's all right, you can stay at the house if you like, but I do think you're brave.'

Phillip fixes me with his tough little almond eyes. 'Why?'

'Well, you are in *bruixa* country.'

'What's that?' he snarls.

'The *bruixa* is the witch of the Tramuntana mountains.'

'You're a baby!' he says contemptuously. 'There aren't such things as witches.'

'As I say, you're a brave boy. Good luck.'

He stares hard at me, a nasty sneer on his face. 'So what does she do, this witch?'

'She steals children with the help of her pack of fierce, flying mountain hounds. Of course the poor children are never seen again.'

I walk towards the door.

'Where are you going? Where's Mum?' he says a tad nervously.

'Well, we're all off now. By the way, when the *bruixa* comes for you, try to keep your eyes scrunched shut and hide under the bed and, fingers crossed, her hounds won't find you.'

He gets up slowly. 'You're lying!'

'I'm afraid not. She loves naughty children with blond hair and brown eyes. The naughtier, the better. Goodness knows how many children she's stolen and gobbled up in the last year.'

He jumps up, his face solemn. 'Will she get me if I come on the treasure hunt?'

'Well, if you're a good boy and stick closely with all of us, it's nigh impossible for her to steal you away.'

He nods his head and meekly follows me down the stairs. I help him on with his jacket and gloves and usher him out into the sunshine. Angel, together with Ollie and his friends, Gunter and Ignacío, are crouching by a tree prodding the ground with sticks where they have discovered an enormous ant's nest. When Phillip appears they race towards him and drag him over to show him their find. Alan and Susie are talking by the gate but she stops, her mouth dropping open at the sight of her subdued and obedient son. We walk across the field together in the direction of a small track that leads into the forests and the mountains beyond. The children race ahead of us. Susie paws at my sleeve agitatedly.

'Will they be safe? Shouldn't we be holding their hands?'

Barraged with frightening stories of child abduction in the British press everyday, I'm not surprised my friends become paranoid about their offspring. I should know, when living in London, I was worse than any of them.

'Susie, up here in the villages, children as young as four walk home alone. It's a different world.'

She sighs and shrugs her shoulders. 'Just the same, let's catch them up.'

The children have stopped to watch a couple of fish swimming in a small stream at the bottom of our field. Phillip is absorbed.

Susie tucks her arm under mine. 'Tell me, what did you say to Phillip?'

'That he'd be gobbled up by the big, bad witch of the mountains.'

She gives a cynical snort. 'Yeah, right! Nothing like that frightens my little horror anymore.'

We walk on silently, the children and Alan beating a noisy path before us. Snow clings to the lower peaks of the Tramuntana range and high above, a solitary rock juts out at the mountain's edge, dark and jagged like the bewitching silhouette of a giant witch's chin.

I am sitting at my old scuffed desk idly scrolling through my e-mails and browsing comments sent by readers of my Saturday column in the *Majorca Daily Bulletin*. I have had a hot, luxurious and scented bath for the first time in months now that the bath taps in my bathroom have been fitted and actually work. Up until now we've made do with a shower. Even the walls have been tiled although the floor is still cement layered with thick grime. Ah well, *poc a poc*. The house is silent now that Ollie's birthday guests have gone home and all I can hear is the velvety, rhythmic purring of Inko as she sits curled under my chair. Outside, an ebullient, mischievous moon peers over the jagged mountain ridge, waits till I look away and then hoists itself up a fraction. No matter how diligently I keep vigil, it continues to rise in small imperceptible moves until it reaches its full height as if by magic and suddenly a luminous bubble of light is hovering outside my window like an impatient peeping Tom. Tonight I pull open the shutters and gaze into the pond below. It is still and the frogs and my friendly toad are nowhere to be seen. Can I blame them on a frosty night like this? I shiver and close the window.

The builders are crashing about in the *entrada* with the front door wide open as they plod in and out with tools and materials. I'm trying not to get over-excited but with any luck our new enlarged stone fireplace will be completed today. Up until now we've made do with a small hearth that doesn't afford much heat beyond the *entrada*. The thought of having a huge blazing fire in the hearth is enough to bring me out in a cold sweat of anticipation. I shiver with the chill knowing that we won't have central heating fitted for some months. The enhanced fireplace will be a start. Meanwhile we will continue to make do with fingerless mittens, thick sweaters, woollen scarves and socks. Catalina is bustling around the builders, breaking up a cardboard box and sweeping up leaves that have blown in through the French doors.

'Always much dirt,' she says accusingly, prodding one of the builders with her brush. He leaps away and cackles with laughter. She turns to me. 'Hey, you forget your Spanish class?'

I look at my watch and realise that I'm running late. Grabbing my exercise books and jacket, I bolt out of the front door. The turf is hard and crusty underfoot as I walk briskly along the lane. Nearing Rafael's house I see Franco sniffing cheerfully in the hedgerows outside his pen. Loud Hispanic music is belting out from the windows of the *finca*. I give the dog a pat as I walk by and plod on. Ten minutes later, deep in thought about my Spanish verbs and nearing the office of Fransisca, I hear heavy panting and am alarmed to see Franco tripping along some distance behind me. Knowing that he is not allowed past our lane, I attempt to steer him back up the road and in the direction of Rafael's house. At the corner of the street, I see Margalida Sampol chatting with some elderly friends. I wave to her and she scrunches up her eyes before the penny drops. 'What are you doing with Rafael's dog?' she asks in puzzlement.

'It won't stop following me,' I reply helplessly.

She confers with her friends who begin calling the dog's name. This achieves nothing given that the mutt is already over-excited and now barks madly at the sound of his name.

Margalida makes the sign of the cross and shrugs her shoulders. Meanwhile several bemused locals stop to watch my dismal attempts at coaxing him home. Have they nothing better to do? I decide to run on and give him the slip but he mistakenly thinks this is a game and bounds along, finally knocking me over and covering me in dirt and spittle. An old lady in black garb starts to cackle and soon various passers-by join in the fray. They all seem to know the dog's name and to my dismay cry out, 'Franco! *Venga! Venga!*' which makes the stupid animal grow even wilder. The big-hipped *duena*, the boss, of our local grocery shop comes out on the pavement and waves to me.

'I see you have a new friend!' she chuckles in Spanish.

Oh very funny. Meanwhile her husband attempts to catch Franco by the collar but the boxer evades him, pawing me frantically and licking my hands in between excited barking. My small band of loyal spectators titter with amusement as I stand helplessly in the street outside Fransisca's office. In a flustered state I buzz her intercom.

'*Si?*'

'Fransisca, it's me but I've got my neighbour's dog down here.'

'*Vale*, OK,' she says. 'Bring him in if you want.'

'You don't understand. I don't want him here at all.'

She struggles to hear me above the barking and sounds a little perplexed.

'Then why did you bring him?' she asks.

'I didn't. Listen, I'm just going to call Alan and I'll be with you.'

'*No problema*,' she says and the intercom goes dead.

Alan is impatient when I call him on my mobile. He asks why on earth I took the dog with me. I try to explain above the din of barking.

'Calm down.' I hear him say. 'I'll get Rafael to fetch him.'

Fifteen minutes later Rafael arrives at the office to reclaim his pet. Franco is lying on the tiled floor listening attentively to the lesson in progress. Grinning from ear to ear, my sporty neighbour bounds over and kisses me on both cheeks.

'*Hola!* Everything good? So you take my dog for lessons of *Español*, eh? You don't think Franco speak good enough Spanish?'

He rocks with laughter while Fransisca enthusiastically recounts the whole tale at my expense. That's one of the keys to life here, being able to laugh at oneself. Anyone with a dangerous sense of self-importance or *gravitas* would be strongly advised to get straight back on the next plane for London. When I first met Catalina's husband, Ramon, I remember telling him rather loftily that I ran a public relations company. He gave me a look loaded with irony and asked whether I could also do anything useful like sewing or cooking, so I'm catching on fast. After much guffawing and belly laughs, Rafael leads Franco from the flat by his collar. At the door, the dog turns and gives me what I take to be a large canine grin, his wet, red tongue lolling out of his mouth as if he too is enjoying the joke.

It is eight in the evening as we arrive at Fransisca and Hans's flat which spreads across the top floor of an apartment block on the perimeter of the town. It is clean and modern with a huge white living space that gives on to a veranda overlooking the busy main road to the port beyond which lie the Tramuntana mountains. I first met Fransisca and Hans, when enrolling for classes at their language school. For several months now Fransisca has patiently persevered with teaching me Spanish despite my erratic timekeeping for I too am falling under the spell of *mañana, mañana*. En route to her office, I am easily waylaid, engaging in gossip with neighbours, and dishing out food scraps to roving dogs and feral cats along the path in the belief that I have all the time in the world. Then there are my frequent hops back to London which mean cancelling lessons, often at short notice, and putting homework on a back burner. While Fransisca and her disciples teach, Hans runs the business, skilfully juggling the diaries of their foreign clients and, on the phone, switching between languages with the speed of a baton in a relay race.

Despite my tutor's efforts I do not feel I have progressed as quickly as I would have liked but this has more to do with my initial naivety in thinking I could be truly fluent in a matter of months, just absorbing the language by osmosis. The reality is that learning a language properly, and by that I mean understanding its nuances and poetry, takes time and dedication. Unfortunately, there is no magic chip which, once inserted, has you babbling fluently in the lingo, and all those feckless friends who merrily tell you on departure that learning a new language is a cinch are what we call in Mallorcan complete *mentiders* – liars. In fact, in most cases, the people who brag about the ease of mastering a foreign language have seldom attempted to do so themselves and often have a dismal grasp of their own. The key to linguistic success of course, is to listen to the locals and attempt at every opportunity to participate in conversation, regardless of how humiliating or embarrassing the consequences might be. However, Alan learned the perils of following this path some months before when at a dinner party he spoke of his love for *pajaras*, slovenly bitches, instead of what he meant to say; *pajaros*, birds. As they say, what a difference an 'a' makes.

But back to tonight. Fransisca and Hans are hosting their pre-Christmas fiesta, an 'at home' which they have organised for clients and friends, and the place is buzzing with chatter. As we enter, engulfed in warm air and light from the small doorway,

I notice out of the corner of my eye a piano and an assortment of musical instruments placed prominently in the centre of the room. What can be the significance of this? Fransisca, face glistening from the heat of the kitchen, greets us with hugs and kisses and shows us into the flat. The drinks are flowing and Hans emerges from the kitchen balancing a tray buried beneath platters of cold meats, rice dishes home-made pies and rich German cakes. He and his wife rig up two pine trestle tables on which they place dish upon dish of food. There is nothing over engineered and the simplicity and homeliness of the occasion takes me back to the buffets once organised by my elderly aunt when I was a child. Various friends dive into the kitchen and open bottles of Rioja which they share round the guests. Far across the valley, stars burn in the sky and the dull rumble of passing traffic can just be heard from the open doorway of the veranda. There's a warm hand on my back.

'*Venga!*' says Fransisca, 'The fun is about to begin.'

I espy Alan and Ollie at the other side of the room, chomping on large plates of paella and pie. At the mention of fun, Alan shoots me a wary look. To our joint astonishment, Hans takes to the piano and Fransisca to the guitar. I am immediately reminded of the singing duo, Peters and Lee. There's a hush as smiling Spanish guests gather round the piano quite obviously anticipating a sing-song. My eyes meet those of Alan and in a moment of self-consciousness of an urban kind, we both scuttle to the side of the room and sit down. Could this ever happen in London? Within minutes the room is filled with singing voices, frenzied guitar strumming and the tinkling of piano keys. Two Spaniards begin to shuffle to the sound of the music, clapping their hands dramatically and *Olé*-ing. Yes, it's true, the Spanish really do say *Olé*. An exotic Spanish woman in a slinky red dress with black hair that snakes down past her waist, beckons to me to join her as she gyrates around the piano. Oh God, how do I get out of this one? I decline demurely and nod in the direction of Ollie, picking him up and pretending that he's sleepy. Indignantly he gives me a shove and demands to be put down. There's nothing for it. I have to join the group. As I sway inelegantly with this happy crowd, clapping to the music, I see Rachel's horrified face swimming towards me as in a dream, her mouth hissing, 'For Christ's sake. What are you doing?' I shake myself out of my stupor and see Ollie watching me from his chair, a smug grin playing on his lips. Alan is to my left now, plucking at the strings of a guitar while a large man, his eyes dancing with excitement, claps him cheerfully on the back yelling, '*Bravo! Bravo!*' An hour later and we are all singing rowdily, Ollie is dancing with an elderly Spanish woman wearing a white caftan and hoop earrings and Alan is playing 'The Maple Leaf Rag' on the piano to rapturous applause.

We leave at midnight, tipsy and warm with red wine and exertion and stroll off along the road back to the *finca*. Several partygoers call out raucously and toot us as they drive by, the tail lights of their cars glowing like cigarette butts in the dusk. Soon we are crunching up the gravel of our track, mutely, engulfed in darkness and the sounds of night in the country. The owls and bats soar overhead and as we reach the courtyard I am at once aware of a huge canopy of white stars blazing above us. There's a familiar scratchy cough coming from the pond and as I peer closer I see the silhouette of my portly toad observing me from a rock at the edge of the water. I thought he'd be gone by now. He creeps out of the shadows, his eyes glinting in the light of the stars, and then, with a sly wink and a full throttle croak, he disappears into the crevice of a rock.

Rafael's cockerel, like an over-excited town crier, is screeching at the top of his voice as Catalina drives, lights blazing, into the dim courtyard. Just in case anyone's still asleep in the house, she stabs at the hooter and yells out of the van's window. I jump in beside her, kitted in mountain gear and thick gloves.

'They're still asleep,' I mutter.

Catalina takes no prisoners. 'But it's half past six. They should be up by now.'

We whiz off down the track and through the quiet country roads. The ghostly light of a *moto* comes towards us on the other side of the road and then I see the familiar frame of Gaspar, the paper delivery man. He gives us a toot and a thumbs up sign and rumbles off.

He must be off to pick up the papers,' I turn to Catalina.

'Yes, Gaspar gets up very early, but he's happy.'

We climb up the mountain roads finally reaching a tranquil spot with wild terrain and forests where the road curves off to the left. Catalina flicks her indicator although at this hour there isn't a soul on the road. Rumbling along a steep track for about a mile, thick forest land on both sides, we turn right into a narrow lane full of boulders and sharp rocks and jolt along for a few miles until we reach a small clearing.

'Thank heavens I borrow Stefan's old van,' she shouts above the noise of the engine. The road widens slightly, enough for a car to park on one side. Catalina stops abruptly and we both get out. In the back of the van, she unearths two large trugs and some sharp little knives and torches.

'OK, we meet my aunt Maria here and then we walk through the forests and up into the terraces. It will be light soon.'

The air is cool and like dragons, our breath is white. I look inside my trug. It's quite big. 'Do you reckon we'll find many *bolets?*'

She shrugs. 'That's the thing about hunting for mushrooms. You never know what you will find until the day.'

The sky is still dark and both of us jiggle about in the chill while we wait for Maria. A headlight hits us before the car struggles up the lane and jolts to a stop behind ours. The door flies open and Catalina's ebullient and energetic aunt, jumps out, talking animatedly. I try to keep up but the stream of Mallorcan linguistic ping pong-ing between the two, finally defeats me.

'*Molt bé!*' she gives me a big hug. 'Now we go searching for gold!'

We take our trugs and set off across the damp field and into the woods. Maria is small and fit and exudes an air of confidence. Up in her local village she and her husband Jaime run an excellent restaurant called Canantuna which even the King of Spain has been rumoured to visit and heavenly fresh *bolets* are always on the menu when in season. She snaps off twigs and bends branches as she strides on, torch in hand, through the obscurity towards her goal. I scramble after her and Catalina, holding my torch in one hand and trug in the other. We're all huffing and puffing as we begin our ascent through the stone terraces where Maria's hidden treasure trove of *bolets*, the much prized local mushrooms, are to be found.

'Do many people come up here for *bolets?*' I ask.

They both swing round and give me a harsh look.

'This is my private land! If anyone dared come here I'd chase them off,' says Maria spiritedly.

'People go mad for them,' adds Catalina conspiratorially. 'You see them searching with torches in the hedgerows at the crack of dawn.'

'Are they difficult to buy?' I'm mystified by the cult and wonder if they have the rarity of truffles.

'You can buy them easily enough, but they cost a fortune and aren't always fresh,' explains Maria.

The science of *bolets* is something unknown to me which is why Catalina and her aunt generously invited me to join them on one of their many seasonal mushroom hunts on Maria's private land. There's a trickle of light in the sky so we turn off our torches.

'Now,' instructs Maria. 'Be careful what you pick and check back with me. There are many poisonous mushrooms around and some are deadly.'

That's cheerful news. I shall certainly not be popping any finds in my mouth before first conferring with Maria.

She takes out a sharp knife and begins scraping the soil beneath a tree. There appears to be nothing there so I'm not quite sure what she's doing.

'Can you see any mushrooms?' she quizzes.

'Not a thing,' I reply.

She raises her eyebrows and like a magician tells me to step aside. With one quick move of the knife, she uncovers two enormous mushrooms on the place where I had been standing. I'm stunned.

'But they looked like half-buried pebbles,' I stammer.

She triumphantly hurls them in my trug. 'Don't be fooled!'

Back under the tree where she was digging, she uncovers a patch of red *esclatasangs*, bloodbusters, so named because of their bright red juice. I fish around in the undergrowth but seem to find nothing but trouble. I hold up a small mushroom.

'*Peu de rata*, rat feet. That one's no good. Throw it away!' she tuts.

A clump of delicious looking grey mushrooms catch my eye. 'No, no,' Catalina yells. 'Those are *bolets verinosos*, very nasty toadstools.'

I notice, a little petulantly, that both Catalina and Maria are filling their trugs effortlessly.

'You develop an eye for *bolet* hunting,' says Catalina sympathetically, 'and my aunt knows exactly where to find them.'

She beckons to me. 'See here? The sheep have beaten us to it. Normally there's a big patch under this tree but they have been eaten. This is why we come early morning.'

An hour later, quite unexpectedly I alight upon a large area of mushrooms. Excitedly as if I've discovered some rare archaeological find, I carefully scrape away the soil and holler for Catalina.

'*Molt bé!*' she says. 'You've found your treasure. Dig carefully and remember to cut at the base of the stem or you'll destroy the next crop.'

Heavens, *bolet* hunting is a tricky business and not for the impatient or faint-hearted. We plod on through the terraces, higher and higher, following in Maria's experienced foot steps. Some hours later we stop for a rest and examine our trugs. Theirs are groaning under the weight of various varieties of *bolet*, while mine is rather thin on substance.

Catalina suddenly claps her hands. '*Bé*, the sun's up and it's time for an early lunch.'

I look at my watch and am disorientated to see it's already nearly one o'clock. The time seems to have flown by and I'm feeling ravenous.

We retrace our steps and head back for the car, rosy cheeked and full of energy. It's been a magical morning and one I will treasure.

'Give me your *setas*,' says Catalina.

'My what?'

She shakes her head. 'Sorry, we switch all the time between Mallorcan and Castilian Spanish. It must confuse you. *Seta* in Castilian Spanish just means *bolet* in Mallorcan.'

'I see,' I reply, realising once again that one day soon I am going to have to get to grips with both Mallorcan as well as Castilian Spanish if I am to enjoy local mountain life to the full.

We head off by car to Balitx d'Avall, a beautiful seigneurial house set in the hills which offers hikers scrumptious Mallorcan fare. Typically, Maria and Catalina know the owners and all the kitchen staff so we are given the best indoor table overlooking the forests.

'Now we cook our *bolets*,' enthuses Maria, patting her stomach. She bustles into the kitchen with one of the trugs and some minutes later, the mouth watering aroma of frying mushrooms, garlic and herbs wafts into the restaurant. I can hardly contain myself as I sit with Catalina quaffing robust red wine and snacking on home cured ham and olives. The platter duly arrives and we all tuck into our booty. I close my eyes and savour my first *bolet*. The taste is incomparable, divine, wonderful and a far cry from mushrooms back home.

'Let's drink to our new apprentice,' yells Maria, with aplomb.

Catalina is gracious. 'Yes, you did well for a beginner.'

We chink glasses and savour the rich ruby wine. Somehow I think this fumbling apprentice will be on the *seta* trail again before long. That's if Maria and Catalina are willing to share their secret treasures once more.

NINE

LONDON: DECEMBER

Sunday night, en route to London

The plane is waltzing about the skies like a possessed ballroom dancer while the cabin crew lurch up and down the aisle, instructing all of us naughty passengers to stay strapped in our seats. We are encountering a little turbulence they say. A little. And the rest. Sitting next to me calmly reading a newspaper and attempting to sip from a gyrating glass of beer is my companion, Jason Moore, editor of the *Majorca Daily Bulletin*. He is tall and lean and a bit of a hustler with a wry countenance and a breezy, laid-back demeanour. Despite his youth, he's more in the mould of an old Fleet Street hack, being sharp witted and pithy with a nose for a story and a fag invariably glued to his lips. As fate would decree we have ended up on the same flight to London. I am back for meetings and a pre-Christmas shopping spree while he is attending a Spanish tourism conference. He gives me a cursory glance as I sit, white-knuckled, gripping the armrests of my seat.

'Not a nervous flier, are you?'

'Just a bit.'

Jason chews on this nugget thoughtfully and slides me a grin. 'You don't look the type.'

How should I look, I wonder: hair standing on end, limbs shaking uncontrollably, mouth open in an expression of abject terror, tears coursing down my cheeks? On the other side of me a middle-aged woman sits clutching a handkerchief, peering into the sullen sky as lightning whips about the wings.

'Do you think we'll be alright?' she asks me anxiously as thunder growls beyond the window pane. I suppress an urge to shriek, 'NO!' and instead, try calmly to reassure her. Jason observes us both and puts his paper away.

'Come on, have a drink, you'll both be fine. Planes nowadays can withstand pretty much anything.' He pauses. 'So, have either of you used a parachute before?'

The woman winces and titters nervously while I knock back the remainder of a lukewarm vodka and tonic. It splashes down my chin as the plane leaps like a bucking bronco in the air. I steady myself on the pull down table.

'Can't take you anywhere,' quips Jason. 'Well there's no sign of Victoria Duvall, our esteemed film director, on the plane.'

'I think she avoids flying over weekends. Spike got on earlier though.'

'Who?'

'He's a travel courier, one of Victoria's commuter chums. He was the guy I was talking to as we were boarding.'

Jason raises a cynical brow. 'That trendy chap spouting to you about some dodgy self-help book?'

'Yes, he's a bit of a hippy. He told me that book, *The Power of Now*, is all the rage in London.'

'Whatever next?' he sniffs with distaste. 'I can't understand why people need these emotional props.'

We bounce about as the plane struggles to rise above the turbulence. A plastic cup skips down the aisle in wild

191

abandonment. I sure could do with a prop or soothing self-help book now. I grip Jason's arm in alarm.

He yawns in ennui. 'Come on, it's only a lick of lightning. We'll be making our descent soon.'

I look at my watch. Another 40 minutes of hell.

Jason turns in his seat. 'So, what are you up to this trip?'

I find his relaxed chatter an unwelcome intrusion in my moment of terror. Limply I take him through some of my forthcoming meetings. He listens enthusiastically, questioning me on every detail. We talk for some time until there's a roar and the plane makes a sharp descent. The time seems to have whizzed by. The aircrew are strapped in and the lights are dimmed. A few minutes later we come to a stop at Gatwick airport. I practically kiss the tarmac.

'There,' beams Jason, punching me on the arm. 'All you needed was a little distraction.'

Monday 8.30 a.m., the Pimlico pad

I shower, get dressed and leave the flat, triple-locking the front door after me. Upstairs the hallway is silent with the musty aroma of old books. Not even Lord Jim Jam is prowling about the place. The mail is neatly stacked on a broad ledge. I flick gingerly through the pile and find three sales circulars addressed to Alan. Junk mail. No one writes to us here anymore because it's no longer our home. I think of my conversation with Pep. Maybe he's right. Why not close the business, get rid of the flat and set up a new enterprise in Mallorca? What have we got to lose?

Shutting the main door behind me, I stroll up the road and into Victoria Station. A Starbucks faces platform one so I buy an Earl Grey tea and sit in a corner sifting through the daily newspapers, undisturbed. Customers pop in and out ordering their coffee and eyeing the muffins and cakes with longing like children in a tuck shop. Several yield to their impulses, shyly indicating the caramel square or chocolate brownie of their choice, and then quickly secreting it inside briefcases or handbags. A small, candied morsel to disguise the bitter pill of the working day. I'm due to meet Michael Roselock in an hour, so I drain my cup and leave, weaving my way through the great tidal wave of commuters spilling out of trains and on to the concourse. They march together side by side; a band of wordless foot soldiers, impassive and resolute in their winter garb. At the front of the station I hop on to a bus and head for Mayfair and to Roselock Fine Jewellery.

5 p.m., Piccadilly

Piccadilly's teeming with traffic as I cross the road and stagger into Waterstone's bookshop with all my shopping bags. Book buying is becoming a serious addiction. I've already plundered Hatchards for new titles and had a quick coffee with Roger Katz before he had to get back to the store. Now I'm on the hunt for books for Ollie and so can't resist the huge children's department in Waterstone's, which is looking particularly festive. After this I will trundle from Knightsbridge to Regent Street in my quest for Christmas crackers, cranberry sauce, stilton, and chocolate truffles to make our Mallorcan Christmas a reasonably British affair. There's still more shopping to be done, not least finding Christmas gifts for Margalida and Teresa, and all our other Mallorcan friends. I scan my watch. Another few hours and then I shall be meeting Ed. I must get going.

7.30 p.m., PJ's, Covent Garden

'I love this place,' opines Ed, chewing on a piece of roast lamb.

'Why?' I ask crisply.

'Well, for one, the portions are enormous, and two, they don't treat me like an alien. That's because it's American owned.'

'Don't be ridiculous.' I toy with a piece of lettuce on my plate.

'It's true, Scatters. Most English restaurants don't understand about the MEK. Here they accept that it's my hot date.' Furtively he pats the heavy bag on the seat next to him.

I roll my eyes. 'There's nothing wrong with being a little eccentric.'

He fidgets with his serviette. 'Well according to Cotton-Georgia there is. We've split up for good.'

I can't disguise my relief. The thought of Ed engaging in a serious Internet romance with the daughter of an American snake handling lay preacher, was giving me palpitations. 'Oh well, there are plenty more pebbles on the beach.'

'That's hardly a comfort,' he sulks, popping a chunk of roast potato in his mouth.

'More ships on the sea, tea leaves in the pot, fish in the pond…'

'Oh be quiet!' He gives a snort of laughter then pulls a blue cordial from the MEK.

'What the hell's that?'

'My doctor prescribed it. It's to help me with digesting food.'

I'd like to meet his doctor once and for all, preferably to give her a taste of her own medicine. He takes a few glugs and then replaces the lid.

'Has it worked its magic yet?'

He casts me a wounded look and turns his head away. A waiter approaches the table and seems delighted to see Ed.

'Sir, how lovely to see you again? How's the food?'

'Marvellous,' replies Ed, nodding happily at the man. 'As always.'

He gives a gracious little bow and saunter off.

'See how nice they are to me in here?'

'Maybe they're all Samaritans in their spare time,' I tease.

'Probably,' he demurs.

'So, when are you coming out to Mallorca?'

'I might pluck up the courage to visit around June.'

'Great!' I say encouragingly.

He ponders for a moment. 'But what if the planes are full?'

'There are loads of flights.'

'But I won't go on one of those no frills airlines. It has to be Bmi or British Airways where they have kind, motherly staff.'

'Oh please..!'

'And then there's the stifling heat to contend with at that time of the year.'

'It's perfect in June.'

'Well, I suppose…'

Another waiter buzzes by our table and refills my glass of wine. He moves towards Ed's glass.

'No!' shrieks Ed as if he's being offered strychnine. He jerks the glass away from him. Politely, the man steps back and rests the half bottle back in its holder.

'Worried I'll get you drunk?' I snigger.

'You know I can only cope with one glass. Don't be provocative.'

My handbag begins vibrating and sure enough my little Judas of a mobile is trilling away. No peace for the wicked. It's Rachel.

'Hi! George has just rung me to say he's brought the meeting forward by an hour tomorrow. He says it will be of a lizardy nature, whatever that means.'

I groan. 'I thought he'd got lizards out of his system?'

'Apparently not. See you at ten then.'

When I've put the phone down I tell Ed about Greedy George's fragrant lounge lizards. He sits in wonder and shakes his head. 'Well, Scatters, I'm relieved to know I'm not the only nutter around.'

Tuesday 10 a.m., Havana Leather

Rachel and I are sitting at the enormous glass table in George's office. A pile of warm mince pies lie sprawled in front of us on an oval plate while Richard, the shop manager fusses with serviettes and coffee cups.

'Push off, Ricardo! God, you're an old woman,' shouts Greedy George, spraying a mouthful of crumbs across the table.

Richard raises an eyebrow, gives a little flounce and leaves the room. Despite the festive atmosphere, I am fretting about the box of leather lizards, each adorned with a miniature Santa hat, that George has thumped down on a chair at my side.

'Santa Lizards,' bawls George, 'infused with frankincense and myrrh.'

'I thought we'd put Christmas to bed some months ago?' I ask pointedly.

'Yeh, well, it's a little surprise product for the festive season.' He averts his gaze and chomps on his mince pie.

Rachel and I await an explanation.

'All right, the truth is our berk of a production manager over-ordered the Lounge Lizards. Sort of added a few noughts on the order so I'm having to improvise to shift them.'

'Are they in the shops yet?' says Rachel warily.

'Yep, and walking out of the door. I've told the staff to say they're a limited edition. Always a good ruse.'

'How much do they cost?' I quiz.

'A hundred quid.'

It stuns me that people in London are willing to part with such a wad of cash for a lizard gizmo. I can't wait to tell Catalina when I get back. She'll be outraged.

Greedy George takes a gulp of coffee and smacks his lips.

'So guv, what's Santa bringing you this Christmas?'

'I was rather hoping it would be a surprise.'

He breaks into a cheeky boy grin. 'Nah. Gotta spell out what you want or you'll get something naff. Last year the wife bought me some horrible sports watch with a million and one dials so I made her take it back and get a refund.'

I look at him reproachfully. 'That's terrible. Bianca must have felt really wounded.'

'Bianca hasn't felt anything for years. Anyway, what do I want with a diving watch worth three grand? Can you see me in a wetsuit?'

Rachel keeps her head lowered.

'God, I hate bloody Christmas. I've got the monster-in-law coming this year. Let's just hope she slips on the staircase. A bit of polish and whoosh!'

'George!'

He gives me an unrepentant grin and crosses the room.

'Well, guv, suppose this year you'll be carving the turkey on the beach and then doing your Mother Theresa bit distributing food to the poor in the hills?'

'Just my stray dogs and cats.'

'I worry about you over there. All this marathon fundraising crap and animal welfare. Hope you're not going soft on me.'

I don't rise to the bait. Inanely he grabs a Santa lizard and yanking its front legs back so they are hidden by his hands, waggles it under my nose, crying, 'Arms for the poor, arms for the poor!'

Rachel tuts, shakes her head and sighs while I observe him coolly from my chair. Satisfied with our respective reactions, he rants on.

'Anyway when's the London Marathon?'

'April. I'm going to have a party afterwards so I expect you to be there.'

'Wouldn't miss seeing you in pain for all the world,' he chortles merrily. 'So, did you see our Michael yesterday? He said you were popping by.'

Michael Roselock and I had indeed met to discuss the idea that I had proposed to him a few months back. With his business folding around his ears, I had made the simple suggestion that he and George collaborate on a leather jewellery range incorporating both their skills. Although unlikely bed fellows, the two of them struck up a rapport and are now working assiduously on Havana Leather's first ever jewellery range.

'Yes I did. Seems to have a new spring in his step. He says you've passed him a lot of business since you met.' I study his face carefully.

'Well, the poor old sod needs some coppers, doesn't he?' He reddens at being caught out doing something magnanimous. He quickly changes tack. 'Is anything going on with him and that Prudence Braithwaite woman?'

Rachel's head bobs up from her notebook in surprise. I am convinced that a romance is blossoming but have no intention of sharing my suspicions with George. 'I've no idea. They've worked together for years. I'd hardly say either of them are the romantic type.'

'Hm, mark my words. There's life in the old dog yet and, as you say, he's been very chipper of late.'

'Well, when we meet him tomorrow, you can ask him what's going on.' I reply.

'Maybe I will.'

Rachel eyes us impatiently. 'Sorry, but we must plough on with the product schedule for next year. Most glossies are working on their April editions already.'

George yawns and sits down heavily. 'OK, OK. By the way how's that flashy client of yours in the States, the American geezer you told me about?'

Rachel turns to us both. 'You mean Bryan Patterson? Funny you should ask because he rang me yesterday. He's in pretty bad shape.'

George and I exchange looks.

'What's up with him?' demands George.

'It seems he's lost Tootsie.'

Who the hell's Tootsie?' he yells.

'His rabbit,' replies Rachel without a hint of irony.

Tuesday 12 p.m., in a cab

As we scurry into a cab, I notice that Rachel is wearing her Santa outfit, a wonderfully cosy, red coat offset by white angora mittens and matching scarf. I wish I were wearing something as warm. By contrast I look like an understudy for Colombo in a scruffy old Burberry mac, which I bought second hand in Greenwich market, and a balding mohair scarf. The dark and murky sky resembles a witch's cauldron and I shiver with the cold.

'You didn't tell me about Bryan Patterson's rabbit.'

'I'm sorry, I thought you might have caught it on last night's news,' Rachel says, slipping me a sardonic smile.

'I know it's just a rabbit but he is besotted with it.'

'Yes, well he'll have to grow up. It's absurd the way he traipses to meetings with Tootsie under his arm. Apparently it disappeared from his Manhattan apartment in the early hours.'

'Poor thing probably fell from a balcony. Are there any suspects?'

We both explode with laughter.

'Yes, well you're no better,' cuts in Rachel. 'I had to hide your *Ally McBeal* dancing baby in a cupboard the other day when a client came in.'

Ah, the dancing baby. Bizarre though it is to have a vibrating, singing rubber baby on my desk, I still haven't found the heart to dispose of it. This hideous toy, which I actually queued to buy at Hamleys, has graced my desk for some years. At the touch of a button, the dancing baby blares out, 'Hooked On A Feeling' and struts its stuff, one arm extended stiffly in what could be mistaken for a left handed Hitlerite salute. It is hugely therapeutic after a phone call from a hysterical client and often has me bopping about the office much to the incredulity of my younger staff. Well, Batman has Robin, and I have my dancing baby.

'By the way,' says Rachel, 'I've left three hundred Christmas cards for signing on your desk.'

'Oh God, do I have to?'

'Well,' she says guilelessly, 'you could always beg a favour of the dancing baby?'

7 p.m., the Ritz

I arrive at the Ritz grumbling at the ten pounds I have just had to fork out on the cab fare. Mind you, the canapés are invariably outstanding here so all is not lost. I enter the wide, gracious lobby which is already awash with guests and make my way to the restaurant where the reception is being held. At the elegant gilt doorway I flick my invitation at a glamorous young PR girl standing by a welcome desk and waltz inside. Delicate violin music wafts through the vast, airy room with its high ceilings, grand mirrors and candelabras. Rachel is already in the thick of the crowd talking to another guest. She beckons me over.

'There you are! You remember Marie from the *Daily Mail*?'

No, but I'll be toast if I don't feign recognition.

'Yes, of course. Long time no see. When was it?'

Marie is a canny Scot, lean and tall with auburn hair and a tattoo on her left shoulder. It looks like a lizard in the half-light or am I becoming delusional?

'The last time we met,' she says archly, 'was when your client George Myers poured a glass of champers down me.'

I see my life passing before my eyes. 'Are you sure? I don't seem to recall the incident...'

She puts a calming hand on my shoulder. 'It was years ago when I was freelancing. You invited me to Hackney to do a feature on Havana Leather.'

It must have been in my salad days.

'I interviewed George and you had to leave for some function or other, so he gave me a lift into town.'

The scene flashes in front of me. 'Yes, that's right, I remember now… you had blond hair then.'

She nods.

'Anyway we ended up going for a drink and George spilled a glass of champagne down my top.'

'Deliberately?'

'I was too drunk to remember!' she howls.

Oh God. At least he didn't make a pass at her.

'Actually he made a pass at me.'

Perhaps it's time to cut this conversation short. Rachel is scrunching up her face into an enforced picture of jollity and is already pulling on my sleeve.

'So lovely to meet you, Marie, but we mustn't monopolise you all evening.'

Rachel steers me hastily into the merry throng. 'What a nightmare. Do you think all that was true?'

'Probably. Don't know what he saw in her, though.'

We push through the crowds of happy imbibers, acknowledging fellow PR and journalist contacts. Waiters discreetly wander about, bearing large trays laden with an assortment of champagne cocktails. I swoop on one and grab us two glasses. 'Remind me why we're here.'

Rachel tuts. 'Simon Drew thought it would be good for networking.'

Networking. Now there's a London term I loathe. I can grasp the concept of networking when it comes to broadcasting, railways, electronics and computers but the social kind leaves me cold. We don't network in Mallorca, just collide with like-minded people by chance, not design. I wave at our host, Simon Drew, and blow him a kiss which he reciprocates over a canopy of talking heads. Simon Drew is the nouveau riche private owner of a chateau in Provence where he has his own wine and liqueur label. He also owns one of London's chicest party catering companies which I have used for many client functions over the years. His company is tonight's sponsor of the Women in Business Awards and in fairness he's pulled in the big fish. Every major journalist worth his or her salt is here, including, alas, a generous sprinkling of PR people and B&Bs, those obtuse skeletal PR women who wear their hair blond and their clothes black.

'Darling!' a middle-aged B&B approaches like a guided missile, air kissing me from a foot away. She rests a critical eye on my turquoise jacket and flashes me a thin, red crocodile smile.

'You look simply divine in bright colours. How are you coping with the heat in Spain?'

No sooner has she posed the question than her gaze wavers, impatiently flitting over my shoulder in search of a UC, what we in the PR world refer to as a useful contact.

'Oh, fine, Letitia, I just keep the shades on and sit in the freezer.'

She's on auto response now. 'Marvellous! Can you get Botox out there?' She fidgets with her little Chanel handbag, desperate to curtail this conversation as quickly as possible.

'I've heard that our local *ferreteria*, that's the ironmonger's, sells a fairly effective rat poison which might do the trick.'

'Lovely!' That thin smile again, slicing through the white face powder like a streak of jam on a plate of tapioca. Distractedly she places a bony white hand on my arm then floats off in the direction of a potentially useful media contact across the room. Sad, lonely Letitia who's still playing the game long after her sell-by date.

'I wish you wouldn't do that,' Rachel frowns.

'Do what?'

'Make fun of them. They can't help it.'

'No one can help being dim, but she's ignorant. That's inexcusable.'

There's a sound of applause and Simon, his face shiny with perspiration, lumbers up on to a small stage in the centre of the room wearing a black suit and purple tie. He takes the microphone, makes a poor joke and begins welcoming the guests.

'Are they announcing the awards now?' I whisper urgently to Rachel.

'No, not for half an hour. We'll creep out before they begin. No one will see us.'

'Phew.'

There's loud clapping and Simon Drew skips down the shallow steps of the stage and is engulfed by an adoring crowd of sycophants, most of whom, I imagine, are looking for a free stopover at his chateau in Provence.

Rachel's mobile rings and she disappears outside to answer it. Suddenly I spy a long-standing journalist friend in the distance and swim towards her through the shoals of guests, my glass raised high. This is Frankie, a journalist of the old school who has edited the feature pages of three national newspapers in her time and who now chooses to freelance. She is always in demand and has to turn away work assignments. From my earliest days in the murky world of PR she gave me a helping hand and in return I gave her several exclusive stories. We've remained firm allies ever since. Tonight she is wearing her trademark Dior glasses and glimpsing the awards programme with the air of a sceptical schoolmistress. I am surprised to see that her mop of thick, unruly brown hair has been cut in to a short, svelte bob.

'Frankie, thank God you're here.'

She pulls me to the side of the room away from the hubbub. 'Who are all these people? Rent-a-mob?'

'The usual hangers on and bimbettes. There are a few cerebral looking types in the corner though. Presumably they're here to pick up awards?'

She smirks. 'Spot on. I've just been over to interview them for *The Telegraph*. They're four pretty impressive women. All in finance and technology and worth a mint.'

'Where did we go wrong?'

'We didn't,' she intones dryly. 'I omitted to say that they're all as boring as hell.'

We share a snigger and are suddenly interrupted by a girl in a tight black cocktail dress and matching knee-high boots.

'Excuse me, are you Frankie Symonds?'

Frankie's eyes narrow slightly. 'Yes, and you are?'

'Hi! I'm Minerva from Jade PR. I'm a great fan of your column.'

Silly twit. Frankie doesn't write one. She stands close to Frankie in an effort to ice me out. I notice that her lips are coated in a thick puce gloss which matches her long talons. I look fleetingly at my bitten stubs and make a futile attempt to mask them with the champagne glass.

Frankie eyes her wryly. 'A good name and are you both a goddess and very wise?'

The girl's mouth drops at the corners. 'I'm sorry?'

'Minerva, Goddess of wisdom. Your namesake'.

'Oh, really?' she tosses back her golden locks. 'Anyway, I just wanted to tell you a little bit about Jade PR. We've just won a major account and I wondered...'

Frankie observes the girl over the top of her glasses. 'Look, dear, I'm rather busy now so why not drop me a line instead? Minerva from Jaded PR, right?'

The girl's face twitches like a frightened rabbit as she fumbles in her handbag for a card which she thrusts in to Frankie's hand. A second later she hops off.

'Ouch, that was cruel. Remember, the blond and blacks are a dying breed.'

Frankie shakes her head in protest. 'Trust me, they're alive and well. Every day they bombard me with crap. Only today, one of them biked me a box of something grim called Hygiene Handies. The little PR was on the phone before I had time to lift the lid asking if *The Daily Telegraph* would be interested in running a story on lavatory hygiene.'

'Oh dear.'

'They simply don't have a clue.'

A waiter flits by and I just manage to snatch a salmon canapé from his tray before it's attacked by a swarm of hungry gannets. I peep at my watch and realise that the awards are about to commence. Frankie opts to stay to the bitter end, but I scythe a path towards the exit and see Rachel's tall form heading there too. As I reach the door, Rachel squeezes my arm and giggles. 'Guess what? Bryan Patterson has just rung to say they've found Tootsie.'

'You mean he'd organised a search party?'

'Stop it! Apparently she fell down the waste disposal chute in his kitchen. God knows how.'

'Well, we can all sleep easy now,' I quip.

'Wait for this though,' she bubbles. 'Bryan's taking her for trauma counselling. Can you believe there's a rabbit therapist in New York?'

My mobile begins trilling. A few heads turn round, irritated at the sound. Rachel and I dive through the double doors and out into the hotel's elegant lobby. A Spanish number appears on the screen.

'*Hola!* Is Rafael. Sorry to disturb but I lose key to Franco's cage. I give you one too, long time ago. You remember? Where is key now?'

The muffled sound of glasses clinking can be heard from behind closed doors as Simon Drew bellows from the stage. Rachel is walking towards me.

'It's normally in the cutlery draw, Rafael. Can you ask Alan?'

There's subdued applause from inside the room.

'No, he look but he no find.'

'Oh for heavens sake! It's always there. Wait a minute, I think Catalina may have moved it to the key rack last week. It's on a string.'

'What is string?'

I try out my faltering Mallorcan, 'Er... *un tros de cordill?*'

'*Molt bé. Gracies.* I see you soon. *Fins a reveure!*'

Rachel is quizzical. 'Who was that?'

'Franco's owner. Looking for the key to his cage.'

She nods sagely and like a wise goddess Minerva, questions me no further.

Wednesday 10 a.m., Havana Leather

'He's a bit of an old woman, guv, isn't he? ' Greedy George is slurping on a large mug of cappuccino and fiddling with a stack of sketches piled neatly in front of him. I presume they are some of the initial designs for Havana's first leather jewellery range.

'Michael Roselock was born an old woman, but he's a first rate jewellery designer', I say defensively.

'Yeh, well we'll find out today, won't we? Shame you've missed the meetings so far, could have done with you around.'

'Why?' I ask sceptically.

'We needed someone to pour the tea.' He wheezes with laughter. 'Seriously guv, I like him but I wish he wouldn't bore me to death about his company going down. I don't give a sod about any of that.'

'It's good to know you still have a heart. Anyway, what have you discussed so far?'

He's biting at a muffin now and scrutinising one of his sketches. 'You inspired us, actually.'

'I'm sure.'

'Don't be like that. Michael and I were talking about what sort of stuff we could do together and hit on a nature range, sand and sea, and all that malarkey.'

'Can I see some designs before Michael arrives?'

He slides some loose sheets of heavy coloured pencil drawings towards me along the table. On each page are hippy chic looking leather pendants, rings and bracelets with shells and feathers and tiny fossils inlaid.

'Where does Michael fit in?'

'He's making them up, isn't he?'

'But where will you get hold of the materials?'

'That's a doddle. A bloke I know in the Maldives is getting me a job lot of shells and some great clobber from an Incan burial site in Peru.'

Alarm bells are ringing. 'What sort of clobber?'

'I dunno. Antique beads and bits of old cloth and stuff.'

'Is all of this legal?'

'Who cares?'

'I hope he's not going to desecrate ancient tombs.'

'Lighten up! They've all snuffed it so what do they care? You worried that the ghosts will come and haunt us?'

'I'm more worried about the authorities, actually.'

'All it takes are a few backhanders, guv. You don't know my mate.'

'No fortunately, I don't.'

Richard, the showroom manager trips up the stairs and pops his head anxiously round the door. 'Mr Roselock's here, George. Shall I take his coat?'

'Depends how much you think it's worth.' He sniggers as Richard shakes his head impatiently and then skips down the stairs.

'Something wrong with that geezer,' he opines.

There's a laboured tread on the landing and in walks Michael Roselock dressed in a grey pinstripe suit and a red tie dotted with blue elephant motifs. He seems apprehensive and jittery.

'Old Bill after you?' greets George.

'Sorry, what do you mean?' Michael's eyes open wide in panic.

'Only a joke, mate. Take a pew. Well we're graced with guv's presence today. The marriage broker.'

Michael gives a relieved smile and comes over and kisses me on the cheek.

'Steady on,' yells George. 'You'll have the staff talking.'

I'm glad he's in merry humour since Michael is obviously nervous in his presence.

'I've mocked up a few pieces for you to look at, George,' he stammers.

'You know, combining leather and the other materials we discussed.' Michael's voice is thin and scratchy.

George listens in silence and spreads Michael's samples out on the table. They look stunning. After a few minutes contemplation, he nods appreciatively.

'Good stuff, Michael. This range is going to be a winner. Feel it in me water.'

Michael's jaw muscle relaxes and his eyes sparkle with pride. He's like a child in class who's just won a house point. We sit for an hour in deep discussion over mugs of coffee. I'm feeling exhilarated that George and Michael seem to have hit it off and have together mocked up such an exquisite range.

'How's Prudence?' George blurts out in a rush.

'Oh tip-top,' replies Michael a tad awkwardly.

'Good girl she is,' says George with a knowing wink. 'worth hanging on to, eh?'

I squirm,

'Quite,' says Michael, pink cheeked and in some confusion.

Before I leave, I hand a small parcel of Serrano ham to George. He sniffs deeply on it and gives me a bear hug. 'You finally remembered. Better be the real McCoy, guv!'

He's still chortling as Michael and I leave the showroom and head for Piccadilly on foot. We both have meetings in different parts of town. He is wearing a heavy brown tweed coat whose collar he pulls up against the bitter wind.

'Must be a bit warmer where you are,' he mumbles into the fabric.

'But it's getting colder, if that makes you feel any better.'

He gives a little chuckle

'How are things?'

'Oh, it's been tough as you know but Prudence and I feel we're getting there'. He manages a lukewarm smile.

'Now the showroom's gone, where are you working from?'

'Sevenoaks. I'm using the stables at the house and Prudence has kindly agreed to commute there from Monday to Thursday. We've got some good private commissions. It'll just take a little time to readjust.'

I touch his arm. 'See it as a new beginning, Michael. You'll never look back.'

As a novice commuter, I've had to embrace change and to accept the new challenges that life, with a glint in its eye, has hurled at me. But that's all part of the fun of it, isn't it?

'And what are you doing for Christmas?' I ask.

He is coy. 'Oh, Prudence and I will probably spend it quietly together in Sevenoaks. Neither of us has much family.'

He hails a cab, courteously opening the door and ushering me inside. He goes to close it but then reaches in and gently pats my sleeve.

'I appreciate what you've done for me with George. It's been a lifesaver. Bless you.' He averts his gaze, slams the door after him and drifts up Piccadilly without looking back.

9 p.m., Le Caprice, Mayfair

Dresden Watts and I are sitting opposite each other at a table in Le Caprice, sipping glasses of Chablis and munching on French bread. There's a sudden commotion as Greedy George blunders in through the swivel doors of the restaurant, holding a fat cigar in one hand and an umbrella in the other which he quickly offloads on to an attendant. The Bolivian manager, Jesus, greets him warmly and shows him to our table.

'Always feel safe in the hands of Jesus.' He winks at us and plonks himself down in the vacant chair.

'Bet you miss all this, don't you, guv?' He gives me a smug grin.

'Miss what exactly?'

'You know, classy places where you can hang out and eat proper grub.' Dresden has a playful grin on his lips but remains silent, observing us both as if we're a pair of fencing partners.

'We do have restaurants in Mallorca, George.'

He puffs on his cigar and gives a scornful laugh. 'Oh come on, guv, they're hardly Gordon Blue are they?'

Dresden makes as if to correct him and then stops, realising in the nick of time that this is one of George's deliberate malapropisms.

'You're probably right,' I say breezily, 'God knows why the likes of the King of Spain, Michael Douglas and Claudia Schiffer keep coming back. Maybe they stock up on M&S beforehand?'

He shakes with laughter and squeezes my arm.

'Actually, guv, it's done you the world of good moving to Mallorca. You're much more laid-back and hippy chic. Must be all the drugs out there.'

Dresden titters politely then points a finger at George. 'You may mock but what she has found is balance and perspective. Isn't that what we all crave?'

'Oh Gawd!' groans George, 'Give him a drink. He's going all cosmic on us.'

Dresden sighs and places his glass with precision directly in front of him.

'Now you two, there is a serious reason why I've invited you both here.'

George and I exchange puzzled looks.

'You're getting married?' quips George.

'I think not,' says Dresden with a frown, flicking a stray black lacquered tendril from his forehead. 'To be brief, I was interviewing the chairman of an American furniture company for *The Times* when he by chance mentioned Havana Leather and an interest in opening a branch or franchise in the States.'

George splutters and grabs at a glass of wine, just poured for him by a tactful waiter. 'Is that so?'

'The chairman suggested I sound you out discreetly when I told him we were friends.'

'Does he know we're meeting here?'

Dresden fidgets with his gold cravat. 'Naturally, since he's footing the bill for dinner.'

'So what's the deal?'

'I don't know. Just that he wants to set up a meeting urgently. He's a cool, immensely wealthy player and the company's products are very chic.'

George runs his fingers through his greying locks. 'I've been thinking about expanding. Just think guv, you could help set up the American operation with me.'

'Fantastic!' I enthuse. Secretly I'm feeling uneasy. If this latest trip to London has taught me anything, it's that I am becoming increasingly disenchanted with the London scene and keen to explore new business possibilities in Mallorca. Flitting back and forth to the States with Greedy George in the future is not in my game plan. Dresden wafts a menu in the air. 'Shall we order?'

George pulls his menu towards him with gusto. 'Imagine. Havana Leather New York. It's got a nice ring to it.'

'It has,' says Dresden. 'It has indeed.'

Thursday 10 a.m., the office, Mayfair

The office is buzzing as I creep in. Throwing my old mac quickly over a chair in the reception area, I dart into Rachel's office before any of my employees has the chance to pounce on me. Rachel has the phone plugged to her ear as always and is chatting away to some journalist contact. She beckons me to sit down in front of her. I look out of her window and into the cold grey sky, wondering how she puts up with this depressing scene every day.

'So, what's new?' She slams down the phone and gives me one of her radiant smiles. Always a tonic.

'Do you know, just now my taxi driver didn't charge me.'

'You're joking?'

'No, honestly. We had a long chat about the London Marathon and when he heard I was taking part, he wouldn't take a penny. Told me to use it as sponsorship money.'

'Wow. What a nice guy.'

'Well, you know my penchant for London taxi drivers?'

It's a strange thing but ever since I've been living in Mallorca, one of my most favourite indulgences back in London has been taking a taxi. What I once took for granted I now cherish, sharing many an animated conversation with the drivers on subjects ranging from politics, house prices to marathon training and how to move abroad. I've recently discovered that many drivers have run marathons themselves and a large percentage already own property in Spain. In the past, like most Londoners, I used to sit sullenly in the back seat of the cab, monosyllabic and stressed, cursing the traffic and irritable if a driver attempted to make conversation. I've discovered that some of the most charming people can transform into monsters on entering a taxi. It's almost as if the internal glass divider serves more as class divider, permitting them to act in a surly, rude and thoroughly obnoxious manner.

Rachel throws me an invitation card.

'It's the Harpers & Queen event tonight. You haven't forgotten?'

'No', I say self-righteously. 'I haven't.'

I pull open my voluminous bag to reach for my diary and a large knobbly object wrapped in toilet paper rolls out on to the floor.

'Urgh!' shrieks Rachel. 'What on earth's that?'

I haven't the faintest clue. Pulling back the paper, I examine it carefully and then as nonchalantly as possible, throw it into her wastepaper basket.

'It's just an old ham bone,' I say casually. 'One I meant to give to Franco. You remember the call I got at the Ritz from my neighbour Rafael? Franco's his dog. Heaven only knows how long it's been lurking in there.'

Rachel observes me for a second and laughs aloud, her shoulders shaking with the effort.

'You're a nightmare!' she says and then pulling a jacket from her chair, clips over to the door in her shiny black stilettos. 'Come on, let's get a coffee while I'm still sane.'

TEN

FOWL PLAY

In Mallorca life is a series of fiestas punctuated by short periods of work. However at Christmas this all changes and the fiesta enjoys an uninterrupted period in the limelight. From Christmas Eve until a full week after New Year, Mallorcans party and eat. In fact, Mallorca probably deserves an entry in the record books under 'Gluttony' for largest amount consumed per capita during a two week period. This is the time when relatives of every generation get together harmoniously under one roof for an extended period without dramas, recriminations, rivalries and the settling of old family scores over the carved turkey. Why is it that this can be achieved in Mallorca but not in England? The secret naturally lies in the stomach. For Christmas in Mallorca is about food, good wines, family and conversation. The word *regimen*, diet, is scorned and anyone vain enough to worry about their *bona figura* is given a cool reception.

It is the day before Christmas Eve, and the sun, a smudge of hot butter in a pale blue sky, spreads its warmth across the valley, tickling the ears of the *burros*, warming the backs of the lazy feral cats and dousing the spire of the town church in primrose light. Snow, like sieved sugar, dusts the mountain tops and the plump and glossy green pines are peppered with dew. I rumble along, the back of the car laden with expectant and empty panniers, ready to gorge on Christmas wares. It's still early and I am keen to make the market before half the townsfolk descend on it in a frenzy. At the corner of the track Margalida Sampol appears. She is in her winter coat and her soft white hair has been cut and set.

'I'm on my way to church,' she informs me. 'Have you time to pop by later?'

'How about tomorrow morning?' I ask, my head jutting out of the car window.

She mumbles to herself in Mallorcan and then nods. 'Tomorrow it is.'

At that moment a car swerves round the corner and with his bumper almost kissing mine, Lorenç the wood man screeches to a halt.

'*Uep!*' he yells from his window. This catchy little Mallorcan word usually denotes surprise of a happy kind. It might have been different if he'd bumped my car.

'Are you trying to kill me?'

His smile is as broad as a melon slice. 'Not today! I've got your wood in the back.'

I soften. We are down to our last dozen logs so his arrival is as welcome as a good fairy at a christening.

'Is Alan at home?'

'You bet. He'll be thrilled to help you unload the truck.'

Alan was still in his pyjamas when I left the house so Lorenç's arrival should buck up his ideas.

'Will you be up in the *plaça* for New Year?'

Lorenç opens his hands wide. '*Segur*. Where else would I be?'

'We'll see you there. Until then *Bon Nadal!*'

He comes over to the car and kisses me on the cheek. '*Molt bé!* You know how to say Happy Christmas in Mallorcan. Every day you learn a new word.'

Margalida listens with her hands on her hips. 'She has a good teacher in me.'

'I'm sure she does,' he grins.

I start the engine and reverse to let Lorenç drive by. Time for my assignation with Teresa.

The market is already humming as I dart through the side entrance, past the fish hall and head for Teresa's stall. She sees me coming and beams.

'Don't tell me you got up early today? *Déu meu!* She's here before nine o'clock!'

'Very funny, Teresa. I'll have you know I've been up a while. Now then, what have you got for me?'

She bustles around her stand, plucking small plastic bags off a row of metal hooks and hurling them at me. 'Fill them up!' she commands. 'Everything's fantastic today. I've even managed to get those *naps* you asked for.' She bends down behind the counter and emerges with a huge bag of parsnips.

'You mean *xirivia*? I'll have you know that *nap* translates as turnip in English.'

'Don't get smart with me!' she barks. 'They're all from beneath the soil aren't they?'

'If you say so,' I shrug, enjoying our banter.

I plunge into the fruit and veg, smelling, kneading, prodding, casting aside the mediocre, and generally behaving in a way that would have me thrown out of any British supermarket. Teresa rolls her head back and laughs. 'Well look how you're becoming a *Mallorquína*! Good girl. I've trained you well.'

Satisfied with my buys I pass the bags over to Teresa who weighs them all and rounds up the total. She stretches under the counter and pulls out two large bottles. 'My home-made cherry *licor* and *herbes*,' she winks. 'and here's a jar of sun-dried tomatoes. *Bon Nadal.*'

I give her a big hug and to her surprise, place a wrapped package in her hands.

'*Un regal* for Christmas,' I say. It's a little gift from London, a box of truffles and a candle holder.

She flaps her arms about and protests vociferously. 'What do I want with *regals?* What do you think you're doing?'

I gather my bags and head off for the square. Before I exit the building I take one look back at her stall. Seemingly unobserved, she is standing marvelling over the present. I feel my eyes water and tell myself to stop being a sentimental fool.

Some minutes later I lurch in to Colmado La Luna. The shop has shelves that rise to the ceiling, each one tantalisingly filled with speciality jams, biscuits, wines, olives and pickles. At the very top, nearly brushing the ceiling, a collection of food tins and metal cartons sporting old fashioned labels from the fifties run the length of the wall, a nostalgic reminder of the shop's longevity. The glass cabinet which serves as a counter oozes the most heavenly cold meats and sausages, Mallorcan cheeses and freshly baked rolls. Carmen greets me with a frown.

'What are you doing carrying all those bags? Where's the *burro?*'

This is Carmen's and my long standing joke. We refer to men as donkeys whose primary purpose in life is to carry our bags.

'He's at home.'

She huffs. 'Typical man!'

Xavier, who finishes serving a customer, gives a heavy sigh. 'Senyor Alano deserves a break. We men are always working. Here, give me those bags and I'll pop them by the *finca* later.'

217

I remonstrate but it's no good. Carmen whisks them behind the counter with a stern countenance. I begin to order my Christmas treats, special *jamon* Serrano, chorizo and *lloms*, cured pork sausage, an assortment of cheeses, local wines, figs and dates, walnuts and cashews. Customers come and go but I'm on a roll.

'Xavier, you'd better deliver her groceries by truck,' mocks Carmen, shaking her head in mirth.

'Well, I have guests coming and I don't want to run out of anything,' I bluster.

'You could feed the whole town!' she bellows.

'Yes but Carmen my new kitchen has been fitted and I want to celebrate this momentous occasion!'

She cackles and shakes her head. It's true. While I was away in London, Alan and Stefan worked like crazy with the builders to have the kitchen completed before my return. Alan knew how much it would mean to me to have a sparkling new kitchen in which to prepare my Christmas lunch. I was in a state of total amazement when I first saw it. Everything was how we'd sketched and designed it. We had a beautiful terracotta tiled floor, gleaming granite work surfaces and buttermilk wooden cupboards. The *pièce de résistance*, though, had to be the big oak table and accompanying eight chairs which I had been eyeing up at Castañer, the local furniture shop in town, for some time. Apparently they had taken pity on Alan when he visited and agreed that we could pay it off *poc a poc*.

When I've settled my bill and left a stack of bags for delivery, I wish her merry Christmas and head off for HiBit to deliver a small gift to Antonia and Albert. Antonia is sitting smoking at the till as I enter. The small shop is heaving with Christmas shoppers.

'You're so kind! I haven't even had time to buy the turkey yet,' she howls. 'Work, work, work. It never stops!'

Albert gives a cough from the back of the shop and swivels round in a chair to see me. 'Hey! How you doing?'

'Fine. I see you're busy.'

'The usual,' he says blithely, as he fiddles with a bundle of coloured wires. 'It pays the bills, though.'

Antonia makes a face. 'Only just.'

I bid them farewell and rush off to the car park. En route I collide with Tolo. 'Can you pop by the bank? I have a *regal* for you. It's a Banca March calendar and diary.'

I accompany him up through the merry *plaça* with its spiky, leafless trees full of tiny white lights. Spanish Christmas carols blast from speakers placed outside the town hall and enormous festive costumed figures, known as *gegantes*, stand on either side of the entrance.

Tolo dashes into the bank and I follow at a more leisurely pace behind him. The manager comes over to greet me and I nod at the small staff, all of whom I know on first name terms.

'Here,' says Tolo, passing me a parcel across his desk. 'They are good quality, you know.'

'I'm sure,' I nod and give him a kiss on both cheeks. 'Alan will be very grateful.'

Back in the square, I see Gaspar waving from behind the windows of Café Paris. He jumps up and opens the door.

'Running girl, come and have a coffee!'

'I must get back home,' I say weakly.

He beckons me inside and draws a chair back from the table.

'A quick coffee won't delay you. I had a busy paper round this morning. *Ultima Hora* had a supplement so my bag was double the weight.'

He orders me an espresso, and digs into a bag underneath the table.

'Here. I've got some leftover newspapers. Take a copy of each. *Ultima Hora, Diario de Mallorca, Veu de Soller, Solleric, Majorca Daily Bulletin...*'

'Gaspar, I can't carry all those!'

'Of course you can. It's not very Mallorcan to turn down a free gift.'

I finish my coffee, wave at José, the terminally cheerful and energetic owner behind the counter, and head off for the car. Gaspar is grinning from the window and waving. Now I mustn't get waylaid by anyone else or I'll never make it home.

Alan opens the front door when he hears the tyres on the gravel in the courtyard. He comes down the front steps of the porch, ready to help carry in the bags.

'No bags!' He looks confused. 'You've been gone hours and nothing to show for it except newspapers?'

I pat him on the arm. 'Don't worry. Xavier, my knight in shining armour, is bringing all the bags up later.'

Alan puts his arm round my shoulder. 'Using your charm again?'

'I've had a lovely time, having a coffee with Gaspar and catching up with everyone. It's so nice not to have to rush.'

'Good for you. Just think how manic you used to be in London.'

'Don't remind me! By the way, where's Ollie?'

'Where do you think? Playing football in the town. Pep and Angel picked him up after you'd left. They're doing some practice and then being treated to hot chocolate and cake with the coaches.'

'It's all right for some!'

We reach the *entrada* when there's tooting from the courtyard. Catalina and Ramon have arrived.

'It's like Piccadilly Circus here,' sighs Alan, striding off to welcome them.

'We've got your turkey,' bawls Catalina excitedly. 'He's in the back.'

For a ghastly moment I imagine our monster turkey is still alive and strutting about on the back seat.

'Is it dead?'

Catalina marches into the *entrada* and the kitchen with some cakes she's made. 'You think we bring him alive? You mad? Ramon killed and plucked him this morning.'

Thank heavens for that. A few moments later Alan and Ramon shuffle slowly into the house, carrying between them the most colossal turkey I have ever seen. They bend under the weight and Ramon is muttering in Mallorcan, no doubt a round of colourful expletives.

They place it on my new oak kitchen table with a thump. I wince. Silence. We look at each other in alarm. I feel like I'm an accomplice to a murder. Where do we dump the body?

'Well then. Shall we see if it will fit in the oven?' I say, a note of panic creeping into my voice.

Ramon chortles. 'You might get his head in.'

We all grapple with the corpse, remove the innards of the oven and attempt to shove it inside. We try it head first, then bottoms up, side on and lastly squash its girth inside by leaning heavily against the oven door but it won't go. After some minutes we all tumble on the floor with the bird on top of us and yelp hysterically. Catalina is laughing so much I fear she might choke.

'We kill another,' says Ramon.

'What?' Alan wails. 'Now?'

'No he is already dead but he is smaller. Ramon will get him from the car.'

No bird's safe on the streets with these two turkey slayers on the loose. This time a more modest bird makes its appearance. It's still huge but with a push and a shove, it fits into the oven.

'*Gràcies a déu!*' says Catalina. 'We'll bring the fat one to Maria's restaurant. My aunt has an enormous oven. She's already cooking our own turkey, so now she can cook two.'

'What will you do with it all?' I'm already fretting.

'Maria can make lots of *croquetes* with the left over meat. *No problema.*'

Ramon and Catalina set off towards the car.

'I made you some cakes.'

'So I see. They smell wonderful. Thanks, Catalina.'

'Yes and thanks for our turkey,' says Alan, who together with Ramon, is struggling to carry turkey number one back to the car. 'I'm sure it's going to be fantastic.'

'Why not rear your own turkey chicks next year?' Ramon pipes up.

'Maybe, Ramon,' says Alan doubtfully. 'I'll sleep on it.'

The walls of Margalida's sitting room are covered in paintings, all the work of her grandson who is a well established artist in Palma. It's obvious which are his early works given their youthful and flamboyant style and flourishes of bright paint. The later *œuvres* are sleek and thoughtfully conceived and far more contemporary. She places a glass of fresh orange juice in front of me on the lace topped coffee table and sighs.

'We all buy so much at Christmas but I think back to the Civil War when we had nothing. You wouldn't believe what it was like.'

It takes me some time to decipher her Mallorcan words. Like a fool, at first I think she's talking about a war in Seville.

'Where were you?' I ask.

'When? In the late thirties? I was parted from my husband. He was fighting in the war. It was terrible and so cold here. I ended up in Menorca. The people were starving and reduced to eating rats.'

As a foreigner it's easy to forget the severity of Spain's civil war and the subsequent Franco Regime until the dictator's death in 1975. Memories run long and the hardships suffered in the Balearic Islands, as a consequence of the war and Franco's reign, are still mulled over by those old enough to remember.

'Under Franco we were banned from speaking Mallorcan,' she tells me. 'We had to learn Castilian Spanish in school and if you were caught speaking the local dialect, there were tough penalties.'

'Well, they wouldn't have had a problem with me,' I jest, trying to lighten the mood. 'I can only manage *Bon dia!*'

She pats my hand. 'At least you're trying.'

I finish my juice and wait while Margalida gets out her photo album. She likes to talk me through all the family ancestors, weddings and events, paying particular attention to her deceased husband.

'God only gave us one child,' she says.

'Well, Sílvia's a credit to you, and you've wonderful grandchildren.'

'True, true,' she concedes.

When we've trawled through the album I get up to go and give her my Christmas gift of a vase and chocolates.

'But I haven't anything for you?' she gasps.

'I don't want anything.'

'Let me get you some oranges from the kitchen.'

I give her a hug. 'Margalida, I have a field full of oranges and lemons.'

She hesitates for a second then grabs my arm and leads me into the kitchen whereupon she fills me a bag of fruit.

'Here,' she says defiantly. 'Your oranges are very poor. Take these. They're really sweet.'

Defeated and laughing, I thank her and head up the track.

I'm in sight of my house when Rafael appears in front of me, biting at an apple. 'Hey what you got from Margalida? Oranges! So now you rob a poor old lady?'

I narrow my eyes at him as he giggles inanely. 'I see you give my dog a Christmas present.'

I feel a bit sheepish. It's true. The night before, Ollie and I entered Franco's cage with a fleecy blanket, a present for Christmas.

'You don't mind?'

He shrugs. 'Why? You silly enough to spend money on my dog. Is OK with me.'

Phew. I invite him up for an early *copa de cava* and he promises to pop by later with Cristian. We have a busy evening ahead, preparing the fireplace for Santa Claus with Ollie, and then driving up to Catalina and Ramon's for their Christmas Eve celebration, hot chocolate and sweet pastries at midnight.

We enter the stone built terraced house in the centre of the village and squeeze into the cosy salon which is teeming with people, Catalina's mother, father, grandmother, three brothers, their wives and several aunts and uncles. Then there's all of Ramon's family. The doorbell rings constantly as neighbours and friends pop by full of cheer and talking ten to the dozen in Mallorcan. Without fanfare, family and friends each bring a contribution to the feast: cakes, cheese, Serrano ham, nuts, cava and wine. There is no petty haggling over who has paid for what, or contributed the most because Christmas here is one big melting pot of goodwill and we, the foreigners, at this most traditional of Mallorcan calorific feasts, are treated as part of the family.

Catalina and Ramon enter the room with trays loaded with mugs of hot, thick *xocolata a la tassa* and plates groaning with *ensaïmadas*, the delicate spiral shaped buns beloved by Mallorcans, *robiols*, jam pastries, and *coques dolces*, a cherry biscuit delight. Ollie tucks into his *ensaïmada*, his face covered in icing sugar, and allows Catalina's elderly relatives to kiss and pinch his face with murmurs of, *'Que guapo!'*, which in Spanish means, How handsome! The front door opens yet again and Sarah and Jack, two Australian friends of Catalina's, who live locally, join the throng.

Ollie pulls at my sleeve. 'Don't forget Father Christmas. We must get home to bed before he comes down the chimney.'

'Leave Santa an *ensaïmada* and a carrot for Rudolph,' says Catalina, putting a spare pastry and a carrot in a bag and handing it to him. He nods gravely.

There's a hush as the village church strikes twelve and then with cries of joy and laughter, everyone hugs and embraces their nearest neighbour. Never have I felt such a sense of belonging, of oneness with a community. I feel an excitement for Christmas I haven't felt since I was a small child. There's the sound of a pistol being fired in the village square: the Mallorcan festivities have officially begun.

The sun is shining in a fierce blue sky, and the mountains are clear of cloud. The patio doors are wide open and I sit outside with Pep and Juana, contemplating the view. Across the field, our local farmer is feeding his sleek black horse and at the bottom of the garden Inko sits in the hollow of our old olive tree, licking her paws. Ollie and Angel are happily kicking a new football around the lawn, one of Ollie's gifts from Father Christmas. Replete and mellow after staggering through a

A LIZARD IN MY LUGGAGE

traditional British Christmas lunch, Juana and Pep continue to discuss the wonders of the Christmas pudding (courtesy of Fortnum & Mason) and the brandy butter (my own devilishly laced version). They have enjoyed the whole dining experience so much that they intend to include various dishes in their own traditional meal the following year to which we are invited. Juana is particularly taken with Christmas crackers and instructs me to bring her back a box from London.

'You won't forget?' she asks.

'Well, I've got a whole year to remember.'

'I liked the smoked salmon,' she muses, 'but we always have pasta soup for the *primer plat*, the first dish. I think we will keep this tradition for next year.'

'Juana, I don't know how you can even contemplate preparation of another Christmas lunch after what we've just eaten.'

Pep laughs and shakes his head. 'She is always thinking of food.'

Juana kicks him lightly under the table. Alan arrives from the kitchen bearing four glasses of brandy.

'Good for the digestion,' he says cheerfully.

I try to visualise how various friends are spending Christmas Day in London but don't believe that anything can better our own blissfully simple and tranquil affair.

'I have something special for you,' says Pep to Alan, producing two missile-like *puros* from his pocket. 'These are especially for Christmas.'

Juana and I share a wince. Alan cannot mask his delight.

'How many of those do you smoke a day?' I quiz.

'I don't know,' Pep drawls. 'It's of no consequence.'

He sits back and admires the Tramuntanas, smoke coiling round his fingers.

'*Quina vida!* What a wonderful life.'

The *plaça* is crowded with happy imbibers and the garishly decorated makeshift stage is besieged with local children while members of the oompah band take five minutes out to enjoy beers in the local bar. Standing in heavy knits and gloves under an enormous bony olive tree, its branches entwined with tiny fairy lights, we chat with a group of friends from the village while Catalina bustles about distributing little bunches of grapes to all and sundry.

'Remember you eat a grape for every strike of the clock, yes?'

Ollie looks down anxiously at the big green grapes she has given him. 'But I don't like them.'

'Well, tonight you must try,' says Catalina, ruffling his hair. She walks off into the throng, self-appointed grape distributor, and is greeted rapturously by scores of locals and neighbours. Ramon drains a can of beer and chats with Alan and Catalina's parents, Paco and Marta. I spy Juana and Pep in the crowd and wave. Moments later they fight their way over to us holding a bottle of champagne and several glasses.

'Here, let me pour you some drinks,' shouts Pep above the human din. He calls to Ollie. 'Can you see Angel? He's over by the stage.'

Ollie rushes off in the direction of his friend. We toast each other and get ready for the eating of the grapes.

The musicians now return to the stage shooing the children down the steps and into the brightly lit square. Then over the microphone, and with great gravitas, they commence their countdown to midnight in Mallorcan. The hands of the church clock creak forward and the chimes boom out above the village. All of us fall on our grapes, manically trying to guzzle them on each strike. There is hysterical laughter and confusion as grapes get squashed underfoot, old men choke on the pips and children, dribbling juice as they cram them in their mouths, cheat by secreting the odd grape or two in their coat pockets. At the last strike the music starts and everyone ambles around the square kissing neighbours and friends, topping up their glasses with cava and shouting '*Molts d'anys*' which roughly translated from the Mallorcan, means long life. We espy some local craftsmen who worked on our house mingling in the square with their families. When they see us they come over to shake hands and we exchange kisses with their wives. Felipe, who runs the football ground, comes over to talk with us and is joined by Lorenç who is complaining about his back given how many log drops he's performed in the last few weeks.

'I need a good massage,' he groans.

'Well don't look at me,' retorts his wife.

'Nor me,' I add, laughing.

'So much for Christmas goodwill,' he laments, giving me a hearty push. I faintly hear Judas ringing from my handbag and trot off to a quieter corner and take the call. It's Ed.

'Happy New Year!'

I can tell by his voice that he's on good form

'Ed, I was just going to ring you. We're up in the square. It's a bit rowdy.'

'Sounds like you're in the middle of a brawl!'

'How's your New Year going?'

'Really well,' he blurts out. 'I'm with a whole load of friends from the BBC. I've just nipped out of the pub to give you a quick ring.'

'You're a star...'

'By the way,' he says coyly. 'I've just met a rather nice nurse.'

'Really? And?' I sniff out a potential romance.

'I'll tell you about it soon. Got to go.'

Hm. That'll make an interesting call.

FOWL PLAY

I see our painter, Luis, pushing through the crowds towards me, his eyes as ever brimming with kindness and warmth. Tonight he is radiant and as we clink glasses he blurts out proudly that his wife is expecting a child. Happy news but more so given his story, for his young first wife died of leukaemia a few years back, leaving him with two small girls to raise alone. Martina, his second wife, a local teacher, stepped into the breach, lavishing the children with affection and gently helping him to rebuild his life. I give him a bear hug, and avoid his eyes since mine are pricked with tears. As the music blares and laughing couples dance around us, I pull at the corner of my eye, pretending to search out a rogue eyelash but he isn't fooled.

'New year, new life,' he says softly, touching my arm.

ELEVEN

ANIMAL RITES

It's New Year's Day and I'm running through the port under a blue and white marbled sky. To my left a restless sea lashes against the rocks and the small fishing boats touch and embrace as the waves unite them in brief moments of passion. The cafés are just beginning to open and the familiar smell of strong bleach assails my nostrils as I sprint by pristine doorsteps freshly scrubbed by women preparing for a new round of guests. From behind, there's the familiar pop pop of Gaspar's *moto* followed by a wild tooting as he levels with me, exuberantly offering seasonal greetings and giving me the thumbs up. I give him a wave and watch as he disappears up a small road. As I pass a mountain of abandoned nets with their briny aroma of stale fish, I hear a resonant voice calling my name and there, pouncing out on the quay, with arms outstretched, is our local doctor, Senyor Vidal. He is portly with greying hair, a large handlebar moustache and eyes crinkled with mirth. He gives me a hug and shouts, '*Bona figura!*' and claps loudly, blowing kisses after me as I resume my run. I turn round and reciprocate the gesture and notice several locals shaking their heads and smiling. Doctor Vidal is a personage, a real character who is greatly respected in the local community and known for his eccentricities. I jog on, leaping over secured anchors and past the trawlers standing tall and impenetrable, their noses to the port, and onwards to the end of the harbour. As I loop back and head for home, a car toots and leaning out of the window and waving frantically is Tolo. I return the gesture and mouth '*Molts d'anys*'. I'm pleased to see that he's having a break from the bank.

The light from the sky hits the masts of the yachts bobbing gently up and down along the side of the quay. Around them the rich blue sea glints and dances and in that split second, with the warmth of the sun on my back, I realise there's no other place I'd rather be.

The sun is dazzling as we finally draw to a halt at the old iron gate leading to Catalina and Ramon's *olivar*, their olive grove. It has been a challenging journey so far with many a precarious bend on a narrow and precipitous mountain road which seemed to curl forever upward like a giant helter-skelter towards the infinite blue sky. Alan gives a genuine deep sigh of relief as we once again study Ramon's hand drawn map offering directions.

'Looks as if we've finally arrived,' he says.

I get out of the car and push back the gate. It gives a squeal of disapproval as it is wrenched open and pinioned against the wall. The air has become notably cooler and the view from up here, high in the hills, is spectacular. Running down from the mountains in all directions are a seemingly endless series of terraces, known in Mallorcan as *marjadas*, on which olives trees are cultivated. Each terrace is protected by a sturdy hand-constructed drystone wall, the *marge*, which serves to keep the soil level and in place. The double wall construction in which rubble is placed between the stones instead of cement, assists with drainage, a godsend in rainy and tempestuous weather, stopping the soil from slipping away and becoming waterlogged. A glut of families in rural Mallorca are lucky enough to own an *olivar* where they spend many a weekend during the olive picking season producing enough oil for their own consumption.

A moment later we drive down a bumpy track surrounded by woodland and find ourselves outside an old stone *porxo*, what might be described as a sort of mountain cabin. It has smoke billowing from a chimney and in the doorway talking are Ramon and Catalina. On the front porch their two daughters, Sofia and Carolina, play with dolls while Catalina's mother and father sit under a tree in the olive grove preparing vegetables. Ramon greets us at the car.

'That was some journey!' Alan cries, stretching his arms in the air.

'The road's a little narrow,' Ramon concedes.

'A little?!' scoffs Alan as he turns to kiss Catalina. 'I need a drink.'

Catalina slaps him on the arm. 'Don't worry. I've got some good Rioja for you.'

'We're not late are we?' I ask.

'You're the first. My brothers and the rest of the family are on their way.'

We all exchange New Year's greetings and stroll off to the olive grove to meet Catalina's parents, Paco and Marta. Her father is cutting thick wedges of lemon and green *pebres*, the Mallorcan word for peppers, which will accompany the paella at lunch. Marta, sublime and smiling, puts down her knife which she is using to cut garlic and gets up to hug us one by one and to talk to Ollie. He shares a few words in Mallorcan and then rushes off to play with the girls on the porch. I notice that the dolls are abandoned immediately in favour of a running game.

We follow Catalina over to the log fire that has been set up for the cooking of the paella on a strip of turf near our car. Inside the *porxo*, the cabin, there are two interlinked small rooms, one with bunk beds and the other with a chimney, sofa, table and sink. A few utilitarian wooden cupboards face the front door and old rugs are thrown over the cement finished floors. There are seldom cooking facilities in a *porxo* and no bathroom. It is akin to camping, and families enjoy the simplicity of preparing food *a fora*, outside, and tending to their olive groves. Ramon lights the fire while Catalina and her mother set about cooking. I have tried numerous versions of paella but in my opinion, Catalina's own recipe takes some beating with its rich blend of succulent *marisç*, shellfish, rabbit and pork, vegetables and saffron rice.

As soon as the cooking begins in earnest, Ollie and the girls come running over, keen to watch the fire spit and spark as the heavy black paella pan is placed aloft and its contents swirled about in hot olive oil. Soon the smell of peppers, onions and garlic rises on the breeze and we all inhale the sweet aroma hungrily.

Paco ambles over to Alan with a bottle of Rioja. 'Here, let's all have a glass before the rest of the family arrive!'

He is filling our glasses when we hear a toot from the track. From the car windows Catalina's brother, Stefan and his wife Cristina are waving and in the back of the car, are some elderly relatives. Another car swiftly follows with her younger brother Marc and his family.

Paco nudges Alan's arm. 'By the way, how was the turkey? I hear it was so big you had to cook it in the garden!'

Ramon enjoys the joke. 'Yes, they only had to dine on one leg. They'll be eating the rest of the bird at Easter.'

I give Ramon a shove. 'Next year we're going vegetarian.'

'Oh you can't do that. I've already started to fatten you a turkey chick!'

I give a mock groan. 'Can you put this one on a diet?'

Paco laughs aloud and pats me on the back. 'Next year we'll save up to buy you a new cooker for Christmas.'

There are explosions of mirth from all sides as Stefan and the rest of the family appear, quickly cottoning on to the joke.

'*Molts D'anys!*' says Stefan giving me a hug. 'So why is my sister cooking paella? We thought you'd be bringing turkey *croquetas* for everyone!'

More giggles and merriment. Somehow I think the turkey joke, like the Duracell bunny, will just keep on going…

We have survived Christmas, New Year and are now on the last lap. El Nit dels Reis has arrived, an event prized above all others by Mallorcan children. In England we have Father Christmas, but in Mallorca they have Three Kings, the Magi, the wise men from the East, who ride into town at dusk on 5 January, bearing gifts. In recent times Father Christmas has some how directed his sleigh towards Mallorca which poses a problem for local families. Do they celebrate both occasions or hold out with the Three Kings? In rural Mallorca at least over-indulging children is frowned upon so Father Christmas finds few takers in the hills.

The arrival of the Three Kings, *Els Tres Reis*, is handled differently all over the island but up in the mountains it is a very intimate affair with three male volunteers from the village playing the kings Caspar, Melchior and Balthasar, and arriving heavily disguised and magnificently attired in Magi dress on horseback with a train of magical creatures and courtiers dancing behind them. Loaded on to a float are presents for every local child. The event is financed by the local *ajuntament*, the town or village council, and is a magical affair. As honorary members of Catalina's village we are invited along and take our seats in the main Square. This is good news for Ollie as he gets to enjoy the generosity of Father Christmas as well as that of *Els Tres Reis* whom Catalina has made sure include him in their distribution of gifts. This year, Catalina's three brothers have agreed to play the kings and they arrive to a great fanfare and screams of excitement from parents and children alike. Ollie, pink cheeked, can hardly contain his pleasure when he sees the cart laden with brightly coloured parcels. Catalina's two little girls are equally ecstatic.

'Will there be one for you, Ollie?' little Sofia questions in Mallorcan.

'I hope so,' he mumbles.

Ramon gives him a hug. 'You've played well at football this year so the kings will be pleased.'

'Really?' he asks.

'*Si, si*. The kings are great footballers.'

Ollie digests this information carefully and looks rather surprised.

Solemnly, the kings dismount and make their way to the stage in the square while a group of elves following in their wake throw sweets to the expectant crowds. Each king has his name etched on his robe. I notice Catalina's older brother Jordi, playing Balthasar, is having problems with his gold turban which keeps slipping over his eyes while her younger brother Marc, playing Caspar, battles to keep a long brown beard in place on his chin. Stefan as Melchior seems to be in good shape and appears to like his silver cape and bejewelled gold crown. As he passes us, Stefan gives a surreptitious wink which we reciprocate. He touches Ollie on the head.

'Did you see that?' hisses Ollie. 'The king touched me!'

The event begins. It is chilly but there is no wind and above the stage the sky is laden with stars. Balthasar attempts to make a speech but the microphone is faulty and so we watch him in mime oblivious to the problem until a technician runs up to the stage and attempts to rectify things. It finally whines into life and he speaks.

'*Benvingut* and *Molts d'anys* everyone!'

There's a huge cheer from the assembled audience and clapping. Caspar sets the ball rolling inviting the children up to the stage, calling out their names one by one from a large gold scroll. As each child approaches the front, I observe Ollie, anticipation and hope etched on his face, listening ever for the sound of his name. Moments later, Caspar looks in our direction and with a smile bellows into the mike, 'Ollie...'

In a flash, Ollie relinquishes his grip on my hand and sprints to the stage where Melchior, with a stealthy nod in my direction, engages him in conversation. Stefan is a good linguist and so I wonder whether he has decided to address our budding footballer in English. Ollie returns to me clutching a large package.

'Those Eastern kings are really clever you know,' he confides. 'They can even speak English.'

The phone purrs and then it connects.

'Ed it's me!'

'Ah, how are you? How's Mallorca?'

'All fine.'

'When are you back in London?'

'Oh, not for a month or so.'

'You don't seem too bothered,' he admonishes.

He's right. I'm rather happy staying here in the mountains away from all the stress and hassle. I decide to change the subject. 'Ed, you didn't answer my last e-mail. Are you OK?'

He coughs. 'I've been a bit preoccupied I'm afraid.'

'What? With work?'

He sniffs. 'Actually I've been seeing rather a lot of Julia the last few weeks.'

'Ah, the nurse?' I've caught him!

'Yes,' he says slowly. 'She's very sweet and seems to be able to cope with my neuroses.'

'Gosh, she must be a saint.'

'Maybe she is,' he says dryly. 'It's quite nice to meet someone in the flesh, I mean rather than through the Internet.'

I decide to resist the urge to say, 'You don't say?'

'So has anything happened?' I ask intrusively.

'Actually, yes, we have shared an intimate moment.'

There's a pause on the line. I'm all agog.

'Well, what was it?' I hiss impatiently.

'I allowed her to look in my MEK,' he says.

It is 16 January, a crisp night up in Catalina's village where the festivities are taking place. We have been invited to join the party in the *plaça* which always happens the day before Beneides de Sant Antoni, the blessing of animals. Pep, Juana and Angel meet us by the water fountain where they are chatting with Catalina and her father, Paco. Angel rushes over to Ollie and they disappear into the crowd on some mischievous mission or other with the local village children. A huge bonfire blazes in the centre of the square, illuminating the ancient olive tree, the centrepiece of the village and tables and chairs are set up around the perimeter for the guests. The local *ajuntament* finances the celebrations, providing a band, wine and copious amounts of meat for barbequing. It's a wonderfully cosy village affair which after the wholesale consumption of warming wine becomes even more entertaining as locals begin singing and telling saucy tales to the gathered guests. Ramon grabs my arm.

'You know Catalina's aunt Maria is bringing her *ximbomba* along. Be warned!'

I have seen one of these bizarre instruments but never watched it in action.

'That's excellent news! I've been desperate to hear the *ximbomba* played.'

'You'll be desperate enough!' he taunts. 'Maria sings very risqué songs while she plays. I hope your Mallorcan's not up to it.'

'Well, I hope you'll translate.'

'You must be joking! They're far too rude for your ears.'

'That's very mean,' I pout.

Juana comes over with Catalina who hands me a huge glass of wine.

'My aunt's coming, you want to play the *ximbomba?*'

Ramon quickly joins Alan and Pep, keen not to be involved in the embarrassing spectacle we women are going to make. I see Maria bustling into the square and pulling her prized instrument out of a plastic carrier bag. She gives me a wicked grin and beckons me over.

'Here, I set it up and you try it.'

I look at the strange contraption which has a terracotta base rather like a plant pot, and a surface covered in taut goat hide. A long, vertical bamboo cane is inserted in its middle which Maria tells me causes friction and a particular sound.

'Here, I also have a wet cabbage leaf. You rub this up and down the cane and it make a good noise. Here, I show you.'

She sits on a chair and with the *ximbomba* held erect between her knees, wraps the cabbage leaf around the cane and begins pushing it up and down. A sound similar to someone blowing a loud raspberry is emitted. People stop to listen and several admiring groups amble over to get a good earful. Someone knocks my arm. It is Pep with a dangerous twinkle in his eye and characteristic *puro* in hand.

'You know this is an important phallic symbol,' he says solemnly.

'Oh please…!' I roll my eyes.

'He pretends to look aggrieved. 'Listen, I can explain the significance.'

'I'd rather you didn't, thank you.'

He giggles. 'Come on Maria, let her try!'

Maria breaks off from her task and gets me to take her place. Rather awkwardly I take up position and begin rubbing at the cabbage leaf. A loud squawk, more an anguished cry escapes from the drum and people erupt with laughter.

'That sounds more like a constipated cow,' yells Pep.

'You do it then!' I growl at him.

'Here, hold my cigar,' he instructs before I can object. Then he leaps up and clasps the stick to his chest and begins singing wildly as he plays. This immediately draws an appreciative crowd.

'He is singing one of the *gloses*,' whispers Maria to me.

'What's that?'

'It's a little bawdy tale. This one is very funny about a nun and a…' she doubles up at the words.

I give her a frustrated nudge. 'A nun and a what??'

She shakes her head and wipes her eyes. 'Oh! It's too naughty. *Molt malament!*'

Alan and Ramon wander over with wry grins on their faces.

'Ever the showman,' sighs Alan.

'He is very funny but his song is a little strong, like a robust cheese,' says Catalina.

The villagers are captivated by Pep's debut. He finishes his piece, stands up and bows, before passing the *ximbomba* back to Maria. The crowd claps as Pep plucks the *puro* stub from my hand and strolls off towards Aina's bar, the oldest bar in the village.

'I need a small medicinal whisky,' he murmurs. 'How about you?'

Alan and Ramon nod and off they go in a pack. Juana has been captivated by her husband's performance and now confers with Maria over what *gloses* they will perform next. Maria decides on her next number and holds forth while a hush falls. As she comes to the end of her tune there's raucous whistling. I lament the fact that my knowledge of Mallorcan can't fathom the naughty nuances of the songs. On second thoughts, maybe it's for the best.

Juana takes my arm and together we go off to enjoy the barbecue and catch up with local friends. I drain my wine glass and am quickly poured another by Lorenç, who has crept up behind me. I notice he's still wearing his log carting gear. Juana and I fill our plates with sizzling meat and sit at one of the tables. Lorenç, with a plate filled to the brim, joins us.

'Do you know,' Juana says with starry eyes. 'My husband may have many faults but I can't deny that he's truly brilliant on the *ximbomba*.'

Aha, that's it! Now I've at last fathomed how Pep won the doughty Juana's heart.

TWELVE

BREAKING NEW GROUND

The last of the snow has cleared from the upper reaches of the Tramuntana Mountains and down in the valley a froth of delicate white almond blossom engulfs the orchards, blanching trees and exuding a fragrance bewitching enough to lure a siren. At the slightest breeze flurries of petals, like diaphanous butterflies, fall to the ground in uneven clusters, as light and fluffy as meringues and as soft as down. Treading air, high in the sky, a lukewarm sun breathes new life into plants and trees, penetrating the smallest green shoot and the faintest of buds.

Leaning on a fork down in the field, Alan looks about him serenely while contemplating how best to work loose the soil that sits beneath his feet in a hard and impenetrable mass. It is the tree-planting season and he is eager to wrestle some saplings into the ground. Slumped against the steep stone wall which separates the field from the courtyard are an assortment of forlorn young fruit trees waiting like evacuees to be given new lodgings. Alan leaves his fork skewered in to the earth and as if inextricably linked, is soon at their side, propping them up and tenderly covering their exposed and skeletal frames with an old piece of hessian. Satisfied with his efforts, he marches up the gravel path towards the house, the soles of his green rubber boots squeaking and squirming in the tiny pebbles and fragments of stone. At the back door, Catalina is remonstrating with Inko about her lack of work ethic.

'You're so lazy! I can't believe it!'

Alan, a Labrador man at heart, gives the sprawling, rotund cat a sideways glance and shakes his head despairingly.

'Just because she's soon to be a mother is no reason to over-indulge her, but of course', he lowers his voice, 'the senyora always knows best.'

Catalina smiles and nods conspiratorially. I watch them from the upstairs window which has been flung open by Catalina in her obsession for fresh air, regardless of the temperature. I'm tempted to startle them with a 'Ha ha, caught you!' but instead tip toe from the pane, leaving them to bask in their mutual disapproval of my habitual spoiling of the cat.

Fifteen minutes later I set off along the track for a run. The London Marathon is less than ten weeks away and my training has been a tad erratic after the Christmas festivities. Training aside, I have also assiduously been collecting sponsorship pledges from family, friends, clients and readers of my column in the *Majorca Daily Bulletin* to the extent that just mentioning the word marathon in a phone call has a contact pleading that a cheque's already in the post before I can badger further. As I reach Franco's run, I hear loud music belting out from the doorway of Rafael's house and then his own tuneless voice trying to sing in tandem. Despite the noise, his radar is acute and he is at the front porch in a flash and clapping his hands loudly. I watch him from the fence of the dog's run where I have slipped one hand between the bars to fondle Franco's ears.

'So here comes the champ, yes? Only few weeks now and then whoosh!'

'Ten weeks, actually,' I say patiently.

'Yes, but time flies. Now you must train hard or you will be in big trouble.' He screeches with laughter and slams a hand on my back.

'I joke, my friend! Come on, you are good runner.'

I often wonder what Rafael did for laughs before I moved in. I wave goodbye, set my stopwatch and sprint up the path. At the end of the track, I turn on to the narrow tarmac road whose surface is milky with frost like a coated tongue. Margalida Sampol is not in evidence so I assume she's wrapped up warmly indoors. Few people are about and I am aware of the sound of my laboured breathing, as I curl upwards towards the main road to the port. A van passes and toots its horn in time for me to see Catalina's brother, Stefan, give a wave from behind the glass. It is rare in our valley to go more than a few yards before meeting someone you know. In London I would find this hugely intrusive and claustrophobic but here it seems reassuring. I turn left at the top of the hill and with relief run fast down a wide stretch of road. There isn't a car on the road and the air carries the heady fragrance of almond blossom. Zipping along, I feel as light as the breeze, an invincible runner in a one-woman race, victory within my grasp.

Inko is lying in her basket by the kitchen door as I squeeze lemon juice into the blender. I am making hummus, one of my weekly rituals. To think I used to spend a fortune buying small pots of the stuff from London supermarkets. I must have been mad or too stressed to care. Having popped in to see the vet earlier I know that my corpulent cat is going to give birth at any time and I am as twitchy as an expectant father. Catalina has left for the day but has promised to pop down to the house to help out if I'm having an emergency of a feline kind. She knows I haven't got a clue when it comes to birthing matters with no idea what to expect, what to do and how to cope with the whole delivery experience. Worse still, Alan is collecting Ollie from school in Palma so my poor feline companion must put her entire faith in my hands. I finish preparing the hummus, take a spoonful, add a little more sesame oil and then put the bowl in the fridge. I get up and soothe the cat, pull her blanket around her haunches and stroke her head. Outside, the mountains are doused in golden sunlight so that they glitter and sparkle like iron pyrites and on the back patio, blackbirds pick their way through the tall grasses in search of worms and grubs. At the far end of the garden, a lean brown rat peeps out of a rock in the craggy wall then scurries off furtively towards the courtyard and out on to the track. It peers back momentarily, sniffing the air and then disappears from view. In a brief moment of self-analysis, I am intrigued by my impassive reaction to this most abhorrent of small mammals living in my own backyard. I shake myself out of my reverie and turn from the open kitchen door to observe Inko. She fidgets and suddenly emits a low anguished growl before hunching up into a ball. To my horror, something more at home on a butcher's blood soaked table plops out of her onto the newspaper covering the floor. I am frozen to the spot. Is it a kitten? No. Then what the hell is it? I inspect it closely. This thing is no cuddly cub. It's earthy red and glistens and to my untrained eye looks like a live organ. Has she expelled her liver? How could she? Trying not to lose my head I grapple with the phone and ring the vet. There's no reply. In desperation I call Alan on his mobile. He is standing in the school playground, his voice drowned by the ecstatic screams of children flooding out of classrooms.

'This is an emergency!' I shout.

'What?' he yells above the din.

'The cat's dropped a thing that looks like a liver. What shall I do?'

'A liver? Don't be silly, it must be the placenta.'

'Is that normal?' I bark.

'How should I know? Ring the vet.'

'He's not there,' I say tetchily, trying to conceal the bubble of emotion welling up in me.

'Look, calm down. I'll take her to the vet as soon as I get back. Keep her warm and make yourself a cup of tea.'

I decide to ring Rachel in London, the voice of calm. With meticulous care I describe the strange object lying on the newspaper.

'Urgh!' she cries. 'That doesn't sound too good. I think she's dropped the placenta.'

'You were brought up in the country, Rachel. What do I do now?'

'Pray?'

'Oh very helpful!'

She gives a snort. 'Sorry, I'm just trying to keep your spirits up. You must get her to a vet.'

I groan. 'Impossible until Alan's home. I've got no car and the vet's not answering his mobile.'

She sighs. 'There's nothing for it but a cup of tea, soothing music and patience. Keep me posted.'

I put the phone down and sit on the floor next to the cat uncertain as to what to do next. Inko's half opened eyes are trained on me as she nestles closer, her head now resting weakly on my right leg. I prop myself up against the side of the fridge, maddened by the cheerful chirruping of a small bird, the sound wafting in through the open window. While life carries on with cold clarity beyond the pane, I remain marooned on my own island of impotence and despondency, bewildered by the vagaries of merciless nature that can transform an anticipated event of great joy into one of total despair. I realise that my successful handling of office and client crises over the years has been nothing more than a pyrrhic victory, leaving me unequipped to deal with the raw and brutal business of real life.

Someone is calling from the front porch. I'm in no mood for social visits and wearily get up from the floor to find old Margalida hobbling into the *entrada* which leads to the kitchen. In our town, no one locks their front doors so it's open house all day long.

'There you are,' she says. 'My daughter picked me a huge amount of flowers so I thought I'd bring some up to you.'

I am incredibly moved to think that Margalida, with her terrible eyesight, has risked walking alone all the way up the rocky track to our *finca*. I give her a hug.

'What's wrong with your cat?' she asks, holding my arm as we walk into the kitchen. I try not to show that both the cat and I are having 'kittens'.

'Oh she's about to give birth but something's just come out of her…'

Margalida bends down and peers at the item on the newspaper.

'That's her placenta. I'm sorry but I don't think her kittens will live. She's too young a cat to give birth.'

'How do you know?' I'm horrified.

She shrugs and sits on a chair, mopping her brow as I bring her a glass of water. 'I've had many cats in my time and the young ones rarely give birth successfully. We have to accept God's will and the law of nature.'

I'm now even more dispirited. 'But she'll be OK?'

She pats my hand. '*Segur*. I'm sure she'll live to have more kittens.'

With her hand clasping her stick, she rises and tells me she must return to the house. I accompany her back down the track in sombre mood. She turns round when she reaches her front door. 'Remember, tomorrow is another day.'

Forty exasperating minutes later, I hear a car tear up the drive. Thank God. Alan leaps out, shoos Ollie into the house, and gently gathers up the cat in its wicker basket and heads for the vet. Ollie sits with me in the kitchen, his little face pinched with concern for his beloved cat. My eyes ache as I try to hold back tears. What's wrong with me? It's a cat. Just a cat. An hour later the phone rings like a death knell. It's Alan. His voice is heavy.

'I'm sorry. Inko's lost her twins. They were just too big for her. The vet said there was nothing we could have done. He's operating on her now and is hopeful she's going to make it. I'll wait here.'

'What colour were they?' I force myself to ask. I notice my voice has taken on huskiness.

He pauses and sighs deeply. 'One black, one white'.

Numbed I put the phone down and hug Ollie. All the months of cheerful expectation and excitement preparing for the imminent arrival, have come to nought. Animals have become such an essential part of our lives now that I don't know how we ever existed without them in London. I walk stiffly down the stairs, Ollie trailing sorrowfully behind me, and on the bottom step sit down and weep. Ollie puts his head in my lap and there we remain, silently, our hands intertwined until Alan and a bandaged and disorientated Inko return home.

Inko has spent three nights lying in her basket in my darkened office making plaintive little murmurs and refusing to eat or drink. Her stomach is a swollen mass of stitches encrusted with dried blood, and her right leg is swaddled in bandages from the anaesthetic injections. Since the operation, I have tiptoed around her, stroking her ears and uttering what I hope have been soothing words. Alan tuts disapprovingly at me but when I'm out of the room kneels down and rubs her ears affectionately. But today she sits up stiffly in her basket, yawns and begins licking her paws. In a state of joy I crawl under my desk to where her basket is and touch her head. She gives me a withering look and turns her back. I pull gently at the bandages on her leg and like a grand dame humouring an impertinent maid, she lies back and allows me to attend to her. When I have removed them, she gives me a warning blink, sups on some water from her bowl and then crosses her paws and sleeps.

The room is cocooned in darkness although it is already seven o'clock. Beyond the window, the sky, like a unwinding roll of soft black silk, gives no hint that morning has arrived. Only the persistent crowing of Rafael's cockerel and the low restless barks of Franco and neighbouring farm dogs, herald the new day. Light suddenly floods in from the doorway and Alan appears bearing a tray of tea, boiled eggs and toast. Ollie follows up the rear clutching his own mug of hot chocolate. I struggle to unearth myself from the bedcovers to switch on the lamp by my side. We sit together munching toast and watching the sky transform from soot to slate until a deep fissure appears in the gloom revealing a vivid turquoise heart. Within a short while, the heavens are a rich azure and the sun has stumbled into view, showering gold light on our orchard and field.

Alan sighs contentedly. 'What a glorious day! By the way, good old Rafael left us a bag of kindling twigs on the porch.'

I drain my cup. 'Maybe it's a goodwill token in return for the hours of mirth he's had at my expense.'

Half an hour later and a roaring fire burns in the hearth. Armed with a wicker basket I leave the warm kitchen and set off to the field with Ollie to pick the new season's crop of oranges and lemons that hang heavy and succulent from the trees. He carries the secateurs with a sense of importance, passing them up to me as I clamber on to a rickety wooden ladder, reaching with my hands into the upper branches to clip off the fruit. We are nearing the end of our task when a loud rumbling fills the courtyard and a huge, grubby blue pick-up truck lurches into view, brakes sharply and stops. I leave the basket overflowing with oranges and stride up the path, Ollie in my train, towards the front of the house. Alan has arrived moments before us and now stands with hands on hips, talking heatedly with the driver whose head pokes through his lowered window. Nearing the truck I see to my irritation that it is Senyor Coll, the rogue builder whom we had originally hired to reform our *finca* and who had left us in the lurch. Senyor Coll is grinning horribly and shouting loudly in Mallorcan. The Scotsman counters in bad Spanish.

'What's going on?' I demand, approaching them both.

He offers me an ingratiating smile and extends a damp, plump paw through the lowered car window. I decline to take it. Alan glares darkly at him and then turns to me.

'He insists that some years back he left a pile of terracotta tiles in our field. He's come to reclaim them.' He points crossly towards a tarpaulin covered heap lying beneath a pear tree.

'Nonsense! We bought those tiles,' I remonstrate.

Indeed the tiles had been purchased by this unscrupulous builder on our behalf at an over inflated price before being unceremoniously dumped in our field when he jumped ship. Never sure where he had really meant for them to be laid, they have remained there ever since, until such time as we might find a use for them. So, filled with rightful indignation, we demand of Senyor Coll how he can dare to show his face at our house given his disgraceful past behaviour. He puffs heavily on a *puro* and shrugs his shoulders, refusing to budge until he has collected what he claims is his property. Keen to despatch with him once and for all, Alan brusquely tells him to take the tiles and never to set foot on our premises again. Obsequiously he mutters, '*Gracies,*' and with a triumphant leer begins driving his jalopy down the steep ramp into our field. I walk slowly back into the house with Alan.

'They don't belong to him, you know,' I say with fervour.

'I know, but let's just get shot of him. As you always say, he'll have no luck.'

He's right and what does it matter? Life's all about letting things go and moving on.

Ollie listens keenly. 'So he's a naughty man, then?'

'Yep. He sure is.' I plod up the stairs, evilly fantasising about buying a box of sharp pins and candles to fashion into a wax effigy of him. Before I've even reached the top step there is an enormous crash followed by the sound of grating metal outside. Shocked, we all race into the courtyard in time to see Senyor Coll crawling out from beneath his overturned vehicle. So voluminous is his stomach that it wedges momentarily under the chassis and I am immediately reminded of a honey-sated Pooh Bear stuck ignominiously down a rabbit hole. Senyor Coll wheezes up the small slope and faces us belligerently as if we are in some way responsible for the dire circumstances in which he finds himself. Although unhurt, he wears the expression of a hunted man, looking fearfully about him as if a posse of secret adversaries is lying low among the long grasses and boulders. Reluctantly he lets us help him up into the courtyard whereupon we fetch him a glass of cold water. He sits by the well, running a nicotine-stained hand over his forehead and coughing into his cotton handkerchief. He is morose and even his big moustache sags at the corners.

'It's ruined,' he cries, his beady eyes darting angrily from side to side. 'The truck is a write off. Look at it!'

'Well, whatever happened?' I ask quietly.

'A wheel went over the side of your accursed slope. Didn't you see it?'

'It all happened so fast. We were in the house.'

He kicks a stone irritably at the wall and curses in local dialect.

'What did you need the tiles for anyway?'

He doesn't answer at first and then fixes me with an unrepentant stare. 'I don't need them. I just want what's mine.'

'But they're not yours,' I say simply.

His eyes simmer with resentment. 'You foreigners always want something for nothing, don't you?'

I observe Senyor Coll thoughtfully, and decide that since he is obviously delusional, it is probably best to leave him to mutter his dark and menacing incantations alone in the courtyard. So, ignoring him, I join Alan and together we scramble down the steep, narrow slope that links the courtyard to the field. It declines sharply and drops about three feet on either side into the field below. It is easy to see how, if driven slovenly, a large truck could lose control and flip sideways over the edge several feet into the mud. Given the severity of the accident, it is miraculous that Senyor Coll escaped injury. Maybe even the damned have guardian angels.

Alan reaches into the truck and manages to switch off the engine, retrieving Senyor Coll's mobile phone at the same time which has fallen from the upturned front seat on to a patch of grass.

'Well he's made quite a dent in the soil,' whispers Alan naughtily to me, as we survey the wreckage. 'Maybe planting the fruit trees won't be so difficult.'

I stifle a giggle and prod him in the ribs. We make our way back up into the courtyard where Senyor Coll petulantly snatches the mobile from Alan, stabbing at the digits whereupon a furious conversation ensues. Then he waits impatiently and in utter humiliation at the gate for his son.

'I've organised a crane,' says his brawny offspring when he arrives in a clapped out old van, 'It will cost a fair whack.'

I notice that the son is developing his father's girth and that two small, shifty eyes puncture his moist, flaccid face like sunken berries in dough.

'Oh dear,' I say. 'That's awful.'

'Get me my *puros!*' steams the father as he laboriously climbs up into the passenger seat of his son's vehicle. I watch his cowed son amble down into the field, squeeze under the wreckage and retrieve what is left of Senyor Coll's packet of cigars. Together they drive miserably away from the house and for a fleeting second I almost feel a stab of pity for naughty Senyor Coll.

Someone is frantically knocking on the door. It is Rafael. He bounds cheerfully into our *entrada* and sniffs loudly.

'I hear about the accident! Terrible,' he says with irony.

'Yes, dreadful,' I reply.

'Everyone is talking about it in the town. What did old Coll want in your field?'

I feel defensive, worried that the locals will side with this vile man who left us in the lurch and ripped us off. After all, he is one of their own kinsmen.

'Our tiles,' I say stiffly.

He clicks his teeth impatiently and pats my shoulder. 'Everyone knows this man. Remember you have many friends here.'

Rafael heads for the hearth and warms himself at the fire. He refuses a drink and says he is just popping by to see the senyor. At the sound of his voice, Alan hurries down the stair and gives him a warm handshake.

'I can't stop,' Rafael says. 'I just want to know you find my rose cuttings this morning OK?'

Alan looks mystified.

'Yes, I leave them in a bag on your porch this morning. A little present for *el jardiner* – the gardener. You no find?'

I exchange horrified looks with my Scottish *jardiner*, whose gardening prowess has obviously failed to make the distinction between kindling twigs and rose cuttings. We both turn to face the raging fire.

'I'm afraid I've made a bit of a blunder...' begins Alan.

It's mid-February and carnival night has arrived. In great excitement we drive up to Catalina's village at about ten in the evening and make our way to Es Turo Restaurant. It is dark outside, and a cool wind whips up the leaves and dust along the cobbled street. Clumsily, like a slapstick comedy trio, we emerge from our car with painted faces and grotesque attire. Alan has two enormous blond plaits dangling from either side of his head, a Viking helmet and a copious yellow beard that has somehow become ensnared in the Velcro fastening of his brown felt costume. His face is covered in boot polish and leather laces run criss-cross up each of his legs. Ollie, in scarlet tights and green bodice, grips a bow and arrow, and is a cross between Peter Pan and Robin Hood. As for me, I'm a hybrid. Korean bride meets gaudy geisha. Back in my twenties, when I worked for a publishing house, I had been sent to Korea on business, returning with a gift of a *Hanbok*, a traditional wedding outfit in pea green and cyclamen pink silk. For good reason, it never left its packing case, but tonight it has come into its own.

As we walk boldly up the street, clamping wigs firmly to our heads in the wind, there is stifled laughter and looks of bemusement from passing locals who greet us enthusiastically but have no idea who we are. It's so wonderfully therapeutic to make a complete fool of oneself and know that nobody gives a damn. We enter the restaurant to the cheers of similarly ridiculously attired friends who have arrived ahead of us. Catalina, Ramon and our Australian friends Jack and Sarah, have cunningly attired themselves in yashmaks and flowing black gowns while a group of young girls dressed as *bruixes* sit cackling together at the next table, swaddled in black and wearing trademark knobbly noses, pointed black hats and blood red finger nails. Weekend trippers and foreign visitors not accustomed to Carnival mayhem, observe us nervously from their tables, desperately trying not to catch our attention. Xisca emerges from the kitchen and lets out a howl of bawdy laughter, calling her husband to come and view the odd-balls gathering under their roof. Mischievously, Catalina gets up and runs into the kitchen like a wild black ghoul, arms outspread, and causes havoc among the backroom staff as they scream and drop saucepans at the sudden apparition in their midst. Peals of hysterical laughter can be heard from within when they see that it is their very own chef. As the hour gets later, more and more heavily disguised locals enter, nonchalantly sitting down at tables and ordering their food. Locals don't give them a second glance. There are Elvis look-alikes, transvestites, popes and vicars, vampires and a good smattering of prostitutes whom we assume are fakes. As we settle our bill and are ready to leave, an earnest, preppy American diner braves approaching our table and whispers confidentially, 'Excuse me, is this what normally happens up here on a Saturday night?'

I keep my face deadpan, although the others have also listened and spoil the effect by bursting into giggles. 'Oh yes, it's just a slice of mountain life. Saturday night is always party night.'

He politely thanks me and heads back to his table, faithfully repeating my words to his unnerved partner. They pay their bill hurriedly, wave goodbye and make a speedy exit. The restaurant erupts into laughter.

Some time after, we make our way in the cold to the underground garage on the outskirts of the village where the Carnival party is being held. It is nearly midnight and the place is already packed with unrecognisable locals. Paper chains and bunting have been strung from walls and ceiling, and large gas heaters now blaze along one side of the dank building. Small fairy lights hang from a flex that has been slung from one end of the garage to the other, but afford little light. Against the far back wall, a jazz band is belting out music and by the entrance a makeshift bar has been rigged up from which three local volunteers battle to take drink orders from the jostling throng pressing against the counter. I see Juan, the village *batle*, leaning against a wall and rush over to greet him. He rears back for a moment, flustered by the vision of a tall black wig, white face and pea green and pink silk swimming towards him. With relief etched on his face, he suddenly twigs it's me when he sees Ollie holding my hand, and gives me a hug.

'Heavens!' he chuckles, 'I can't believe it's you.'

I upbraid him for not having dressed up himself but he tuts and gives me a little frown. 'But I'm the *batle*!'

I am, of course, forgetting village protocol which would probably regard a costume-clad mayor with the same derision as it would a middle-aged senyora wearing a miniskirt and fishnets.

I spy the local traffic warden sitting on a chair by the bar, who, with a nice touch of irony, has dressed as an angel. She puffs on a cigarette, her fluffy wings squashed back behind her, and talks closely with a chunky Julius Caesar who blows me a kiss, but I can't for the life of me think who it is.

Catalina's mother and father, Marta and Paco, now make their appearance at the party. Both are wearing thick jumpers, jackets and scarves and grinning broadly. Paco greets Alan and shakes his head with mirth when he sees me standing behind him. I greet him and his wife, trying not to smother them with white face paint as I bend to kiss them.

Marta gives a little laugh. 'I hope everyone makes the most of tonight because they've got forty days of *Cuaresma* to look forward to now.'

The end of the Carnival always signifies the beginning of Lent. A distant childhood memory floods back to me when my sister and I were banned sweets for what seemed like an eternity, all in the name of Lent.

'Does everyone fast in the village?' I ask with surprise.

'Heavens no!' cuts in Paco, 'Things have changed, few people fast now. Many years ago we all used to give up meat for Lent but the wealthy in our village gave a backhander to the priest and carried on as normal.' He finds this amusing and tips his head back and laughs raucously.

There's a sudden cry of joy and a frisson of excitement as a tall, ample bosomed woman appears dramatically in the garage doorway wearing a Marilyn Monroe blond wig, a devilishly figure-clinging red dress and a pair of lethally high black stilettos. Her lips are lavishly coated red and she dangles a cigarette holder between two exquisitely manicured fingers. Despite the perfectly applied make-up and disguise, the villagers are not fooled, for this is clever, quick-witted Cati, mother of three, owner of a local *bodega*, wine store, and one of the liveliest *personatges* in the area for whom chutzpah is a byword. To my delight I got to know the voluptuous Cati through the village holiday school attended by Ollie in the summer. With great aplomb, she struts to the centre of the garage, hand on hip, haughtily surveying her audience. The crowds gape at her in awe and there is a sudden hush when she raises her hand for attention.

'Well,' she drawls with a wicked grin. 'I take it I'm just in time to win the best costume award, or is there,' she purrs provocatively, 'anyone who'd like to challenge me this year?'

There is applause and wolf whistles but no one dares step forward. 'Good,' she says crisply.

Satisfied that she is to remain Carnival Queen for another year, Cati takes a bow and with a flash of white teeth, saunters off to talk to some friends.

Up in Catalina's village, we sit drinking coffees in Aina's cosy bar by the square. Several wooden tables and chairs have been set up outside but despite the blue skies, it is chilly and everyone huddles inside. As always the place is a hub of activity with children running noisily up to the counter for packets of crisps and sweets while Aina attempts to dish out coffees and plates of *pa amb oli*, a traditional Mallorcan plate of bread, rubbed with garlic and olive oil, to various regulars. Catalina pushes open the door, engages in a lengthy and animated conversation, punctuated by gales of laughter with a table full of villagers by the window, and then comes over to join us.

'What was all that about?' I ask.

'Everyone is talking about the English man who bought the restaurant on the other side of the square. I told you about this man.'

'The one who everyone hates?'

'Well, he doesn't like any of us. Anyway, yesterday he closes his bar forever so everyone is very happy.'

The tale of the snooty Englishman and his fanciful Polish wife who the previous year took over the running of a local restaurant and then proceeded to alienate everyone in the village, is a story which has done the rounds. This couple, like a pair of lost aliens, had landed, unannounced, in the village one balmy summer's day and taken up residence at the erstwhile abandoned restaurant. They had previously, so rumour has it, run a small bistro in the Home Counties, and decided to bring their interpretation of cordon bleu to the mountains probably in the same way that missionaries attempted to bring Christianity to remote Amerindian tribes. At their opening party, they had exclusively invited only English speaking residents, dismissed the local clientele as a bunch of *pagès* and disastrously attempted to launch an English-speaking residents' club. Not only did this have the effect of enraging all the locals but also the long established English-speaking residents – American, British and Australians – who were utterly appalled at their boorish behaviour, having for many years been assimilated into the local community themselves. From that moment onwards the restaurant was doomed to failure. No one set foot in the place except the odd unsuspecting tourist and soon it was obvious it would have to close. The villagers went about their business, listening with satisfaction to the gossip of the delivery men who, privy to the dwindling orders placed by the restaurant, predicted that it would soon be on its uppers.

'So, if the restaurant's closed down, does that mean the couple will leave the village?'

Catalina regards me thoughtfully. 'Of course. There is nothing for them here. They have no friends. Yes, they will go.'

'What about the restaurant?'

She shakes her head. 'Another foreigner will buy it and lose money and then another. It has always been like this. No Mallorcan will touch it.'

Given its ill-fated past, I find it peculiar that outsiders are willing to jack in their life's savings to buy the place.

'The thing is,' says Catalina, using her most endearing of favoured English expressions, 'Foreigners come here wanting to live their dream. They open bars and restaurants and they behave as if they're on holiday. But they're not. Work is work and bills are bills wherever you are. We work hard but these people, they believe it's all sitting in the sun, drinking *vino*. Look at Aina,' she tilts her head towards the bar. I watch Aina cleaning down the laminate work surface by the sink. She seems tired and careworn, but still manages to share a joke with a customer hunched over the bar. How she juggles running the bar with family life and caring for her children, I will never know.

'She hasn't had a holiday for years. She takes maybe two mornings off a week. This is real life not a holiday.'

Alan puts down his copy of *Ultima Hora*, gives Catalina's arm a squeeze and says jokingly, 'So you don't think it's worth our making them an offer, then?'

She looks momentarily confused, and then with a growl of laughter, elbows him in the ribs.

THIRTEEN

TOAD IN THE HOLE

Alan is standing in the garden, sleeves rolled up with his nose in the air and his eye fixed on the verdant hills. There is a sniff of spring and the *burros* are braying madly from a nearby field while Rafael's cockerels with their harems of hens strut up and down on the track having made an earlier bid for freedom and just squeezed their way through a hole in his orchard fence. One comes to inspect our courtyard, goose-stepping around its perimeter, sniffing at the gravel in apparent disapproval and cocking its head from side to side. It squawks at Inko who surveys it with disdain before slinking off to the back terrace in search of a good spot for sunbathing. It is already warm enough to don shorts and sunglasses and so it isn't long before Alan finds an excuse to appear in the kitchen for a glass of water. Catalina regards him harshly.

'Water already? You've only been digging for an hour. When are you planting the vegetables?'

'That a girl!' I taunt.

'If you must know, I'm finishing weeding in the garden then I'm off to plant the summer veg. I never get a break around here.'

'It's a hard life!' chuckles Catalina. 'Anyway out of my way or I'll brand you with the iron.'

Alan skips around the flex as water sizzles and steam rises as she pounds at the ironing board.

'It's a good day for drying,' she murmurs to herself. 'This afternoon I pick up the girls from my mum's house and we go to the Fira de Fang.'

I wonder if this is some Dracula Fest for kids.

'What on earth's that?' I ask in trepidation.

'It's the annual pottery fair in Marratxi. You should go. They sell wonderful handmade plates and cups.'

'Don't encourage her to spend money,' growls Alan. 'We'll visit next year. Let's just get the house straight first.'

He has a point. We still have work to do even though we've got used to wires spewing from walls and exposed light sockets. I've stopped dreaming about owning a dishwasher. We can't have one because its designated place is currently home to the washing machine and we have nowhere else to put that. Stefan is going to build a small *casita* off the patio which will house all our washing paraphernalia and the dratted machine and dryer but until then, it must stay in the kitchen. As for the swimming pool, it's possible we can start work on it next month if we can squeeze a little more goodwill money out of our indulgent local bank.

'*Poc a poc*', says Catalina cheerfully.

A car draws up to the house and we look at each other in puzzlement.

'Were you expecting anyone?' asks Catalina.

'Ah!' says Alan in a state of angst. 'I forgot… my lesson with Paula. She's having her flat repainted so asked if we could do it here instead. Damnation!'

Paula, clad in a floaty red floral dress which covers her rather ample girth, wafts into the kitchen and studies Alan carefully.

'You haven't forgotten our lesson?' she says sternly in Castilian Spanish.

'No! Of course not. I was looking forward to it Paula.'

He plants a kiss on her cheeks and at the same time shares a surreptitious grimace with me. Paula shakes hands with Catalina and gives me a peck on both cheeks. She is wearing bright red lipstick and I feel a sticky layer deposited on my skin. I smile and offer her a coffee.

'A *café solo*. No milk,' she barks, running her pink talons through her mane of thick grey hair.

'Where are your books?' she says suspiciously.

'Er, just upstairs in the office. I'll go and clear the table.' Alan bolts up the stairs while Catalina tries to hide her amusement.

'He loves Spanish with you,' she says mischievously. 'He talks about how much he's learned during the year.'

She baulks at this. 'That's surprising to hear. He always seems to have an excuse for why he hasn't done his homework. He's got to be more disciplined.'

'Absolutely!' I nod. 'Maybe he needs more lessons.'

'I agree. One hour a week isn't enough. We could up it to two perhaps?'

'Good idea,' I add.

Alan is halfway down the stairway, his eyebrows knitted in horror.

'It's a lovely thought, Paula, but I'm just too busy. Come along and let's leave them to their work…' He gives Catalina and me a meaningful, nay, threatening look. We keep our heads down and snigger. Paula seems oblivious to it all, takes the coffee cup from me and sweeps out of the kitchen like a proud galleon behind Alan.

He turns on the bottom stair and hisses, 'I shall speak to you two later.'

And with that, he stomps up to the office to suffer his fate.

It's Saturday and Ollie returns ecstatically from the local football pitch where he has scored a critical goal in a friendly match. Angel has his arm draped over his shoulder as they slope up the drive, having walked home, covered in mud and with grubby knees.

'Hi Angel! Were you playing today too?'

'*Si*. We had a match but we lost.' He runs his tanned fingers through his unruly black hair and tuts. 'The other side were very mean.'

'Too bad. Well, come and have some orange juice.'

He pulls a face. 'Do you have Coca-Cola?'

'Why drink delicious, freshly squeezed orange juice from the field when you can drink coke, eh?'

'Exactly!' says Ollie energetically and they dive for the fridge. They sit chatting in Mallorcan discussing animatedly the two matches both have played. Ollie drains his glass and thumps it down on the table.

'We're going next door.'

'To see Helge and Wolfgang? But they've only just arrived from Berlin.'

He gets up. 'I just saw her and she's invited us for a game of football.'

The woman must be a saint. 'Alright but don't overstay your welcome.'

They disappear in a flash, leaving me to finish setting the table. Juana and Pep are joining us any minute for lunch and Alan has hinted that he and his accomplice will be unveiling their plans for the whisky shop. Juana and I have had many a furtive discussion by phone and neither of us are keen to encourage the notion further. The thought of those two running a shop every day and commuting constantly between here and the capital seems unrealistic to put it mildly. There are far better, less tying ways to earn a crust, me thinks. Alan bounces in from the back patio.

'They're here.'

I follow him into the courtyard where Pep is parking the car.

'Come in,' yells Alan. 'Time for a cava!'

In the kitchen Alan pours them a drink.

Pep raises his glass. 'Here's to spring! Are the boys back?'

'They're playing with our gorgeous German neighbour.'

Pep's eyes light up. 'Ah *sehr gut*. Maybe I should go and introduce myself. I speak excellent German.'

'Why am I not surprised?' I give him a stern look. 'And so modest too.'

I usher them into the sunny garden where Alan enthusiastically begins showing them his plants and vegetable patch.

From beyond the open French windows in the *entrada*, I can hear a loud croaking from the pond in the front garden. I tiptoe over to the door and peer out. Can it be true? I am overcome with joy to see that the *granots*, my frogs, are back for the spring. And what of Mr Toad? I lean over the pond and peer in. Silence. Perhaps I've scared them all away. There's a splash and a rasping sound.

It's him, large as life and fat as ever. Dreamily, I begin inventing a new script for us but maybe this time he could be a Hispanic toad?

'*Hola amiga!*' he rasps. 'You comma here often, *si?*'

No. That doesn't work. I like him better as a fast talking American. I start again.

'Hey, you look well!' I smile.

'You mean fat,' he says caustically.

'Who wants to be thin anyway?'

He blinks at me. 'How's tricks?'

'Oh everything's fine.'

'You seem different. Much less stressed out. The island suits you.'

'Thanks. That's good to hear.'

He suddenly plops into the water. Mystified I search for him. 'Was it something I said?'

'I don't know,' Pep says wryly, having wandered quietly up the path. 'Who were you talking to?'

Caught in the act. 'Oh just imagining I was talking to a friendly *calàpet*.'

He lights a *puro* and studies me. 'You know when I was ten I used to have a pet toad called Jorge.'

'Is that so?'

'He taught me a lot.'

I wonder where this is leading. 'Such as?'

'Well never to judge by appearances for one thing...' He is about to continue when the boys run into the courtyard. Helge appears behind them, waving. 'I'm exhausted but we had a good game. It's so lovely to be back. Anyway, enjoy your lunch... we'll catch up later.'

Pep's eyes bulge. 'Wait for a second,' he calls after her. Then he taps my arm. 'This charming lady, I have to meet.'

An hour later we are working our way through my homemade lemon tart and ice cream when Pep raises his glass again.

'Here's to new ventures!'

We all exchange glances. Alan has obviously been primed.

'Yes, maybe it's time to discuss our whisky enterprise to you all.'

Juana gives a crooked smile. 'We're all ears.'

The boys groan. 'Can we go and play?'

I nod and watch as they rush into the garden in some relief.

'Well we've found a shop site in Palma that looks quite promising.'

'Where?' I quiz.

'Around Jaume III.'

'That would cost a fortune!' shrieks Juana. 'How would you fund it?'

Pep sips at his white wine. 'One or two people might like to invest. We're having another meeting with the bank next week.'

I decide to bide my time. Once their plans are a little more concrete I shall seek advice privately from Terence Panton, a savvy Palma property agent I met some months back through one of the parents at Ollie's school.

'Just keep us in the loop,' I say brightly. 'If it's meant to be, I'm sure it will happen.'

The two men eye me quizzically while Juana throws me an inscrutable look.

'Anyone for coffee?' I ask.

There's the sound of foot steps on the gravel at the front and suddenly Helge appears, this time with Wolfgang. They pop their heads round the front door. 'Can we interrupt?'

'Of course, Helge. Come in, have some coffee,' says Alan in Spanish.

'Your Spanish is getting better. How are the lessons going?'

'Oh Paula and I commune regularly. It's the highlight of my week,' he says dryly.

They join us at the table whereupon Pep makes his introduction to Juana in German. Wolfgang gives him a broad smile. 'You speak excellent German.'

'*Ein bissien*,' he replies modestly giving me a wink.

'So, tell me about the whisky shop…' says Wolfgang.

I express surprise.

'I was just telling Helge about it earlier,' confesses Pep. 'In German, of course. She mentioned that Wolfgang enjoyed *puros* too…'

Juana gives him a swipe on the arm. 'You're incorrigible!'

'By the way,' says Wolfgang with a glint in his eye. 'Those wretched frogs of yours are making a terrible racket. Mind if I shoot them?'

He knows of my soft spot for small amphibians.

Helge gives him a push and tells him off.

'Well, if you want us to maintain good Anglo-German relations, you'd better not!'

'Only pulling your leg,' he says, punching my arm. 'Whatever happens, we don't want to start another war.'

It is the week of Setmana Santa, Holy Week, and here in our local town the occasion is celebrated with great gusto, not maybe on the scale of a city on the Spanish mainland but it's significant nonetheless. During the nights of Maundy Thursday to Easter Sunday, locals collect in the centre of the town to observe the lively nightly procession which with great ceremony forms a slow, faltering loop from the cathedral in the *plaça*, round the town and back again. We decide to meet Pep and Juana for a drink at Café Paris on the second night of the procession. Pep is at his happiest in Café Paris because it's where the heart of the townsfolk beats on a Saturday morning and where Mallorcan is heard above all other languages. In the tourist season, visitors sit at its tables under parasols on the front patio drinking orange juice and licking on ice creams, relishing the hustle and bustle going on around them in the square. But for the most part, locals and foreign residents huddle inside with newspapers, playing cards and iced coffees, enjoying the shade of the bar and familiar chatter in Mallorcan.

Juana gets up to greet us as we approach the table.

'Let's order some drinks and then find a good position for the procession.'

Pep shrugs. 'We could always sit here and watch it go by. What's the rush?'

'The children will want to get a good view. You and Alan can stay here with your beer.'

'Now you're talking,' adds Alan helpfully.

'Let's all stay. The kids can go and watch. We can see perfectly well from here.'

For once Juana seems to defer to him and we order our drinks. Within a few minutes José arrives with a tray of chilled wine, beer and cokes. Angel and Ollie drain their glasses and run into the busy square in anticipation of the big event. Pep touches my arm.

'You know the significance of Setmana Santa?'

'Somehow I think you're going to tell me anyway,' I say.

'Correct,' he yawns. 'We good Catholics celebrate the passion, death and resurrection of Jesus, what is known as the Paschal Mystery. You knew this?'

'I was brought up a Catholic.'

'That doesn't mean anything. So was I and do you see me in the procession?'

'I doubt you'd be invited.'

'Very true!' cackles Juana. 'Only pure of spirit can take part.'

There is suddenly great activity outside the church, a brass band strikes up and the procession slowly wends its way through the square. I notice that one of the leaders of the band is the son of the toy shop owner. To his left is Rafael's son, Cristian, a talented young singer. The *capella*, the priest, leads the way followed by a long line of spookily clad men who are covered from head to toe in triangular hoods and long flowing coloured robes.

'Here are the *caparutxes*. They look like the Klu Klux clan, non?' jokes Pep.

Juana swipes his arm. 'People might hear!'

'So what? Oh, yes, now behind them are all the *confradias*.'

'Who?' asks Alan.

'They are religious groups from different neighbourhoods who bring their own religious icons and statues along to the procession. You see each group has its own colours?'

I stand up to get a better view. 'Yes, and who are the women dressed all in black?'

'They are local women who wear antique traditional costumes and follow the procession. You can't see their faces because I suppose they are modest.'

'It's quite complicated,' says Alan.

'Not really. It follows the same pattern every year. Ah, here comes good old Jesus with his cross.'

Juana puffs out her cheeks and eyes her husband warily. 'If you're going to start being sarcastic…'

He ignores her and narrows his eyes. 'Hey, you know who it is this year? Poor Pedro. I bet he'd rather be having a drink.'

Juana tuts and turns to me. 'That's complete rubbish. He's a lovely man, our electrician in fact. He's so committed and devout.'

I watch this muscle-bound would-be Jesus carrying the hefty piece of timber representing the cross and wonder how he's going to manage the four mile circuit. He's only just started off on the procession but he's already huffing and puffing behind the women in black. A small man in a dark suit, one of the leaders of the *confradias*, is holding a sizeable painted porcelain effigy of the Madonna aloft. His aspect is serious as he marches to the music. I hope he doesn't trip.

Does this happen everywhere on the island?' I ask.

'Yes, in most towns and villages. How about another beer, Alan? You two want another *rosado?*'

The chilled rosé is rather good here and another glass wouldn't go amiss. Juana nods her head and chews thoughtfully on some nuts. 'I always like this event. It evokes so many memories from my childhood.'

'Juana came from a good Catholic family. Mine wasn't quite so religious. But despite that...' he trails off, momentarily distracted. 'Look, here come the boys.'

Ollie and Angel rush up to the table panting.

Angel touches his father's arm. 'They're going up the hill now. By the way, dad, Pedro whispered to me that once he's shot of the cross, he'll be around later for a beer.'

Juana's eyes flash. 'How can he even be thinking of such a thing when he's playing Jesus?'

'The priest volunteered him to do it. He didn't want to play Jesus at all!'

Pep taps his *puro* on the side of the ashtray and nudges a laughing Alan. 'As Juana says, Pedro is a very holy and committed man.'

Alan appears at the kitchen door with a trug brimming with *faves*, broad beans in Mallorcan.

'How's that for a nice crop?' he beams.

'Wonderful, but we'll never get through them all. Can I pop some in to Margalida?'

'Please do. I hope she'll be impressed with my efforts. I told her I was planting a crop.'

Catalina wipes her hands on her apron and comes over to inspect the trug. 'Hm, not bad for an Englishman.'

He gives her a frown. 'Scotsman, if you please!'

'You know, it might be nice if you gave some to Paula,' goads Catalina.

'Don't even think about it! I haven't forgiven either of you for your behaviour the other day. The wretched woman is nagging me to have extra lessons because of you two.'

'She obviously thinks you have potential,' continues Catalina.

'Money you mean!' he puffs.

'Oh, how cynical of you.' I pat him on the sleeve. 'I think you're her star pupil.'

The phone rings. Catalina slams the iron down and answers.

'Hello, can I help you?' She listens and then giggles. 'No, she isn't sun bathing. Not yet anyway. I get her now. One moment.'

She hands me the phone. I hear Greedy George's naughty chuckle on the line.

'Hi guv! Did I catch you with your feet up on the terrace?'

'Oh very funny.'

'I had a meeting with Rachel the other day and she said you wouldn't be back this month. You OK?'

I wonder if he's beginning to rumble me. The truth is that I'm enjoying life here and each trip back to London is becoming harder and harder.

'I'm fine, Just had a lot on with builders. I'm back in a couple of weeks.'

He drops his voice. 'Thing is, I've held talks with this American furniture company and they seem really keen to finance a Havana Leather in New York. I need to talk it through with you soon.'

I hope my voice doesn't have a hollow tone. 'That's great. Fantastic! Can you send me through anything to look at?'

He hesitates. 'No, it's at a sensitive stage. I'd rather wait till you're over. We can talk about the marketing aspect.'

'Sure. Let's do that.'

He prattles on about a new lap dancing club he's discovered and then rings off.

'What was that all about?' asks Alan.

'Oh, just the usual. George wants to catch up with me soon,' I lie.

I'm feeling uneasy about Havana Leather's possible expansion plans because I'm not sure I want to be sucked into a major project in the States and yet the financial rewards would be tempting. I've come to a crossroads sooner than I had thought and am seriously toying with the idea of changing direction, possibly starting a new venture in Mallorca. But what? I haven't discussed any of this with Alan yet. It's all a question of timing and first, I need to have a few concrete ideas.

'Dreamy woman!' exclaims Catalina. 'What are you thinking about?'

'The complexities of life.'

'Ah,' she says. 'What you need is *pastis de xocolata* and tea.' And together we sit and demolish half a cake and put the world to rights while an exasperated Alan regards us in disgust and strides off into the garden to continue his planting.

In a pizzeria in the local port, Catalina and I sit wedged between two ample bosomed, laughing *avis*, grandmothers, who in this group of Mallorcan women ranging from 25 to 80 odd years of age, are probably the most senior. It is the village school's annual mothers' night out and I have been invited because Ollie attended its playgroup during the Christmas holidays. I feel privileged since I am the only foreigner at the event and the ladies are keen to include me as one of the *chicas*, the girls. As a courtesy they switch from Mallorcan to Castilian Spanish when they attempt to share jokes with me and I am relieved that Catalina is at my side to steer me through the subtle nuances of the language. The waiters approach the table nervously, panicked by this scene of Bacchic revelry which has transformed demure village housewives into Beryl Cook blueprints. Drawing deeply on cigarettes and sipping at strong red wine, these women follow the tremulous movements of the young male waiters with eyes dancing with mock lust and amusement.

'He's got a good pair!' yells one.

'Ah, but can he use them?' shrieks another.

Much raucous laughter follows and then someone recounts a tale about her husband which has the entire table wobbling with mirth. I sit mesmerised by these women. They are fearless, gutsy and know their own minds. They are out to have a good night without husbands, children, chores or outstanding commitments and nothing is going to dampen their evening, not even the sharp chill that penetrates the restaurant.

'Order some more wine!' someone calls, when one of the *avis* complains about the draughts. Shrieks of laughter ensue when a doe-eyed youth in a white apron arrives at the table and can't work the bottle opener.

'Give it to me, little boy!' says a kindly hour-glass shaped senyora, a fag dangling from her crimson lip. Then with a stealthy thespian wink in our direction, she rasps at him, 'I'll name my price later.'

More hoots of laughter. He leaps back and allows her to work loose the cork. As it pops into life, everyone applauds. I watch with some sympathy as the young harassed man scampers back to the kitchens, one hand mopping at his forehead with a linen napkin.

At one o'clock in the morning, everyone pulls back their chairs, the bill has been split evenly between the ladies and it is time for the cackling Cinderellas to wend their way home. Tipsily we hug each other good night and spill out into the semi-lit street. The sky is embedded with tiny stars that quiver and blaze above us like miniature lighthouses and in the hazy moonlight, the restless sea glistens rich and viscous like black molasses, smothering the rocks with a briny glaze. Catalina and I stroll along the sea front, our shawls wrapped tightly around us, in search of a taxi. The cold sea spray stings our lips and the wind nags at our hair and clothes so that we are forced to huddle by a shop front until a sharp-eyed taxi driver dives towards us, with the car's front lights flashing. Once ensconced in the warm interior of the vehicle, we sweep the hair from our faces, rub our eyes and with fits of giggles recall anecdotes and jokes shared at dinner. We agree that it was indeed a great night out.

'You're lucky to have such good friends,' I say. 'They really are such a fun bunch.'

'Yes', says Catalina proudly, 'The best.'

FOURTEEN

LONDON: APRIL

Friday, en route to London

We are sitting three abreast in the plane, Ollie closest to the window, Alan in the aisle seat and me sweating it out like piggy in the middle. However this trip has so far been less fractious than some I've experienced, thanks to the presence of Ollie. Should a couple ever be in any doubt about whether to have a child, they should contemplate what future budget airline trips might be like without one. On a budget airline, as any shrewd parent knows, having a child in tow automatically entitles you to embark the plane ahead of fellow passengers. This means that you can arrive at the airport at a leisurely pace, and carry ticket number 210 or more and still get on the plane before the smart alec with ticket number one. This, of course, is hugely satisfying for us parents who are nervous fliers and is also a cunning way of punishing those childfree individuals who all their lives have probably enjoyed blissfully peaceful evenings undisturbed by peevish small creatures that go bump and burp in the night.

Before boarding the plane, I decide, for Ollie's sake, not to make a fuss. I have dutifully downed a double vodka and tonic at Palma airport and have selected a Bill Bryson book to turn my habitual terror into laughter. As we make ourselves comfortable in our seats, I feel someone touch my arm.

'Excuse me? Do you write for the *Majorca Daily Bulletin*?'

I'm a little nonplussed. An attractive woman in head-to-toe linen scrutinises me closely. 'I thought it was you! I read your column every week but I didn't agree with you last Saturday…'

'Oh dear, that's a pity,' I murmur, feeling under siege.

'Oh don't worry. I won't stop reading the column.'

'Excellent, thanks.' How gormless I sound as butterflies swoop and dive around my solar plexus. I really must conquer this flying phobia once and for all. She smiles and passes my seat whereupon I find myself facing none other than Victoria Duvall. 'Still haven't been up for supper yet,' she snaps as she dips her head towards me.

'But you haven't invited us…'

She frowns then roars with laughter. 'Ah, that must be the reason then! Ha ha!'

She shakes hands with Alan and manages to block the aisle for several minutes until she is moved on by a long suffering member of the cabin crew.

'Let's get together when we're all back…' she yells robustly down the plane.

'She's a character,' says Alan admiringly. 'Can't help but like her.'

As the plane rumbles along the tarmac, I sneak a look at Ollie and grasp his small hand.

'Oh no you don't,' he says brutally. 'I'm not scared so you shouldn't be. You've just got to grow up.'

He snatches his hand back and avidly peers out of the window as we speed along. Once the plane lifts into the air, he lets out a 'Cool!' and begins pointing out everything he can see from the air. I screw my eyes shut waiting until the plane is on an even keel.

'Open your eyes, Mummy. You're just being pathetic.'

I give him a sulky look. 'I'm just sleepy, that's all.'

He rolls his eyes. 'No you're not. Come on, let's play soldiers.'

Actually, engaging in battles of an Action Man kind with six-year-olds can be a good distraction for fretful fliers although I find stickers and colouring books more therapeutic.

A vodka and tonic later, I'm feeling fairly relaxed and skimming through a copy of *easyJet Inflight* magazine when a man taps me gently on the shoulder. It's James Grant, a member of the ECC. He proffers a hand to Alan over the seat and introduces himself.

'Back for work?' asks Alan.

'I'm writing a script for a new television cop drama. We've got a meeting to discuss the series. I'll be back tomorrow.'

'Interesting stuff. So how often do you commute?'

'About every two days.'

'What?' I hear myself shriek. 'I'd be a nervous wreck.'

He gives a laid-back shrug. 'It's just like catching a bus. Besides, it pays the bills.'

He wanders up the plane, his happy hunting ground, to catch up with another contact.

As we make our descent into Gatwick, I suddenly focus on the main reason for our return: the London Marathon, and with a touch of uneasiness, wonder whether despite the months of training, I will be able to complete the course and raise a packet for my chosen cause, a remote Amerindian tribe in Guyana. Then I think of the party I have arranged at our flat afterwards and the many friends and contacts I will see once again and suddenly running 26 miles doesn't seem quite such an ordeal after all.

Wednesday 7 p.m., One Aldwych

George and I have agreed to meet for a drink at a discreet hotel called One Aldwych which is conveniently close to one of his favourite hamburger joints. The sky is already dark and an icy wind blows as I walk quickly from Covent Garden tube, down Long Acre and turn right into Drury Lane in the direction of the Aldwych. The street is full of stressed individuals hurriedly heading for home, theatre land or the many bars and restaurants that suffocate this part of the West End. Traffic has snarled up and taxis are wedged nose to bumper on one side of the street, their red tail lights a blur in the sudden downpour of rain. I grapple around in my handbag and realise that once again I've forgotten to bring an umbrella with me. Fool, you're not in Mallorca now. I sprint across the road and a car brakes sharply and toots as it misses me by an inch. The driver gesticulates wildly from inside; an angry, distorted face through the pane which seems to sweat rain from every pore. I hurry on and finally see an oasis, the familiar floodlit exterior of the hotel. A doorman has already seen me crashing towards him, face obscured by the upturned collar of my coat, and gallantly rushes forward with an umbrella. I walk through the towering glass front doors and into the enormous lobby with its huge vaulted ceiling, arched windows and sleek white interior. Straight ahead but some way off, lies the bar and sitting at a small round table with a pile of papers in front of him is George.

I cross the vast expanse of white marble, stopping at a pillar to push back my wet hair. I am momentarily thrown by a gigantic sculpture of a naked man squeezed into a boat with enormous oars jutting out at right angles. The place is littered with cool, contemporary sculptures so that it has more of the feel of a gallery than a hotel. As I approach the table, George rises cumbersomely from his seat to greet me. He's not in stand-up comic routine today because he doesn't have an audience, and wears a serious expression.

'Let me get you a drink.'

A waiter appears on cue and George orders two glasses of champagne.

'So, still enjoying life in the sun?'

'Immensely.'

'No regrets?'

'Only that I'm not there enough.'

He fiddles with a small vase in the centre of the table.

'Old Campbell Gray's got good taste.'

'Yes, he has.' I look round the lobby momentarily reflecting on the owner's inimitable style which penetrates deep into the very pores of the building.

'Cards on the table, guv,' George bashes on. 'I've had three meetings with this American company and agreed to carve a deal. We'll be launching Havana Leather in the States in the next year.'

'Wow, this has all happened very quickly.'

'You know me, don't like to hang about. Point is, I need to know that you're on board to sort out the marketing and PR with me. I don't want you wobbling off.'

'I never wobble off.'

'Sorry, I didn't mean that. I just want to be sure that you're around to help. You know the brand inside out.'

'I'll be honest with you. I'm not sure how long I want to carry on working in London.'

His eyes pop wide open, just as the waiter places two fizzing glasses gently in front of us.

'Are you mad? What, you're just going to vegetate in the sun?'

'Of course not. I might want to think about some new venture.'

'That's all pie in the sky. See this as your new venture. Our expansion plan is going to be the best thing you've ever worked on.'

Hm. I'm not sure about that, but I'll humour him for now.

'Listen, I'll give it serious thought. I'm flattered you want me around.'

'Give me a break,' he puffs impatiently. 'OK think about it but don't mess me around.'

I raise my glass and he breaks into a grin.

'Oh, got something in my bag for you. A little good luck charm for the bloody marathon.'

He pulls out a small and chic turquoise box with a white ribbon. 'A gift from Tiffany?'

'Don't get carried away,' he moans.

I pull open the ribbon and lift the lid. White tissue paper flutters as I peer between the folds. A bejewelled designer silver lizard stares back at me, with tiny green eyes. It hangs from a chain.

'What can I say? It's beautiful.'

'I was worried you might get homesick while you were over,' he clinks my glass. 'Here's to the marathon.'

'And here's to Havana.'

He takes a long sip. 'Yep, so just make sure you're on board.'

Sunday 2 p.m., London Marathon day

The sky is streaked with sunlight as I arrive at my Pimlico flat, a marathon royal bedecked with a medal and draped in a warming silver foil sheet, the runner's equivalent of an ermine stole, courtesy of the marathon sponsors. I can hardly believe that I have just run for nearly four hours solidly around London, clocking up 26.2 miles, and have still managed to walk a further two miles back to my flat afterwards. It has been a spectacular day and my fellow participants and the crowds of well wishers who lined the route created such a cocktail of energy and goodwill that it was nigh impossible to fail. Now it's party time and Rachel is at the flat, playing host to family and friends who've popped by to share a celebratory glass. Alan is fumbling with the door key.

'It's funny but this all seems so alien now. It's just not home anymore.'

I nod. 'You're right, so why don't we sell up?'

He looks astonished. 'You mean it? What, pack up everything in the UK?'

'I'd have to do something else but why not? New challenges and all that.'

'Let's talk about this later,' he whispers.

At the bottom of the stairs, the door flies open and warm light from the flat pours into the corridor. Rachel welcomes us in and Prudence Braithwaite stalks out of the kitchen and places a cool glass of bubbly in my hand. There's the sound of loud laughter and champagne corks popping. The party appears to be in full flow without us.

'Come on,' she says robustly, grabbing my left arm and pulling me towards the living room. 'Everyone's waiting to welcome the champ.'

Michael Roselock comes over to greet me and is keen to inspect the medal. 'Not very good quality', he says, inspecting it carefully. Prudence laughs. 'Really, it's just a memento, you silly sausage.'

I'm amused at this term of endearment. She catches my expression and when I've done my round of greetings with friends and family, she beckons me over.

'I wanted to let you know,' she says shyly, 'that Michael and I are going to get married. Nothing extravagant you understand. A small affair in Sevenoaks next month.'

'That's fantastic!'

'Well, we're pleased,' she says, trying to hide her pleasure.

Ed comes over. 'By the way Scatters, I've decided to visit you in Mallorca. I really mean it. This June.'

'Well book your flights before you bottle out.'

He sighs heavily. 'Mid June is best for me. I'll e-mail you with dates.'

There's loud banging at the front door and a moment later Alan appears with George in tow, a glass of champagne in his hand. He swans into the room, gives me a thump on the back and goes over to talk to Michael. My mobile rings and I rush into the corridor to escape the din.

'Did you make it?' Catalina is yelling excitedly into the receiver.

'How nice that you called. I did it.'

'Congratulations. I will let Ramon and everyone know.'

George is yelling for me. 'Go,' she says. 'Enjoy your party. We'll see you home soon.'

I switch off the mobile as George bounds towards me forcing me back into the living room. He breaks into a reptilian smile and tells everyone to charge their glasses.

'A toast to guv,' he says, raising his own flamboyantly in the air before adding with a vulgar cackle, 'and to the Queen and all who sail in her!'

A week later, Thursday 8.30 p.m., en route to Mallorca

I'm sitting in the aisle seat of row one because, quite simply, my preferred aisle seat of row two is occupied. My copy of *The Fearless Flier's Handbook* is open on my lap and I have only three pages left to read. Passengers are filing by, and once or twice someone smiles at me and I recognise them as a fellow commuter. Spike, one of my ECC pals, passes my seat and we share a few words. It's a comforting moment. Just as I dip back into my book, one of the air hostesses approaches me and squats down conspiratorially at my feet.

'I have a very nervous flier coming on the plane. Since we recognise you as a regular commuter, would you mind if we put him next to you?'

Him. Can there be neurotic male fliers? I thought Ed was a one off. I am about to tell her that I'm the last person on the plane he should sit next to but find myself curiously tongue-tied.

'So is it OK with you if he goes by the window?'

'Yes, of course,' I hear myself saying calmly. Have I lost my mind? Between us we could bring down the plane. A few minutes later she guides a tall, ashen faced man, somewhere in his thirties, towards me. He gives a half-hearted greeting then ducks his head to avoid the overhead locker and slips into the window seat. He hunches up and peers out at the darkening sky beyond. I notice he's biting the inside of his mouth by the little puckers forming at the sides of his lips. The air hostess stands at the front of the plane like a teacher, willing me to act. I feel like the form prefect with a new school recruit.

'It still seems like a nice day out there,' I say lamely.

He turns to face me with terror in his eyes. 'Why shouldn't it be nice? Is there supposed to be bad weather?'

I can tell this is going to be a fun flight. 'No, not at all.'

He breathes deeply. 'I don't like flying.'

You don't say?

'Oh really? I'd never have guessed.'

He gives a snort of laughter. 'I don't believe you.'

The door is now closed and the air hostess is speaking on the intercom to the cabin crew at the back of the plane. She takes her seat and clips the belt shut. He strains to see her when the lights are dimmed.

'She's still there,' I say, 'If she heads for the exit, I'll let you know.'

He is horrified. 'That's not funny,' he says.

'No, it wouldn't be,' I reply.

He leans back in his seat, teeth clenched, hands gripping the armrests. God, is this what I look like normally?

'Are you familiar with the bings and bongs?' I ask casually.

283

The plane is starting to gather speed.

'What?' he says in panic.

'There's a series of bings and bongs. If you're a nervous flier, it helps to identify them.'

'What comes first?'

Chicken or egg?

'Well, normally there's a BING about now.'

He stares hard at me. BING.

'See?'

'What next?'

The plane has raced up into the air and my head lolls back against the seat with the force. My companion puts his head in his hands.

'Right, the BONG BONG is coming up soon.'

He lifts his head, and dares to look at me but I can tell by his panicked expression that he's not sure what to fear most, the lunatic at his side or the flight itself. Nevertheless, he listens carefully. Sure enough there's a BONG BONG. My companion sits frozen in his seat, ever attentive.

'Now wait for the final BING in a moment,' I say cheerfully.

It comes a minute later. The air hostess unclips her seat belt and the lights go on.

'What's happening?' he gasps.

'She's getting out of her seat.'

The sheer stupidity of the questions we nervous fliers ask, never ceases to amaze me.

'What now?' says the wreck next to me.

'Hopefully we can order a drink.'

He sighs deeply and runs a shaky hand over his face. 'I used to be as relaxed as you until I was on a plane that had engine failure.'

'What happened?'

'We had to return to the airport. It was terrifying.'

'Did everyone survive?'

'Miraculously, yes.'

'That's the point then.'

The drinks trolley arrives and I order a vodka and tonic. 'What would you like? My treat.'

He opts for a red wine and thanking me, tells me his name is Mike and that he is coming over to Mallorca for a job interview with a hotel group.

'I'm on the final shortlist, but if I get the job, I'll have to commute back and forth each month,' he says dejectedly. 'If I tell them I'm a nervous flier, I won't stand a chance.'

'Do you really want the job?'

'Yes.'

'Well, don't tell them anything. If I can commute each month, so can you.'

'But you can't possibly understand,' he pleads.

'Hey, listen,' I whisper, 'I'm going to give you a little gift because I'm about to graduate.'

'From what?'

'The Fearless Fliers Club.'

I hand him the book. He opens it in surprise and gawps at me.

I slap my plastic glass against his. 'Here's to happy landings.'

FIFTEEN

ORANGE GRIND

The two men are sitting in the kitchen drinking dark coffee shots with whisky. Catalina observes them critically despite their having dutifully deposited their muddy boots and gardening tools outside the back door. Alan licks his lips and salutes Catalina's father in Spanish.

'Well, that should be it for another year,' he says contentedly, warming his hands on the hot mug.

'*Si, si,*' nods Paco, his weathered face breaking into a smile. 'The oranges should grow well now but you need to put fertilizer down.'

'Of course. I'll get some in the town later.' Alan is reverential to this shaman of the soil, who can coax dry earth to breathe new life with just the touch of his hands.

'So,' says Catalina, 'Have you pruned every tree?'

'More or less,' enthuses Alan. 'I'll just have to do a little more trimming later. Your father has done a fantastic job in the field. You won't recognise the trees.'

She looks at them both and tuts loudly. 'OK then, maybe you deserve your whisky.'

I walk into the kitchen, my feet muffled in sheepskin slippers bought from the local market.

'Ah!' cries Paco, 'Here comes the senyora.'

I bend down to kiss his cheeks. 'Sorry, I didn't hear you come in. I've been up in the office sorting out e-mails.'

'Better to be in the kitchen sorting out hungry stomachs,' he says with a chummy wink at Alan.

'Oh, but that's my relaxation at the end of the working day,' I say warningly.

'Your husband has been telling me about his idea to start a whisky business,' Paco says. 'But you know, I think he'd be better doing garden design. He's very good.'

I shoot a look at Alan, impressed with Paco that he's speaking his mind. I have been keen to encourage Alan's horticultural leanings rather than his and Pep's madcap whisky shop caper. During our last two years in London, Alan had masterfully juggled consultancy work with studying for a landscape gardening diploma, and for the last six months, has been quietly cementing his plans down in his garden *abajo*. Well, at least I think that's what he's been doing in between *puro* smoking and dreaming about whisky shops with Pep.

'What do you think?' I say archly.

'I'm exploring a few things at the moment,' Alan rejoins with a secretive smile.

'I think the gardening idea's got huge potential as long as you get on with it,' I say with meaning.

Paco takes this as a quite unintended hint for him to leave and slaps his mug down on the table. 'OK. I must go. Work to be done.'

Alan lets out a wail of disappointment like a child at a birthday party watching the magician perform his last trick. 'You can't go yet! Go on, have another drink.'

Paco casts a furtive glance at his daughter who raises her eyebrows sternly and continues to scrub at the interior of the oven.

'Oh, well, maybe one for the road,' he says, nudging Alan.

Despite his years, Paco is as strong and wiry as a man half his age and has a handsome profile. Of the generation when women were manacled to the kitchen and the children, he manages with disarming charm to hark back nostalgically to the old days while fervently supporting the notion of young women's emancipation as far as his daughter is concerned. I wonder what he really thinks.

I leave them discussing the merits of manure over compost, and walk out to the pond. The air is warm now and the sun penetrates a fallen mass of mimosa flowers floating on the surface casting golden light into the watery depths. I bend over the edge and with delight see huge drifting bubbles of frogspawn. Tiny fish flit around the rocks and the water quivers and throbs with the excited exertion of the many insects and hidden creatures going about their frenzied business in minute movements between plants, water lilies and deep fissures in the rocks. The frogs have withdrawn to their waterside cave and my companionable toad is nowhere to be seen. I can only surmise that he's off on important business of an amphibian kind. I linger for a moment by the water's edge and with some irritation rise when I hear the phone bleating plaintively in the kitchen. Is nothing sacred?

This is as close as Mallorca gets to London. Palma, Mallorca's capital. The traffic is stationary, exhausts are panting heavily in the midday sun and the horns have already started to blast. Smugly, for I am on foot, I skip along the cobbled pavement and past the town hall en route to lunch at La Cuchara, a favourite haunt, with Jason Moore. I'm having a day in town and for once I've abandoned jeans and am wearing city garb. It still feels strange clopping along in dressy shoes and a fine wool suit, for they are dressing up clothes normally strictly reserved for London. I pass the *sobrassada* sausage shop, a small cave of a place whose large interior belies its minute frontage. It is impossible to resist the sweet aroma of fat juicy tomatoes piled up by the front door and peering into the depths of the shop at the plump, red garlicky sausages and threaded red and yellow chilli peppers hanging from the roof's wooden beams.

'Can I help you, senyora?' enquires the cheery shopkeeper rather primly until peering into my face she quickly realises that I am a regular visitor and a gourmand to boot. 'Ah! I recognise you now. What's happened? Look how chic you are today.'

She is entitled to express incredulity since I am usually attired in clothes more suited to the countryside. This is a curious phenomenon since I am most particular about my wardrobe when in London. Perhaps it's just that I am happily always in a state of dressing down while in Mallorca. I explain to her that I'm on my way to a restaurant but that a small package of garlic sausage might just squeeze in to my handbag. She gives a throaty laugh and begins slicing me some rich tomato chorizo.

Out in the street I breeze along until a deep rumbling sounds from above and a spot of rain kisses my hand. Have I brought an umbrella? Well of course not. This is Mallorca in April, for heavens sake. The sky is suddenly in an ugly mood, the clouds swarm together in shades of grey, thunder growls and water reigns down. I leap off the pavement and into a linen shop just as the electricity and street lights die. Torrents of rainwater now spew from the drains forming two rivulets that gush down both sides of the street. The senyora behind the counter welcomes me in and shakes her head at the sudden inclement shower. A few minutes later three clucking women with shopping baskets burst into the shop, followed shortly by a middle-aged business man. We are now a party of damp individuals not in the slightest bit interested in purchasing linen tablecloths or pillowcases. I feel somewhat guilty about clogging up this hospitable lady's shop but when I make a move towards the door, she shoos me back in with a frown and points to the torrential rain hitting the narrow street outside. I smile weakly and huddle with the others. Soon jokes break out and the waggish businessman suggests we wear pillowcases as hats. The owner takes a frilly one from the window and places it on his head. This causes general merriment all round. Two ladies from the flamenco-wear shop opposite watch what's going on from their window and in response, take a giant mantilla from a showcase and drape it over their heads and begin dancing. Our lady giggles, opens the door and yells out 'Olé', while a young man from the chemist shop next-door gallantly pops by with a paraffin light for our gloomy interior.

'We should all be dancing in the street!' announces our senyora, flinging open the front door again. There's a general titter.

'Or perhaps singing in the rain?' I suggest.

She squeezes my arm. 'I like that tune. You are English, *si?* Sing us the song.'

I try and imagine this scene unfolding in Mayfair knowing that in reality it never could. Everyone turns to me.

'Well come on!' shouts the businessman good-naturedly stepping into the rain splattered street. 'What are you waiting for?'

My Spanish isn't proficient enough to explain that I am far too embarrassed to start singing in front of a bunch of strangers in a linen shop, so in small voice I begin humming the tune.

'What about the words?' says the robust senyora.

'Louder,' chirps one of the matronly women.

'OK, OK...' I say quietly.

And that was how I spent the next ten minutes prior to arriving at my luncheon appointment-singing and dancing in a rainy street with a bunch of Mallorcan shopkeepers, a chemist, a businessman and three housewives. Would I ever have done this back in England? In a nutshell no, but now I'm not so sure. The spontaneity of life here is addictive and compelling, more so because gregarious behaviour is positively encouraged. So could this scene be reciprocated in London perhaps? With a little artful persuasion I am sure I could have half of Bond Street on its feet, doing the conga. On second thoughts...

It's still spitting outside but the sun is out and as I walk down Passeig Mallorca towards La Cuchara, I can just glimpse the port and a pinch of turquoise sea. I arrive at my destination in good spirits albeit a bit damp, and carrying a pillowcase above my head. The maître d' leads me to a table. Jason eyes me quizzically from his seat and, as if needing fortification, takes a sip of beer.

'Novel umbrella,' he says, indicating the pillowcase with his eyebrows.

I squeeze it into my handbag where the smell of garlic sausage has become overwhelming.

'Yes, it's the latest trend,' I reply, pecking him on the cheek, 'A gift from a shopkeeper for services rendered.'

He smirks, 'Oh yes?'

'For entertaining the troops.' I whisper.

'I don't think I want to know.'

'Best not.'

Jason narrows his eyes and tilting his head back a touch, surveys me with wry suspicion. He says nothing. A waiter bustles over and offers me an aperitif. And why not? A Martini *rojo* on the rocks would do nicely. Approvingly, the man saunters off, arriving moments later with a fat glass crammed with ice and a slice of lemon over which he pours a lake of dark red liquor from a full bottle. He gives a little bow, smiles and passes me a menu. I peer round the restaurant at the tables full of relaxed looking diners clutching menus like prayer books. Several share jokes with the waiters as they discuss the menu *del dia* and the extensive wine list. For most Mallorcans a menu holds the same thrill as an action-packed blockbuster and small talk and niceties are put aside until the food has been selected with great care. Wine lists are treated with equal reverence and a lively debate about the merits of a particular *vin negre* can absorb much of the meal. In Mallorca, business can always wait. The tables are filling up fast and at intervals a gust of cool air from the front door heralds the arrival of more diners. All are welcomed graciously on arrival by the avuncular maître d'. There's no ticking of names on lists in here. Mallorcan restaurateurs know their customers by sight.

Moments later a pile of roughly hewn brown bread is placed in front of us on the red gingham tablecloth, together with a bowl of black olives, thick golden olive oil and a plate of *ramellets*, the local Mallorcan tomatoes, which are often used to make *pa amb oli*. Jason chews on a piece of bread and gives me a round up of the day's news. Local Mallorcan elections are looming and the political mud-slinging season has officially begun, promising to provide endless column inches for a newspaper like his. I lean back in my chair and yawn.

'It doesn't matter where you are, you can't escape politics.'

Jason sniggers. 'On well, it'll be the celeb season soon. That'll liven things up a bit out here.'

Mallorca has its celebrity season from June to August when shoals of European household names (most unknown to me) arrive at the airport or by luxury yacht and turn a blissfully peaceful island into a living copy of *Hello!* magazine.

'I don't recognise half the supposed celebs that come out here,' I say sniffily.

'Yes, well if you bothered to watch some British soaps, you might,' he scoffs. Fair criticism. Since living here I rarely glimpse television and return to London each month like Rip Van Winkle, rising from a blissful slumber, disorientated and bemused by the volume of tittle-tattle in the media and the public's desperate desire to exist vicariously through celebrities' lives. Surely there has to be more to life than that?

A waiter bounds over and takes our order – fresh calamari, chargrilled artichokes and rosemary-infused lamb.

Jason suddenly raises his glass. 'Heavens, I nearly forgot! Well done on the marathon. That was a result. Under four hours, right?'

'Three hours and forty eight minutes of hell but it was worth it for the party afterwards and hopefully I'll have raised several thousand pounds for charity.'

'Great stuff. You're so lucky,' he muses, 'Living here and flitting back to London. You really have got the best of both worlds, haven't you?'

'Perhaps.' I drain my glass and put it down gently in front of me. I rarely stop to think about it but Jason's absolutely right of course. Ostensibly, island hopping each month holds many attractions but is that what I really want? Aye, there's the rub.

I'm rushing along the Borne in Palma to the estate agency, Engel and Volkers. My contact there, Terence, has offered to give me some off the record property advice about Pep and Alan's whisky venture. He beams as I walk in to his white pristine offices. 'Come, let's have a quick catch up.'

He seems amused at the thought of Alan opening a shop. 'It's not cheap on Jaume III,' he says. 'And can you imagine these two semi-retired guys driving from the mountains each day to open up shop?'

No, in a simple word.

'I think he'd be better following the garden consultancy idea you mentioned.'

Join the club. 'Could you maybe have a word with them?'

'Sure. Why don't I invite them in and we can chew the bit.'

My mobile chirrups. It's Alan. He's just taken Ollie for his weekly treat to an English bookshop near his school. Having recently discovered that there are two British bookshops on the island, it has become a ritual to visit the Universal Bookshop on a Tuesday and the Bookworm when we're ever in town on a Saturday. Now the boys are en route to pick me up from Cortès Inglès, the large department store, a stone's throw from the Borne.

I get up to leave, having only a few minutes to jog up the road to our appointed meeting place. Terence scratches his chin thoughtfully. 'Joking apart, have you ever thought about the holiday rentals business? Very profitable if you buy the right properties. I could help you.' Ever the good salesman.

I laugh. 'A really interesting idea but first we need to knock the whisky shop on the head and decide what we're doing about our London flat.'

'Don't worry,' he says tranquilly. 'It'll all come together. You'll see.'

You never know, he could be right.

SIXTEEN

STONE WALLING

Alan orders me an espresso while I finish a conversation with Ed. I ring off and plop the mobile back in my handbag and glance round at the other tables. As usual Café Paris is full of the usual suspects. Gaspar the paper delivery man is grinning at me from the other side of the bar and Tolo is finishing a *cortado*, a small strong coffee laced with milk, while he catches up with the news. He flicks his newspaper down and gives us a smile from across the room.

I glance at Alan. 'Good news! Ed's booked his easyJet flight and he's arriving mid June.'

'He might be in time to christen the pool with us,' laughs Alan. 'By the way, I've given the go ahead to Stefan to get on with it. Should take them about two months to remove the soil and get building.'

I'm ecstatic. 'But what about the cost?'

He waves his hand in the air. 'We'll just have to tighten our belts for a while.' He lights up a cigar but I'm too pleased about the pool to chastise him. 'So, is Ed alright about flying?'

'No, but we'll deal with that nearer the time.'

'Still with Julia, the nurse?'

'Apparently so. I can hardly believe it.'

He yawns and looks at his watch. 'It's eleven o'clock. Do you want me to drop you back at the house?' His eyes rest on my two bulging baskets beneath the table.

'No, the walk will do me good. Besides, I don't want you to be late for your lesson with Paula.'

Alan is quiet for a second then he sighs. 'Well, I might as well tell you. I've finally decided against the whisky shop idea. Actually Pep and I have both been getting cold feet about the cost and time involved.'

I nearly choke on my coffee. 'What?'

'It's just that I had a surprise call from Terence the other day and he gave me a lot of food for thought about the property market. I still think it's a great idea but there are other things we could do.'

Good old Terence. I owe him one. 'Such as?'

'Well, I've talked to Pep about working on a landscape design business with me and we could think about the holiday rental business. It's very profitable apparently.'

I try to feign surprise. 'We should do a bit of investigation then.'

He takes a bite of his croissant. 'You and Juana always hated our whisky shop scheme anyway.'

'Well we worried that you and Pep would down most of the product before it actually hit the shelves.'

'As if!' he cries. 'So have you thought any more about London? I mean maybe we really should sell the flat and move on.'

I decide now is the time to discuss George's expansion plans for Havana Leather. Alan listens intently and then draws a *puro* out from his pocket.

'Why on earth didn't you tell me about this before?'

'I don't know, I thought you'd tell me I'd be mad not to accept.'

'You're wrong. It might well be lucrative but is that what you want to do?'

'I don't think so. But what about the money?'

He sits back in his chair. 'How much money do we really need? We hardly live in the fast lane. Don't let that cloud your vision.'

His mobile rings. '*Vale, vale. Me voy!*'

He says he's on his way so it has to be Paula calling.

'I've got to run. Paula's waiting for me at her house. After that, Pep and I are off to view some nurseries and garden centres.'

So, they're on to the next venture. Plan B.

'Listen, we don't need London anymore. Don't make money the excuse for not letting go.' He ruffles my hair, drops some coins on a plate and strides off to meet his accomplice in crime.

As I turn wearily into the stony track leading up to our *finca*, I pause for a moment outside old Margalida's house to readjust the two heavy baskets of vegetables I am carrying. Like a merciless sniper stalking his victim, the sun has kept pace with me from the town, its burning rays trained unflinchingly on my middle back with the precision of a laser beam. Ahead of me, crickets are leaping about the path and a mass of butterflies flitter past, their golden wings iridescent as they catch the light of the sun. It seems that summer has at last arrived in Mallorca.

Placing the bags down against Margalida's rocky wall that is ablaze with scarlet bougainvillea, I examine my red and swollen hands and wonder why I stubbornly chose to walk rather than drive to the market. The reason, of course, is that I love the leisurely walk to and from my small market town when I have the opportunity to meet friends and neighbours along the way to catch up on gossip of a rural kind. Everyone, from the local garage attendant and his family to the buxom matron who polishes the local church brass, greet me like a long lost friend even though in reality they may have exchanged news with me as recently as the night before. Neither am I fobbed off with a brisk *Hola!* No. People here like to talk and there are never any constraints on time.

When foreigners first arrive in Mallorca, they are often appalled at the atrocious time keeping of the islanders and cannot understand how they can be an hour or more adrift for meetings or social events. The simple reason for this is that everything is done in a spontaneous manner and it is very easy to be distracted on the way to an engagement. It might be that a neighbour suddenly invites you to view his new orange tree irrigation system, another to partake of a glass of *herbes* liqueur with him in the local square, or a friend pops by with a newborn baby over which you coo dutifully for some considerable time. In a similar vein to the aberration suffered by Little Red Riding Hood en route to her grandmother's house, there are more than a hundred respectable excuses for being side-tracked and why you may indeed turn up shockingly late for a preordained appointment. However, when you do eventually arrive, the best approach is to act cheerfully and in a relaxed manner so that your host is made to feel that it is he or she who has confused the time and that you are innocent of any social blunder. In those circumstances where you play host yourself, it is best to avoid unnecessary angst and heart palpitations by setting the time of your appointment or function at least one hour ahead of the time you would like to greet your guests. That way, everyone can relax.

I pick up my bags and am about to continue along the path when there's a faint twitch of a lace curtain and suddenly Margalida is opening her front door and hobbling out on to the steps. She holds one hand over her eyes and squints at me while the other hand searches out her wrought-iron grab rail. Today her short white hair is uncombed with small clumps rising up from her head in soft meringue peaks. I give her a cheerful '*Hola*' but she eyes me with suspicion and grasping her wooden stick perched against the bottom rail, approaches me haughtily, one firm step at a time, like an aged Queen Victoria, swathed in black, and disdainful. I almost feel I should bow. When she is a gnat's breath from my face, she breaks into a smile.

'Ah, it's you, senyora! How young you look! I didn't recognise you.'

I put an arm gently round her shoulders. 'Margalida! Where are your glasses?'

She waves her stick impatiently in the air. 'Pah! What's the point of glasses when you're half blind?'

There's tooting at the front of the house and a young man with raven black hair emerges from the passenger seat of a dusty red car with a young toddler in his arms. Who on earth is this? I stand on the porch smiling inanely without the faintest clue who he is. To my relief the driver of the vehicle bustles out and I see that it is Rosa, the local curtain maker. She waves and ducks into the back of the car to retrieve something. Her companion strolls towards me, smothering the child with kisses and smiling broadly. He introduces himself as Rosa's son. He explains that he is here to assist her with hanging our curtains. Our curtains? Somewhere in my head a distant bell is ringing, a memory of an order placed some many months ago.

'*Hola!*' wheezes Rosa, her ample bust rising and falling like the giant swell of a wave as she hauls two bulky bags on to the porch. 'I finish the curtains. You are pleased, yes? Have you met my son and Gabriela, my granddaughter?'

'Yes, indeed. Well, what a surprise! It seems ages ago that you first came to measure our curtains.'

She is offended and rears backwards like a defensive cobra ready to strike. '*Home!* Is only eight months!'

I nod my head quickly and attempt to pacify her. Indeed, what is eight months between friends? In Mallorca everything takes time and soon the pain and irritation of not having what you want when you want it subsides into a form of apathy and then complete nonchalance. It is only when guests visit and comment innocently on a missing tile on the patio, a gaping hole under a rug, a mass of electric wires lying abandoned under a sofa or a leak under the sink that you hazily recall the time when you requested these things to be fixed. In London I would be snarling threats down the phone receiver of a hapless plumber or builder but in Mallorca I have learned the art of patience. There is a good chance that one day the errant ironmonger, electrician, phone engineer, or curtain maker will arrive quite out of the blue and when least expected, rekindling faith in the Mallorcan term *poc a poc*, little by little. All good things come to those who wait. So, Rosa, the curtain lady, follows me into the house while her son deposits little Gabriela on the floor of our *entrada* and bounds outside to the boiler room to find the stepladder. An hour later, thick cream linen curtains hang above the French doors in both kitchen and *entrada* and buttermilk cushions adorn the kitchen chairs. The introduction of textiles really does have a startling effect on the appearance of our *finca* and the unexpected pleasure I feel at having achieved this small step towards domestic rural bliss is immeasurable. The phone rings and I leave Rosa and her son scrabbling around on the kitchen floor playing with his toddler. It is Rachel.

'I sent you a couple of press releases this morning. It's pretty urgent. Could you check them?'

'Ah, of course. Sorry Rachel. I'm just having some curtains fitted so I'm a little distracted.'

She strikes a cautious tone. 'Are you serious?'

'Why ever not?'

'Never mind. Look, I've got a stack of meetings today so if you could e-mail any corrections through later, that would be great. By the way, Michael Roselock's a dark horse. He's getting married tomorrow to guess who?'

'Oh that's a tough call. Let me think...'

'Did you know?' she asks.

Gabriela has crawled over with a big grin on her face and is pulling at the laces on my docksiders. 'I had a small inkling. Just because I live in the sticks doesn't mean I'm out of the loop.'

'You could have told me,' she sounds aggrieved.

'It slipped my mind Rachel. You know what I'm like these days?'

'I'll let you off this time. By the way, can you give George a call. He rang this morning but won't tell me what it's about.'

Thinking of George makes me feel edgy. I have been stalling him. Avoiding his calls. Avoiding the big issue. Avoiding simply saying, NO. What am I afraid of? Finally severing the chord with London? Rachel's voice on the end of the line pulls me back to reality.

'Well, must dash. Speak to you later.'

I turn round and smile at Rosa. She and her son have been waiting patiently for me to end my call. Once again, Rosa's son is holding Gabriela and showering her with kisses because in Mallorca it is cool for men to show public affection for their children and most enjoy any excuse to parade their offspring especially on market days.

'We go now,' says Rosa, much appeased now that the curtains are up and the senyora of the house is overcome with gratitude. 'But first I have something for you.'

She disappears to her car and returns with a small, crimson silk cushion infused with local herbs. 'A little house warming gift,' she says without ceremony. The strong smell of rosemary and lavender pervades the sunny *entrada*, and as I stand there breathing it in, I am thankful that the little cushion bears not the slightest resemblance to a lizard.

Catalina walks into the kitchen from the back garden carrying a huge trug full of *faves*, broad beans, and a healthy pile of baby potatoes, their skins caked in rich red soil. She thumps the trug down by the sink and washes the mud from her hands.

'It's very hot out there now,' she says, slightly short of breath. 'The Moro is still out there picking *faves*.'

I rise from the kitchen table and fetch her some cold water from the fridge. 'Well I hope he doesn't pick too many or we'll have beans coming out of our ears. I think you've picked more than enough there.'

She nods. 'Yes, but he is worried the builders will accidentally drive over the vegetable patch with their machines.'

'Well they'd have to be blind to miss it.'

We both laugh. Catalina, opens the back door to let in the fresh air and stalks out to talk to the builders. She returns with a look of excitement on her face.

'My brother thinks the pool may be finished in June.'

In truth, we haven't got the money for such an extravagance. Alan's preference had always been to buy a rotavator, a powered soil-tilling machine, which he felt was a much more practical purchase and one which wouldn't cost us dearly. However, I impressed on him that the dubious pleasure of using a rotavator under a scorching sun could never replace the delights of swimming in a cool pool so, begrudgingly, he acquiesced.

'When they finish cementing the hole, we wait some weeks for it to dry and soon the men will tile it,' continues Catalina. 'Then we have big party to celebrate.'

Once the pool is finished, the builders will down tools and leave for the summer and will not be returning until at some stage in the future we have funds enough to embark on phase two of our building work which might see patios and paths being laid in the gardens, the courtyard tiled and a front gate fitted. Until that time, we will be grateful for what we have: heating, running water and a roof over our heads.

I leave Catalina ironing sheets in the kitchen and slip out to the pond by the courtyard. Peering into the dark water I spot the first of our baby frogs swimming in and out of the rocks. Somehow, observing the evolution of tadpole to fully formed frog in my own front yard has proven far more captivating than I ever recall it being so during my school biology days. I am concerned that our resident toad is not in evidence but comfort myself that he'll be back soon. There's the sound of heavy footsteps in the yard and Rafael appears in running shorts and a T-shirt. He strides over to me, a big smile on his face.

'Ah, there you are! I have invitation.'

I step forward to greet him and take the card he proffers.

'My son Cristian has First Communion. You must come.'

I am touched that he should include us at such a family event. 'We'd love to. When is it?'

'Saturday. First there is church and then dinner. You meet all my family.'

I promise that Alan and I will attend. 'Is the church easy to find?'

'*Si, si,* everyone knows it. It's two minutes from town. Ask anyone.'

I watch Rafael cheerfully jog up the track for his morning run while I walk back into the house. I have a pile of e-mails and work to do on my desk but am being seduced by a warm sun and a mountain view so mesmerising that I can hardly tear my eyes from it. It seems a criminal offence to be hunched up over my computer in the house when I could be gainfully employed sitting on a rock and contemplating life and the universe. Catalina beckons to me when I enter the kitchen but first, like the villain in a pantomime, she places a finger to her lips and steps out of the kitchen door, peering exaggeratedly this way and that in a thoroughly farcical manner.

'What on earth are you doing?' I ask.

'The Moro was just here. I just wanted to make sure he was back down in the field. We need to discuss his birthday party.'

Alan's forthcoming birthday is a subject of much discussion amongst our local friends. Although still a month away, the restaurant, Cas Marroig, has been booked, the wine list scrutinised by Pep, connoisseur of all things, and the invitations to twenty friends have been sent. Catalina and I have already held surreptitious meetings with Pau, the maître d', checking out the private room, inspecting the veranda, and mulling over appropriate menus. The young, and much revered, chef has joined us at these clandestine think tanks and has already solemnly declared that the birthday cake should be on a gardening theme. Meanwhile, Alan suspects nothing and is cheerfully anticipating a quiet dinner à deux on his birthday at Cas Marroig.

'We must choose the menu soon,' hisses Catalina as if Alan may burst into the kitchen at any given moment. 'You think lamb is good or not?' she persists.

I realise that my hesitancy about the main course is probably causing both Catalina and the maître d' sleepless nights so I decide that the situation must be resolved now.

'Let's go for the lamb and start with the roast artichokes and Serrano dish as planned.'

'And the fish course?'

'Local catch of the day. Whatever Pau recommends.'

'Good. Now we need to think about flowers and what to wear. I will need to go on a *règim*.'

'A diet? Don't be silly! No sane Mallorcan would diet.'

She shrugs. 'Well, maybe I have just one croissant in the morning for the next few weeks otherwise I cannot fit my dress.'

The door flies open and in steps Alan holding a trug brimming with beans. He catches the expression on my face and blurts out quickly, 'A few beans for your mother, Catalina.'

Offering beans to Catalina's mother is like carrying coals to Newcastle but Catalina has the good grace to hide her smirk and show gratitude. 'Well, my mother has all the family coming for dinner tomorrow night so she can make a very big bean soup. Would you like to join us?'

The thought of yet more beans, having lived on them for the last two weeks, fills me with dread.

'*Quina llàstima!*' What a shame, I exclaim. 'We have friends over tomorrow night.'

'*No problema*,' says Catalina playfully, 'I'll make sure we keep some soup back for you and I'll bring it over on Thursday morning.'

I narrow my eyes and give her a knowing look.

'Unless of course,' she says with a wink in my direction, 'we cannot help ourselves and eat it all up.'

What does one wear to a First Holy Communion? It's all very well if you're the subject of the occasion because all you have to do is turn up in white. For young Spanish girls, with a penchant for dressing up, the First Holy Communion service is a dream ticket allowing them to live out their fairy-tale fantasies with white polyester Barbie frocks and frothy, voluminous Cinderella style ball gowns drowning in frilly lace. They wear big floppy white bows in their hair or tiaras and veils, and clip along to the church in shiny little white shoes and oversized lacy white tights which they are forever hoisting up because they sag woefully around the ankles. By contrast, Spanish boys have a more sober time of it when it comes to attire, many wearing black suits with white shirts although the *Saturday Night Fever* white, all-in-one is always an option for the rugged individualist and sailor suits for the nautical types are proving popular. As a guest you are expected to turn up in smart, but casual, attire.

So, at six o'clock in the evening, Alan, Ollie and I, make our way to the outskirts of our local town where we confidently expect to find the church in which Cristian is to receive his First Holy Communion. Knowing how Mallorcans despise punctuality, we have set off rather late never thinking that the service will actually start on time. Besides, Rafael has given us a scruffy hand drawn map which looks straightforward enough. We follow his instructions as best we can but are confused by the appearance of a steep hill looming up to our left, and a junction just beyond which doesn't appear to be indicated on the map. We cross over it and a see an old stone church rising up before us along the road.

'I'm not sure about this,' I sigh, 'Rafael's map has a squiggle going to the left so maybe we should have gone up that hill?'

'Look this has to be the one,' says Alan. 'It's called the Church of the Immaculate Conception and that's the name given on the invitation and the map.'

We arrive to find the car park abandoned and the church devoid of life. A mantilla clad elderly senyora who is praying in the nearby graveyard, gets to her feet and comes to our aid.

'*Mira!* Look! You want the Church of the Immaculate Conception,' she instructs, holding the invitation card to the sunlight. 'You've missed the turning. You must go back and take the one up the hill. It's in a small lane on the left at the top. You can't miss it.'

'But this church has exactly the same name,' I say with exasperation.

'Yes,' she says, shrugging her shoulders philosophically. On that note, I take my leave and trail after Alan to the car. We turn round and head back, take the hill turning and carry on up, as instructed. Although there is a strong wind, the sun continues to smoulder in the sky like an enormous red coal, and the lining of my dress begins to weld itself stickily to my skin. I shift around irritably in the passenger seat wishing I'd chosen to wear a kaftan instead. Rather ominously en route up the winding road, we count at least three more churches. It could be my imagination but as we pass one, I could almost swear it too has the name, Church of the Immaculate Conception.

We reach the top of the hill, and to our relief see a road leading off to the left where an old stone church sits plum in the middle of a pretty cobbled courtyard. Better still it has the name, Church of the Immaculate Conception. As we drive slowly past its frontage, a group of young girls in white veils and fluttering white skirts frothed with lace, walk with deliberation across the courtyard towards the entrance, an old, arched wooden door. As the soft breeze catches at their veils and delicate white gowns, the petticoat layers billow up around them, so that for a second, they resemble celestial beings or exquisite swans in flight. We park the car on a cobbled, tree lined street across from the church and step into the cool, intimate interior, scanning the pews in the hope of glimpsing Rafael and his family but they are nowhere to be seen. There are small clusters of parents in modest but smart attire, talking loudly and in a relaxed manner to one another as if they were sitting in a local café, while their offspring giggle and run about the pews waiting for the priest to arrive. First Holy Communion is an occasion much prized by Mallorcan families. It offers them the opportunity to parade their children in their finery, to dress up themselves and enjoy family and neighbourly gossip over a celebratory dinner after the service.

'This must be the wrong church,' I whisper crossly.

'Well, this is where the old woman told us to go and it has the right name,' mutters Alan.

'Can we go to a restaurant instead?' Ollie chips in.

We get up and quietly take our leave. A few heads acknowledge our departure but no one looks remotely interested in us. We get back to the car and examine the invitation.

'The problem is that these churches all seem to have the same name,' I say impatiently. 'We might as well be looking for Larry the Lamb in a sheep cloning lab.'

We set off back down the quiet hill we have just driven up and suddenly see Rafael emerging from a small lane to our right with his mother, Cristian and what appears to be some elderly relatives. We stop the car at its junction and in great embarrassment call out to them from the window. Rafael runs over to the car, full of smiles as I get out to greet him.

'We couldn't find the church,' I say pointedly. 'Have we missed the service?'

He howls with laughter. 'You English! The church is here on this lane like I put on the map. The service is over now so let's go celebrate in the Puerto. *Vamos!*'

I peer up the lane he has indicated and to my annoyance see that only a few yards on the right is an elegant stone building with a small steeple and spire. Rafael sees my disappointment.

'Don't worry,' he says. 'Only family come to church. Is very boring so everyone else goes straight to restaurant.'

Just in case we get lost again, we agree to stay where we are until he fetches his car so that we can go in convoy to the restaurant in the port. While we wait, I stroll down the lane to the church. To my astonishment the board at its entrance announces its Parish name as Santa Agnes, not the Immaculate

Conception. When Rafael returns I challenge him about its name.

'It's true,' he says nonchalantly, 'The church is called Santa Agnes but many years ago it was known as the Immaculate Conception. Some of us still call it that.'

'Well no wonder we couldn't find it,' I say crisply. 'You put the wrong church name on the invitation and map. We've spent the last forty minutes at all the other Immaculate Conceptions around here.'

'I don't believe it!' he says in mock surprise, reaching out and clasping my shoulder, 'and to think in the Bible it says there has only ever been one.'

SEVENTEEN

RESTORATION

The windows of my office are flung wide open and at the side of my desk an old metal fan whirs monotonously, unsettling papers and teasing my hair. A lizard scurries up the white wall in front of me as I tap away on the keys of my computer, then stops dead. I glance up at its vertical frame and marvel at how it remains upright. The powerful rays of the sun brush my shoulders and then, like burning wax, slide insidiously downwards to my arms and fingers so that I flinch with the pain. I get up and walk around the room. The lizard remains suspended, its glassy eyes frozen wide, its little squat legs and webbed feet pushed out at right angles. I wonder what it's waiting for, why it hasn't scampered to a safe darkened crevice in the wall. I pour myself a glass of tepid water, cool just moments ago, and stare out over the mountains. The high and distant peaks of the Tramuntana range rise sharply into the sky, their rocky tips emblazoned with sunshine. Down in the valley, our small town is suffused with light, and the curved terracotta roof tiles of the houses glint in the sun like the scales of a ruby basilisk.

I flinch when the telephone rings and drawing back from the window, pick up the receiver. It's Ed.

'I'm at the airport but I don't think I can get on the plane,' he says breathily.

'Calm down, Ed. You'll be fine.' My worst fears have come true. 'It's only a two hour flight. Have a drink and try to relax.'

'I've got palpitations. I just don't think I can do this.'

Now what do I do? I study my watch. He's got another hour before the plane takes off from Gatwick. 'Where's Julia? I thought she was going to the airport with you?'

'She did, but she had to go. She's on duty at the hospital.'

'Why not call her for advice. After all she is a nurse?'

He flinches. 'She'll be cross with me.'

'Good. Call her.'

There's the sound of a hollow voice speaking over a tannoy.

'They're calling my flight!' he yelps.

'Call her now. Ed, and make your way to the plane.'

'OK. I hope I'll see you soon.'

The line goes dead. Whether Ed will ever appear remains to be seen.

I'm still reeling in shock as I pull out from the arrivals car park at Palma airport. Ed is sitting next to me in the car, suitcase safely stowed away in the boot. I never thought this day would come.

'It's all thanks to Julia,' he enthuses. 'When I called her she gave me hell and told me to get straight on the plane.'

'I'm glad you listen to someone.'

'Anyway, there was a nice air hostess who looked after me the whole flight. She even gave me a paper bag to breathe into.'

I can just picture the scene. The traffic is heavy so I'm relieved when we hit the fast Cintura road and are heading for the hills.

'It's jolly hot,' says Ed, pulling at his threadbare shirt collar. 'I might need a nap when we arrive.'

'Don't be such a geriatric. This is mild compared to the heat in August.'

As we leave the busy roads and skim past orchards of oranges and olives, the golden mountains shimmering in the sun, Ed sits spellbound. 'Wow, this is so beautiful! I still had this image of Mallorca being full of pubs and British yobs.'

'That's the trouble with stereotyping,' I sniff.

'I can see why you don't miss London. Anyway, what's happening with George?'

Ed and I have spent many a clandestine phone call discussing the matter in the last few months.

'I've really got to talk to him. I've been using delaying tactics.'

Ed gives a diplomatic cough. 'So, why are you still wavering?'

'He's offering a serious financial package.'

'But is money the issue or is it really something else?' he says pointedly.

I turn off the main road and into our town centre, nearly home now. Perspiration is clinging to my skin, as I run my hand over my face. He's right. This isn't about money at all, but about being lured by flattery and misplaced ambition towards a spiritual blind alley which could prove my nemesis. Money is always just a red herring. Even I know that.

I turn up our rocky track. Ed looks down at the steep orchards to his right with a pained expression. 'Just remember,' he manages to say as he claws at the sides of his seat. 'Always follow your instincts, old thing.'

Inko has arched her back and is dabbing at the coiled greeny-brown intruder in our *entrada* with a curious paw. Ed stands some feet away watching in abject terror.

'It's only a *garriga*, Ed,' says Catalina calmly. 'A field snake. The marble is nice and warm for him. I take him up to the forest and let him out.'

I can't say I'm good with snakes either but I do as I'm instructed by Catalina. In the summer snakes often slither through the French doors into the hallway. 'Get me a broom, newspaper and a waste paper basket.'

I return dutifully with her homespun snake removal kit. 'OK. Now I push him in bin.'

Quickly she shovels the snake into the bin with the broom, and then claps the newspaper on top. 'Good! Now I take him up the road in my car.'

Ed is a quivering heap. 'You're not seriously going to drive with a live snake sitting next to you?'

She regards him with wry humour. 'Of course, unless he asks to drive.'

With the snake in its basket, she sets off. 'I'll drop it off in the forest on the way up to the village.'

Ed stands on the porch shaking his head. 'She's utterly bonkers!'

'It helps if you live here.'

'You didn't tell me you were surrounded by dangerous creatures.'

Alan saunters into the courtyard. 'A bit of rural life for you, Ed.'

'Great,' he replies faintly, mopping his brow. 'Can we go into town for that coffee now?'

Teresa is full of smiles as I bustle about her stall. She's fascinated by Ed.

'He's very white,' she remarks critically. 'And he could lose some weight.'

'Thanks, Teresa. I'll tell him.'

Ed listens uncomprehendingly. 'What did she say?'

'Oh, just how nice you seem.'

He gives Teresa an appreciative nod.

She tuts. 'And why is he wearing a jumper? No wonder he's sweating.' She gesticulates to him to remove the offending item and he finally twigs. 'Ah, yes, I am a bit hot but in London the weather can suddenly turn.' He pulls off his jumper and places it over his arm.

'That's much better,' she says.

I hand her over some notes and then bend down to pick up my baskets. She grabs one and thrusts it towards Ed but he has already picked up his MEK. Teresa frowns. 'What's he carrying in that big bag.'

He guesses what she's saying. 'Tell her it's for any medical emergencies.'

I translate and watch as she roars with laughter. She's obviously decided that he's a hopeless case. We leave the market and head for Café Paris where Pep is joining us for a coffee. He is puffing at a *puro* and reading the local paper.

'So, Ed, we finally meet. Please, let me get you a coffee.'

One of the waiters takes our order. 'And how are you enjoying your stay?'

'Well aside from the heat and snakes, I'm enjoying it.'

Pep shows great interest. 'Wonderful! You have seen a snake already. What about a scorpion?'

'What?' splutters Ed. 'You're joking surely?'

'No, quite to the contrary. We have many small scorpions around here so examine your bed carefully at night. Oh and the bats…'

'Bats?' exclaims Ed, his eyes as wide as a couple of CDs. 'I won't sleep a wink!'

I give Pep a kick under the table. 'Stop it, you meanie.'

He slaps Ed on the leg good-naturedly. 'Just a little Mallorcan humour.'

'Right,' says Ed uncertainly.

'You're lucky,' Pep touches Ed's arm. 'There's a folk dancing display in the square in a few minutes. You can have a go.'

Ed gives a nervous whinny. 'I think not, Pep. I'm not a great mover.'

'Nonsense! I'll show you.'

Poor Ed sips on his *café amb llet*, his milky coffee, seemingly lost for words.

'So you've had a good morning,' says Alan as he sits bottling orange juice.

'Well, the folk dancing nearly gave me palpitations. That Pep is a forceful fellow, wouldn't let me off the hook and of course your sadistic wife,' he trails off and stabs a finger in my direction. 'just stood on the sidelines doubled up, taking photos while I was twirled around by endless big Madonnas.'

I guffaw. 'Every man's dream, Ed!'

'I'm not sure about that, Scatters. Besides I have Julia now.'

Alan gives Ed a sympathetic look. 'I think you were a damned good sport. I heard you made a few fans in the town.'

Ed toys with his glass of juice. 'I did like Colmado La Luna and the guys at HiBit. That Albert knows his onions and I can say that as a computer buff.'

While they're talking, I slope off upstairs. In less than six hours we shall be celebrating Alan's surprise birthday party and there's much to do before then.

There is a narrow, cobbled side street in the town used as a cut through by motorbikes and boy racers on a Sunday afternoon. Tall, stone-built terraced houses run the length of it, and appear rather sombre and gloomy by night, but when the sun is shining, they take on quite a different hue. As soon as bright light floods the sky, the inhabitants spill out of their homes in a cacophonous scramble to face the working day. Doors are opened, shutters pulled back and rugs are hung from windows to air. Whining *motos* and rumbling trucks advance slowly along the road and on the cobbled pavements, laughing children clatter about on bikes, dogs bark, and elderly senyoras drag wicker chairs on to their doorsteps where they sit and crochet or gossip loudly with passing neighbours until night fall. There is nothing remarkable about any of this, since this scene mirrors that of many a street in the rural towns of Mallorca. Still, only this one can lay claim to Cas Marroig, arguably one of the best restaurants in the North West of the island. Situated on a corner of the street, this modest building, with its graceful windows and nut-brown shutters could easily be mistaken for a private home. Only a small, subtle brass sign on its exterior indicates that it is, in fact, a restaurant. It is here that I have chosen to hold Alan's birthday dinner tonight, a quiet and idyllic oasis in the middle of the busy town.

Beyond the heavy wooden front doors, there is a wide, cobbled *entrada* that gives on to a large and stunning stone terrace with distant views to the hills. Draped in white linen, dining tables are placed at discreet intervals, shrouded by vast stone urns overflowing with flowers, while high above, small lights twinkle from hanging terracotta pots. Tonight, friends of various nationalities have secretly gathered on the terrace for drinks awaiting the arrival of Alan who innocently believes he is coming to Cas Marroig for a quiet supper with me. Catalina and I have planned everything meticulously. Unbeknown to him, she and Ramon are not at their home making dinner for their daughters, but have instead gone ahead to the restaurant and met up with all our other friends there. Neither is Ed babysitting Ollie at our home because they too have joined the others directly there.

By the time we roll up, everyone is assembled out on the terrace. Suspecting nothing, Alan bounds into the restaurant's hallway and chats cheerfully with Pau, the maître d' who lures us out to the terrace. A second later, Alan rears back in shock at the vision before him. Standing and laughing, with glasses of cava raised in their hands, are all the people who have made our transition to the mountains possible and also so special. There is Catalina and her family, Pep, Juana and Angel, Tolo from the bank and his wife Rosa, Albert and Antonia, Rafael, Fransisca and Hans, and Jason Moore and his wife, Jack and Sarah and many others. Flushed and overcome with emotion, Alan grips Ollie by the hand and together they greet the guests. I slip off with Ed to talk to Pep and Juana, who, being such good friends, have been party to every detail of the birthday plot from the beginning.

'How are you enjoying your stay?' asks Juana.

'It's been an eye opener,' says Ed. 'Magical. Up here it's like a lost horizon.'

Juana sips at her cava and turns to me. 'I can't believe you've been here a year already. Think you're going to stay forever?'

'I can't think of anywhere else I'd rather be,' I answer.

'What's there to go back for?' snorts Pep. 'You have all of us and you live in Eden.'

Juana rolls her eyes at me. 'At least we don't have to worry about the whisky business.'

'Let's not discuss that,' says Pep. 'Alan and I have bigger plans.'

I squeeze his arm. 'Heaven help us!'

After aperitifs on the terrace we adjourn upstairs to a private room for a four course dinner. The room is wood panelled and imbued with soft light from the candles lining the walls and twinkling on the table. An antique wrought-iron candelabrum sits in the middle of the dark oak table, and oranges and lemons, their leaves intertwined, spill down its centre. The evening passes raucously and at midnight everyone sings Happy Birthday in English and Mallorcan. Alan rises to make his speech and is interrupted constantly by banter, jokes and loud clapping. Catalina takes control, instructing him to open his gifts. She stands protectively behind his chair, placing the gifts in front of him, one at a time, so that they can be seen and appreciated properly by the assembled guests. He unwraps each one carefully, embarrassed to have so much attention thrust upon him but delighting in it all the same. His presents include a bottle of one of Mallorca's finest wines from Tiffany, an American friend in Palma, a rare Mallorcan bonsai from Catalina and Ramon, a sack of almonds from Rafael, goblets from Pep and Juana and from Catalina's parents, a strong, hand made wicker basket with rope handle and hook for collecting oranges from the trees. I think of the elaborate sort of presents we give in London, and how simple, unaffected and practical the ones are here. Many have been made by hand and must have involved hours of work for their creator.

Alan, Ed, Ollie and I wend our way home on foot, full of laughter and good cheer. We have left all the gifts at the restaurant and will pick them up in the morning. Pau waves to us as he shuts up the restaurant and ambles along the road towards his home, singing as he goes. The night is balmy and the sky is crammed to bursting with bright stars. Several guests hoot as they pass us in their cars and a group of laddish fan-tailed dogs saunter past and then all is still. Gloriously still.

The next day I walk out, barefooted, on to the hot terrace to inspect progress on the pool. It is already half tiled and, with any luck, will be finished before Ed returns to London. At the far end of the garden I see the last of the builders packing up his tool bag for the afternoon. He gives me a cheery wave and disappears down into the field. Alan, Ed and Ollie sit on the terrace at the back of the house, playing Scrabble and hardly notice when I pass by them en route to the kitchen where I pour myself a glass of wine from the fridge. I take a sip and quietly make my way to the courtyard and the pond. The frogs are quacking and squawking as usual and my portly toad has returned and sits passively in the centre of the pond on a large craggy rock. As I approach, the frogs dive into the water but he remains still, studying me intently. I slide on to the pond's broad ledge and observe him closely. Silence. After a few seconds he opens his mouth as if to speak, then slams it shut. His throat is moving imperceptibly and for an insane moment, I imagine he's actually chewing gum. The heat of the sun warms my back and I close my eyes, listening to the sound of the gurgling water of the pond's small fountain. I imagine my companionable toad clearing his throat and launching into conversation.

'So, you're still here?'

My eyes click open. 'Oh, I thought you were ignoring me.'

He puffs up his chest. 'No, just collecting my thoughts. You know, it's getting on for a year since you came here.'

I nod thoughtfully and give him his next line.

'I have to tell you straight up, I never thought you'd hack it.'

I look at him in surprise. 'Why ever not?'

'I dunno, put you down as a bit of a townie, but now I'm not so sure. I think you're maybe a country girl at heart.'

I laugh. 'Well, I'm a bit of both.'

'You know,' he says provocatively, 'everyone comes here either to lose or to find something. I can't work out which camp you're in.'

'Well,' I say warily, 'Maybe I'm not in either.'

He gives me a sardonic smile. 'Oh yes you are.'

Would he really say that? Maybe. I pause to contemplate the tiny spasms his throat makes, the delicate veining under the translucent, mottled skin and his all seeing, inky-black eyes and decide that he really is quite handsome. The shrill sound of the telephone ringing makes me jump. Irritably, I turn towards the house. My corpulent friend blinks. I could almost swear he says in a gravely voice, 'Saved by the bell. Go on Miss Busy, don't you want to get that?'

'No.'

A door bangs and Alan strides into the courtyard. He calls over to me. 'It's George. He says he needs to speak with you urgently.'

'Tell him I'll ring him back.'

I feel the toad's penetrating gaze. Just follow your heart, he seems to be mouthing.

Alan eyes me steadily. 'You should speak with him today.'

'I know.'

'When will you call?'

'Later. Just say later.'

He nods slowly and plods back into the house. An apple, vermilion in hue and perfectly formed, floats in front of me. Its fragrance is alluring, irresistible. Eve, it calls, just one bite. That's all. I snatch at the air. It evades me. Ever higher, safely out of reach. Gone forever.

I steal a glance at my silent companion, and trail a finger in the cool pond water, watching the small fish dart beneath the glassy surface. Slowly I get to my feet and stretch. Beyond the courtyard, the front garden, with its rich, silvery green lawn and myriad of brightly coloured Mediterranean flowers, beckons. Huge crimson roses, their parched hearts laid bare, sag on the far stone wall by the gardening shed. Their season is nearly passed. The smell of rosemary clings to the air and the rhythmic clicking of the cicadas merges bizarrely with the loud buzzing of a passing hornet. With a spring in my step, I leap up the small stone stairway by the pond that leads to the front garden.

'Hey, wait up!' My amphibian friend croaks in bewilderment. 'Where you going?'

I throw him an inscrutable smile. 'Where do you think? I'm off to smell the roses.'